Apologetical Aesthetics

Apologetical Aesthetics

Edited by

Mark Coppenger,
William E. Elkins Jr., *and*
Richard H. Stark III

WIPF & STOCK · Eugene, Oregon

Wipf & Stock
An Imprint of Wipf and Stock Publishers
199 W. 8th Ave., Suite 3
Eugene, OR 97401

www.wipfandstock.com

PAPERBACK ISBN: 978-1-6667-1508-8
HARDCOVER ISBN: 978-1-6667-1509-5
EBOOK ISBN: 978-1-6667-1510-1

04/27/22

Contents

Preface

In the fall of 2019, the three of us were part of a teaching mission to Christian schools in Southeast Asia. All of us had been in the worldview program at Southern Baptist Theological Seminary—Coppenger as a prof, Elkins and Stark as students. More specifically, we'd done work together in the theology-and-the-arts doctoral program as dissertation adviser and advisees. With Coppenger freshly retired from Southern and with Elkins and Stark, PhDs in hand, engaged in ministry, we looked back at our studies in aesthetics, recalling the others who'd done doctoral work in this area. Soon, the idea of "getting the band back together" surfaced, this time in the form of a book featuring the thought of fellow students in this vein, and then we moved to the notion of apologetics as the binding theme.

As we made contact with our compadres in the program—Ahrens, Blackaby, Cabal, Crawford, Halla (as a prof), Raley, Scondras, Watson, Williamson—we thought of others at SBTS, who'd done work in aesthetics—Haykin, and Warnock—as well as Christian aestheticians outside the program—Shockley and Miller. (You can read their bio notes in the back of this book.) Yes, there was an element of fond reminiscence, but the main point has been to encourage fresh work in this field, both from the contributors and from our readers.

Mark Coppenger
William E. Elkins Jr.
Richard H. Stark III

Introduction

IN RESTAURANTS AROUND THE world, "fusion" cooking is popular, even though the concoctions may sound doubtful, whether sushi pizza, kimchi quesadilla, or country benedict (with sausage gravy instead of hollandaise). You see the same sort of thing in academia, with, for instance, the emergence of "aesthetic theology" (to which we'll give attention) and "virtue epistemology" (applying the canons of moral excellence to the definition and pursuit of knowledge). We think that the fusion expression, "apologetical aesthetics," is a helpful one, identifying a Christianly-strategic field of inquiry.

To be sure, we're far from the first to enlist artistic and aesthetic phenomena in the cause of apologetics. Alvin Plantinga and Richard Swinburne are just two of the names that spring to mind. We're just walking in those paths with what we hope are fresh insights and applications. And we're not reluctant to give credit to non-believers when their thought and work advances our case—all truth being God's truth.

In this volume, you'll see the seventeen essays in five groupings—critiques of naturalism, divine signs in nature as well as in the Way, connections to various art forms, and a critical survey of the field. Most of them grow out of dissertations, whether completed or projected. Others reflect fresh study by those with doctorates already in hand. Some complement the others; some conflict with the others. Such is the way of serious scholarship.

To help engage your reading, we've provided a brief synopsis at the head of each essay, plus illustrations by Harrison Watters, as well as the one George Scondras did for his piece. Also, we have Steve Halla to thank for the photos accompanying his piece.

Please take a look at the bio sketches at the back of the book. They'll give you a sense of the remarkable friends we've met in this enterprise, cherished Christian brothers—and a sister—all. And we trust we'll gain new friends and counselors in the work outlined and exemplified in this volume.

The Doubtfulness of
Naturalistic Accounts

Everyone knows evolutionists have provided a comprehensive and compelling account of human constitution and proclivities. The schools, museums, and media assure us this is so, or that good answers are right around the corner where puzzles might remain. But even Charles Darwin knew aesthetic values were a special problem, and he's had some distinguished critics to remind him this is so, critics whose perspective resonates with ancient wisdom.

A Peacock's Tale

The Darwinists' Art of Making Stuff Up

WILLIAM E. ELKINS JR.

"THE SIGHT OF A feather in a peacock's tail, whenever I gaze at it, makes me sick!" wrote Charles Darwin in a letter to the American botanist Asa Gray (April 3rd, 1860).[1] The peacock's tail sickened Darwin because the intricate design seemed far too complex to explain by natural causes. It was after the publication of *On the Origin of Species* in 1859 that Darwin became increasingly aware of the problem of beauty. Aesthetics was a common philosophical topic in intellectual circles at the time, and most naturalists (many of them pastors) believed that the beauty of nature was evidence for divine creation. This perspective was consonant with the prevailing biblical worldview in the West, bolstered by such Christian thinkers as William Paley.

Paley's textbook, *Natural Theology*, was required reading at Cambridge in the early 1800s and had a profound influence on Darwin's theory. In his book, Paley likened the complexity of creation to a watch which, upon close examination of the gears and springs, bore all the marks of having been designed by a watchmaker. When considering the topic of beauty, Paley understood that two things were at play—the real presence of beauty and the ability to perceive it. He concluded that the pleasure received by the senses should be understood as evidence of a benevolent Creator, a Creator who designed life to be experienced with a

---

1. Darwin, *Life and Letters of Charles Darwin*, 2:90.

certain measure of pleasure and happiness.[2] After all, why would nature, apart from God, care if human beings enjoyed food, the sunset, or the smell of a rose? However, after Darwinian evolution began to take hold in academic circles, what once seemed clear—if there is design, there must be a Designer—no longer seemed obvious to all. But this left Darwinists with the difficult task of explaining the presence of design and beauty in the world without a divine Designer.

In chapter 15 of *On the Origin of Species*, Darwin acknowledged this challenge:

> How it comes that certain colours, sounds and forms should give pleasure to man and the lower animals, that is, how the sense of beauty in its simplest form was first acquired, we do not know any more than how certain odours and flavours were first rendered agreeable.[3]

At this point, Darwin did not make a clear distinction between the aesthetic sense of man and animals, but his answer was the same: "We do not know." Darwin acknowledged that many of his critics believed that the beauty of nature was intended to "delight man or the Creator," but he quickly dismissed the idea as "beyond the scope of scientific discussion."[4] However, he then added, "Such doctrines, if true, would be absolutely fatal to my theory."[5] Darwin admittedly did not know why beauty existed and why certain pleasures were connected to the perception of beauty, but one thing he knew for sure was that he had to come up with a non-theistic answer to the problem if his theory was to survive.

As Darwin sought to dismiss the need for a "watchmaker" to justify the existence of the proverbial watch, critics like John Ruskin continued to press him on the problem of beauty. Ruskin was a well-known author, artist, art critic, and outspoken detractor of Darwin despite their mutual friendship. After reflecting on Darwin's theory, Ruskin suspected that he was motivated by a latent atheism because he refused to consider the slightest possibility of a Creator.

The peacock's tail was Ruskin's favorite example to counter Darwin's atheistic theory. He argued that the colors and intricate design in the tail feathers were so complex that even if natural and sexual selection could

2. Paley, *Natural Theology*, 299–300.

3. Darwin, *On the Origin of Species*, 352.

4. Darwin, *On the Origin of Species*, 147–49.

5. Darwin, *On the Origin of Species*, 147–49.

produce them, doing so would have squandered too much precious evolutionary energy.[6] Eventually, Ruskin's question of the peacock's tail became such an iconic counterexample to Darwin's theory that, when Darwin visited Ruskin's home in 1879, the peacock was a major topic of discussion. Art historian Phillip Prodger concludes,

> Ruskin, who had a penchant for touching raw nerves, had put his finger on one of the most sensitive elements of late Darwinian science. The beauty problem, and the question of the peacock's tail in particular, typified a new phase of research that confronted the traditional view of humans as being unique in their ability to express emotion.[7]

In *The Eagle's Nest*, Ruskin wondered which came first: Did the hen arbitrarily develop a taste for the as-yet nonexistent, colorful peacock's tail, or upon seeing an existing peacock's tail, was she suddenly attracted

6. Prodger, *Ugly Disagreements*, 49.

7. Prodger, *Ugly Disagreements*, 56.

to it? Ruskin understood that Darwin's theory required one choice or the other. Perhaps this is why, in the same section, Ruskin quipped, "Very positively I can say to you that I have never heard yet one logical argument in [Darwinism's] favor, and I have heard, and read, many that were beneath contempt."[8]

Darwin was not the only one focused on the problem of beauty. Alfred Russell Wallace, who formulated the theory of evolution through natural selection around the same time as Darwin (Darwin beat him to the punch), also wrestled with the problem of beauty. But unlike Darwin, Wallace was not afraid to entertain the possibility of a divine Creator. Focusing on the human ability to create and enjoy beauty in the arts (i.e., music, literature, and painting), Wallace could not see any direct relation to the survivability of the species. He wrote, "The inference I would draw from this class of phenomena is that a superior intelligence has guided the development of man in a definite direction, and for a special purpose."[9] Philosopher Anthony O'Hear explains,

> Alfred Russell Wallace, the co-discoverer of the theory of evolution, argued that our . . . love of beauty could not possibly be explained in terms of survival promotion. He concluded that this must mean that there was more to human nature than evolution could account for and . . . looked for the answer in divine intervention.[10]

Darwin was not happy with Wallace's suggestion of the divine origin of beauty and the aesthetic sense: "I hope you have not murdered too completely your own and my child."[11] However, despite his rebuke, he sympathized with Wallace's struggle. In *The Descent of Man*, he wrote, "Since neither the enjoyment nor the capacity of producing musical notes are faculties of the least use to man in reference to his daily habits of life, they must be ranked amongst the most mysterious with which he is endowed."[12] The same could be said for all human artistic expressions.

8. Ruskin, *Eagle's Nest*, 199.

9. Barash, *Homo Mysterious*, 143.

10. O'Hear, *After Progress*, 67.

11. Barash, *Homo Mysterious*, 143.

12. Barash, *Homo Mysterious*, 143.

The Darwinian Attempt to Solve the Problem of Beauty

In the midst of repeated criticism, Darwin continued to work on the evolutionary problem of beauty. In his first few additions of *On the Origin of the Species,* his discussion focused primarily on birds, including the peacock. Without specifically addressing Ruskin's question of which came first—the peahen's desire for beautiful plumage or the beautiful plumage itself—Darwin did lean toward the theory that the peahen had a secret sexual attraction for the flamboyant. In story form, the development of the peacock's tail would go something like this: Once upon a time, there were plain brown pheasants frequenting a small field near some trees. One day, a young male pheasant, about three years old, developed a small blue patch on his otherwise plain brown tail. This blue spot got the attention of all the lady pheasants, who then snubbed the rest of the plain brown boys during mating season. Decades later, the Blue Spot clan was all the rage—that is, until Mr. Blue-and-Green Spot was born and dominated for years to come. But, of course, he and all of his boys were later replaced by Mr. Blue-Green-and-Black Spot. And so on and on the story goes for thousands of generations, until we arrive at the masterful design (without a master designer) of the proud peacock's plumage we all enjoy at the local zoo. (And, of course, all this assumes that the offspring of the bird with a colored-spot mutation would manifest that same development, which is far from genetically persuasive.)

Darwin seemed to know that this argument from sexual selection was weak when he wrote,

> It may appear childish to attribute any effect to such apparently weak means: I cannot here enter on the details necessary to support this view, but if man can in the short time give elegant carriage and beauty to his bantams, according to his standard of beauty, I can see no good reason to doubt that female birds, by selecting, during thousands of generations, the most melodious or beautiful males, according to their standard of beauty, might produce a marked effect.[13]

Darwin was quite happy, without explanation, to equate an intelligent man's overseeing the process of making his birds beautiful with the deliverances of thousands of generations of random mutations working within some standard of beauty that the peahens just happened to possess. But

---

13. Darwin, *Darwin,* 392.

for his theory to be right, this same scenario would need to be replicated throughout countless species on the planet, including colorful roosters and male mallards as well as lavishly antlered deer.

Darwin believed that natural selection and sexual selection were the two main driving forces in biology. Natural selection attempts to explain how organisms survive and flourish by developing certain physical features or abilities through random mutations. Sexual selection, on the other hand, attempts to explain why certain features in a species develop to allow greater opportunity to attract a mate. Even though Darwin saw natural and sexual selection as two distinct forces, most naturalists after Darwin followed Wallace in reducing sexual selection to a subcategory of natural selection; that is to say, they recognized natural selection as the driving force, with sexual selection playing only a minor role. However, with a renewed interest in the question of beauty, some modern evolutionary thinkers have returned to Darwin's clear distinction between sexual selection and natural selection. This fresh focus has not been without controversy as a host of recent journal articles and books can testify—many of them replete with fantastical stories of their own. Some of these narratives range from "selfish-genes" that control everything to accidental "spandrels" that became really useful to artistic skills (developed for the purpose of "group-cohesion") to the emergence of imbedded collective memories of "shelter-finding instincts" from the Pleistocene Age. For instance, Ellen Dissanayake suggests that the aesthetic sense and artistic expression developed in humans for the purpose of enhancing cooperation, thereby contributing to the social cohesion of the community.[14] However, Denis Dutton thought Dissanayake's theory of group-cohesion was too weak.[15] Dutton preferred natural selection and sexual selection along with Steven Pinker's version of the selfish-gene. Citing Pinker, Dutton states that people do not

> selfishly spread their genes; genes selfishly spread themselves. They do it by the way they build our brains. By making us enjoy life, health, sex, friends, and children, the genes buy a lottery ticket for representation in the next generation, with odds that were favorable in the environment in which we evolved.[16]

14. Dissanayake, "Arts after Darwin," 9.

15. Dutton, *Art Instinct*, 224.

16. Dutton, *Art Instinct*, 43.

Helena Cronin, observing the altruistic and cooperative behavior of sterile worker ants, believes that natural selection and sexual selection are outdated holdovers from the nineteenth century. She, too, favors the "selfish-gene."[17] However, David Stove not only rejects the selfish-gene theory, but declares it a new religion:

> Everyone knows this, except certain religious people. A person is certainly a believer in some religion if he thinks, for example, that there are on earth millions of invisible and immortal non-human beings which are far more intelligent and capable than we are. But that is exactly what sociobiologists do think, about genes. Sociobiology, then, is a religion: one which has genes as its gods.[18]

David Rothenberg rejects most of these theories, particularly that sexual selection alone is sufficient to explain all expressions of beauty in nature:

> Though the qualities we find in natural forms do not always make adaptive sense, I have not been happy with the idea that every living thing evolves as the result of random mutations and the play of adaptation and aesthetic/sexual selection . . . Why is the cardinal red? Sexual selection. Why does the nightingale sing tirelessly through the darkness instead of relaxing in sleep? Sexual selection. Why do butterflies come in so many dizzying colors? Sexual selection. Are there any specific qualities of beauty that hold all these traits together? Sexual selection has no comment about that.[19]

Rather than embracing any of the popular theories, Rothenberg puts forth one of his own. He believes that evolution is whimsical and creative, it simply likes to try things out. Although he's not a theist, he also allows for the possibility that beauty is a universal concept infused into the very fabric of the material world.[20] Many more examples could be given of one group of evolutionists criticizing the creative stories of other evolutionists. We could say of

17. Cronin, *Ant and the Peacock*, 60.

18. Stove, *Darwinian Fairytales*, 248.

19. Rothenberg, *Survival of the Beautiful*, 27.

20. Rothenberg, *Survival of the Beautiful*, 34.

them what Basil the Great said about the ancient materialists: "It is vain to refute them; they are sufficient in themselves to destroy one another."[21]

Some of these stories are so outlandish that social scientists and philosophers have weighed in against them, as in *Alas, Poor Darwin*, edited by Hilary and Steven Rose, and *Darwinian Fairytales* by David Stove (mentioned above).[22] Along those same lines is the critique made popular by Stephen Jay Gould in the late 1970s, when he called these narratives "just-so" stories, a reference to Rudyard Kipling's stories for children that attempted to explain in wild fashion the origin of certain distinctive features of animals.[23] For how the camel got its hump, Kipling tells the story of "when the world was so new and all" the camel refused to work for the first three days. The horse, the dog, and the ox tried to get him to work, but all he said was "humph." Later, since all the camel would say is "humph," a Djinn gives the camel a "humph" on his back so he could store up his food and work for three days without eating.[24]

In another story, Kipling tells why the elephant has a long trunk: One day, a little elephant, full of curiosity and a bulgy nose like a boot, wanted to know what crocodiles had for dinner. After searching all around for the answer, he finally finds a crocodile more than eager to show him. The crocodile clamped his teeth down on the little elephant's nose, which caused the little pachyderm to pull, and pull, and pull until his nose stretched really long into a useful trunk that could do all sorts of useful things.

And then there's the one about how the giraffe came to have a long neck. Long ago, there were many little giraffes with very short necks happily eating the leaves from the lower branches of the trees. But soon—because there were so many giraffes and other animals—all the leaves on the lower parts of the trees were eaten up, which left them very hungry. So, they stretched and strained at the leaves that were too high to reach, but they still couldn't reach them. One day there came along a giraffe who had a longer neck than most, so he was able to eat the leaves that were much higher than all the other giraffes could reach. This happy accident allowed the longer necked giraffe to grow stronger and stronger while the other smaller giraffes grew weaker and weaker. Over time, the strong,

---

21. Basil, "Hexaemeron," 53.

22. Rose and Rose, *Alas, Poor Darwin*; Stove, *Darwinian Fairytales*.

23. Gould, "Return of Hopeful Monsters," 581–98.

24. Kipling, *Just So Stories*, 17–29, 65–85.

long-necked giraffe had lots of children and grandchildren, and with each generation, their necks continued to get longer and longer (after all, there were always more leaves just a bit higher out of reach), until they became taller than a two-story building . . . oh, wait! This last one wasn't a story by Kipling, it was a story told in my college biology class in 1987. Nevertheless, you get the idea of "just-so" stories.

In philosophy, the "just-so" story commits the *ad hoc* fallacy: It amounts to nothing more than a fanciful, imaginative tale hatched to try to explain how certain internal or external qualities evolved. The real problem with most of the explanations, as plausible as a few may sound, is that they can never be scientifically verified or falsified. Was it *group cohesion*? Was it *mate selection*? Was it *choice of habitat*? How do we decide? And if multiple explanations can be constructed with no way to adjudicate between them, how can we call them "scientific"? Is it merely because scientists are spinning them out?

An Appeal to Ancient Wisdom

The objection being made is not against all stories, for surely there is one correct story that can be told. The objection is against stories told by those who are committed to reducing it all to natural and sexual selection. It objects to the approach of those, like Darwin, who have an *a priori* commitment to atheism. Are we really to believe that the splendor of beauty observed throughout the world can be reduced to such banal origins? Are we to believe that the peacock's tail and human artistic expression evolved for the same reason? Should we just blindly accept these stories and ignore the countless voices throughout the ages (e.g., Plato, Augustine, Edwards, and Scruton) who have recognized a transcendence about beauty that is beyond pure materialism?

Some will likely accuse critics of these Darwinian stories of being unscientific, but the problem is not with science; it is with scientism. It is with those who foolishly think that the only way to discover truth is through the scientific method. Such an approach is foolish because the so-called truth of scientism cannot itself be established by the scientific method; it can't satisfy its own demand. It's self-defeating, and yet many scientists continue to propagate this preposterous standard.

The real problem is not with science, but with the fallen humans who are all too willing and able to skew it. As Anthony Esolen insists,

"We do not have other gods before God. We refuse to place our hope in magic 'science,' which amounts to placing our hope in *scientists*, who are men as we are: frail, vain, ambitious, stubborn in error, prone to going along with the herd, eager for power over others, apt to believe themselves to be wiser than they are."[25]

The puzzling reality of beauty in the world and the human ability to perceive it should call everyone, including scientists, to exercise a little humility when contemplating its origin. Scientists and philosophers should continue to do their work even as they, like Wallace, leave open the possibility that a God exists who created all things beautiful. Nothing about science requires atheism. Historians of science have noted that the biblical worldview was one of the factors that gave rise to modern science, and if the biblical worldview was a science starter, then the accusation that it is a science-stopper is unfounded. As the historian of science James Hannam writes, "Christianity was a necessary, if not sufficient, cause of the flowering of modern science."[26]

Perhaps, though, we will discover that the truth about beauty has been around much longer than modern science. The *Wisdom of Solomon* was a well-known text among the ancient Jews.[27] It was likely written in the first century BC by a Greek-speaking Jew living in Alexandria.[28] In chapter 13, the author addresses the foolishness of idolaters who refuse to recognize the divine artisan through his works. The writer undoubtedly believed that beauty in the world is conclusive evidence for the Creator, stating,

> 1 For all people who were ignorant of God were foolish by nature; and they were unable from the good things that are seen to know the one who exists, nor did they recognize the artisan while paying heed to his works; 2 but they supposed that either fire or wind or swift air, or the circle of the stars, or turbulent water, or the luminaries of heaven were the gods that rule the world. 3 If through delight in the beauty of these things people assumed them to be gods, let them know how much better than these is their Lord, for the author of beauty created them. 4 And if people were amazed at their power and working, let them perceive from them how much more powerful is the one who formed them.

25. Esolen, *Out of the Ashes*, 187 (emphasis original).

26. Hannam, "How Christianity," 8.

27. Although not considered canonical, the *Wisdom of Solomon* has often been esteemed within various Christian traditions.

28. Elwell and Comfort, "Wisdom of Solomon."

5 For from the greatness and beauty of created things comes a corresponding perception of their Creator. **6** Yet these people are little to be blamed, for perhaps they go astray while seeking God and desiring to find him. **7** For while they live among his works, they keep searching, and they trust in what they see, because the things that are seen are beautiful. **8** Yet again, not even they are to be excused; **9** for if they had the power to know so much that they could investigate the world, how did they fail to find sooner the Lord of these things? (13:1–9 The Holy Bible with Apocrypha)

Of course, the apostle Paul sounds this theme in Romans 1:18–23, where he says that God's "invisible attributes, namely, his eternal power and divine nature, have been clearly perceived, ever since the creation of the world, in the things that have been made. So they [unbelievers] are without excuse." In the case of the *Wisdom of Solomon*, the thing that should not escape everyone's notice and the very thing that will render everyone without excuse for not believing in God is the "greatness and beauty" of creation.

Several centuries after the *Wisdom of Solomon* was written, many early and medieval Christians likewise used beauty in their apologetics. Clement of Alexandria (AD 150–215) concluded that "God is the cause of everything beautiful."[29] Marcus Minucius Felix (died AD 250), one of the first of the Latin apologists, argued in *Octavius* that the obvious order and beauty in the world is sufficient evidence for those in their right mind to conclude that God is the "artificer."[30] In *A Treatise of Novatian Concerning the Trinity*, Novatian (AD 200–258) maintained that God is the source of objective beauty in the world and the human ability to perceive it, which should lead humanity to worship Him.[31] Dionysius, the Bishop of Alexandria (AD 248–64), maintained that the mark of God's providence is not just the creation of useful or functional objects, but also their beauty.[32] In the medieval period, both Augustine and Thomas Aquinas had much to say about beauty. To Augustine, God is beauty, and the beautiful things he created were intended to draw mankind to himself.[33] Similarly, Aquinas understood the beautiful as "shining form,"[34] which he thought was a fitting description of God's glory. Therefore, Aquinas

29. Tatarkiewicz, "Great Theory of Beauty," 170.
30. Felix, "Octavius of Minucius Felix," 4:182.
31. Novatian, "Treatise of Novatian," 5:611–12.
32. Dionysius, "Works of Dionysius," 6:114.
33. Cilliers, "Beauty of Imagined Meaning," 40.
34. Martin, *Beauty and Holiness*, 25.

understood God's glory to be the source of all order and beauty in the material world.[35]

Since some of the great Christian thinkers of the past didn't hesitate to use beauty as evidence for God's existence, today's apologists should at least question why beauty is often underestimated and underutilized in modern apologetics, particularly in response to naturalistic evolution. Contra Darwin's theory, a more likely explanation for the beauty of creation (even in the peacock's tail) is that it was designed by God for his and our enjoyment and to point all humanity to himself. Beauty should not be understood as a random accident of nature but rather the very signature of God on his creation. If this idea is true, then no Darwinian fairy tale will ever be able to explain it away.

Bibliography

Barash, David P. *Homo Mysterious: Evolutionary Puzzles of Human Nature*. Oxford: Oxford University Press, 2012.

Basil. "The Hexaemeron." In *Nicene and Post-Nicene Fathers*, vol. 8, edited by Philip Schaff and Henry Wace, 51–107. 14 vols. Peabody, MA: Hendrickson, 1995.

Cilliers, Johan. "The Beauty of Imagined Meaning: Profiling Practical Theological Aesthetics." *Practical Theology in South Africa* 24.1 (January 2009) 32–47.

Cronin, Helena. *The Ant and the Peacock*. Cambridge: Cambridge University Press, 1992.

Darwin, Charles. *Darwin: The Indelible Stamp*. Edited by James D. Watson. Philadelphia: Running, 2005.

———. *The Life and Letters of Charles Darwin, Volume 2*. Edited by Francis Darwin. 2 vols. New York: Appleton and Co., 1887.

———. *On the Origin of Species by Means of Natural Selection*. London: Arcturus, 2012.

Dionysius. "The Works of Dionysius: Exegetical Fragments." In *Ante-Nicene Fathers*, edited by Alexander Roberts and James Donaldson, 6:111–20. 10 vols. Peabody, MA: Hendrickson, 1995.

Dissanayake, Ellen. "The Arts after Darwin: Does Art Have an Origin and Adaptive Function?" In *World Art Studies: Exploring Concepts and Approaches*, edited by Kitty Zijlmans and Wilfried van Damme, 241–63. Amsterdam: Valiz, 2008.

Dutton, Denis. *The Art Instinct: Beauty, Pleasure, and Human Evolution*. New York: Bloomsbury, 2009.

Elwell, Walter A., and Philip Wesley Comfort. "Wisdom of Solomon." In *Tyndale Bible Dictionary*, edited by Walter A. Elwell and Philip Wesley Comfort, n.p. Wheaton, IL: Tyndale, 2001.

Esolen, Anthony. *Out of the Ashes: Rebuilding American Culture*. Washington, DC: Regnery, 2017.

35. Martin, *Beauty and Holiness*, 25.

Felix, Minucius. "The Octavius of Minucius Felix." In *Ante-Nicene Fathers*, edited by Alexander Roberts and James Donaldson, 4:173–98. 10 vols. Peabody, MA: Hendrickson, 1995.

Gould, Stephen Jay. "The Return of Hopeful Monsters." *Natural History* 86 (1980) 22–30.

———. "*The Spandrels of San Marco* and the Panglossian Paradigm: A Critique of the Adaptionist Programme." *Proceedings of the Royal Society of London*, Series B, 205.1161 (1979) 581–98.

Hannam, James. "How Christianity Led to the Rise of Modern Science." http://www.equip.org/PDF/JAF3384.pdf.

Kipling, Rudyard. *Just So Stories*. Garden City, NY: Doubleday, 1907.

Martin, James Alfred. *Beauty and Holiness: The Dialogue between Aesthetics and Religion*. Princeton: Princeton University Press, 1990.

Novatian. "A Treatise of Novatian Concerning the Trinity." In *Ante-Nicene Fathers*, edited by Alexander Roberts and James Donaldson, 5:611–12. 10 vols. Peabody, MA: Hendrickson, 1995.

O'Hear, Anthony. *After Progress*. London: Bloomsbury, 1999.

Paley, William. *Natural Theology*. 12th ed. Chillicothe, OH: DeWard, 1802.

Prodger, Phillip. *Ugly Disagreements, the Art of Evolution: Darwin, Darwinism, and Visual Culture*. Hanover, NH: Dartmouth College Press, 2009.

Rose, Hilary, and Steven Rose. *Alas, Poor Darwin: Arguments against Evolutionary Psychology*. New York: Harmony, 2000.

Rothenberg, David. *Survival of the Beautiful: Art, Science, and Evolution*. New York: Bloomsbury, 2011.

Ruskin, John. *The Eagle's Nest*. London: George Allen, 1905.

Stove, David. *Darwinian Fairytales: Selfish Genes, Errors of Heredity and Other Fables of Evolution*. New York: Encounter, 2007.

Tatarkiewicz, Wladyslaw. "The Great Theory of Beauty and Its Decline." *The Journal of Aesthetics and Art Criticism* 31.2 (Decemebr 1972) 165–80.

To cite gorillas who sign as an argument for the evolutionary development of human language is like climbing a tree and saying you're on your way to the moon. And whatever difficulties the Darwinists face in tracing day-to-day communication back to supposedly vestigial expressions, according to the justifiably ridiculed "pooh-pooh," "ding-dong," and "bow-wow" theories, they multiply and expand exponentially when it comes to great literature. How much more sensible it is to ground sublime, poetic writing in the special creation of the God of the Bible, who is himself a literary being in whose image we are made.

Darwin's White Whale

How Literature Points toward the Existence of God

DANIEL BLACKABY

An Answerable Problem

IN HIS 1901 POEM "The Problem," English novelist and poet Thomas Hardy grappled with how to live in a world that had been changed by Charles Darwin's evolutionary theories:

> Shall we conceal the Case, or tell it—
> We who believe the evidence?
> Here and there the watch-towers knell it
> With a sullen significance,
> Heard of the few who hearken intently and carry an eagerly
> unstained sense.
> Hearts that are happiest hold not by it;
> Better we let, then, the old view reign;
> Since there is peace in it, why decry it?
> Since there is comfort, why disdain?
> Note not the pigment the while that the painting determines
> Humanity's joys and pain.[1]

Unbeknownst to Hardy, a resolution to his problem was hiding within the very poem he used to pose the question. The answer is not in the message but in the medium. Poetry possesses a transcendent quality that has never fit comfortably into the naturalistic confines of Darwin's theory.

1. Hardy, "Problem," 120.

Indeed, the existence of sublime literature ultimately points toward a reality beyond the natural world.

Evolutionary biologist Richard Dawkins retorts that Shakespeare's sonnets "are sublime if God is there and they are sublime if he isn't. They don't prove the existence of God; they prove the existence of . . . Shakespeare."[2] Like a student who reads *The Great Gatsby* and perceives only the surface-level plot, Dawkins overlooks the problem literature poses to his naturalist worldview. The creations constructed within a sandbox matter little unless one can explain the existence of the sandbox. The real challenge to Darwinian theory is much larger than one or two sublime works of literature; it is the concept of literature itself.

The Three Pillars of Literature

When applying aesthetic philosopher Morris Weitz's "family resemblance" definition of art to literature,[3] three foundational pillars emerge: language, aesthetics, and literary meaning. These elements loosely correlate to the *how, what,* and *why* of literature. An account for the existence of literature must provide an explanation for each of these three foundational pillars. Each one requires a lengthy and nuanced discussion far beyond the scope of this essay, so a brief overview of the central challenges must suffice.

The Challenge of Language

In the ancient world, people assumed language was of divine origin—a gift bestowed on man from the gods. Darwinism created the need for a new explanation. So voluminous were the attempts to provide a naturalistic justification, and so meager the results, that in 1866 the Linguistic Society of Paris banned all future papers on the topic. These early Darwinian theories leave much to be desired, emphasized by the so-called *pooh-pooh, ding-dong,* and *bow-wow* hypotheses. More sophisticated theories were required to bridge the chasm between bleating goats and Shakespeare's *Macbeth.* Evolutionary biologist Eörs Szathmáry admits, "The origin of the eye, once considered one of the hardest problems for

---

2. Dawkins, *God Delusion*, 110.
3. Weitz, "Role of Theory," 33.

evolutionary science, now looks almost trivial compared with the problem of the origin of human language."[4]

Modern scholarship has further compounded the problem. The uniqueness of the human language ability, the prevalence of so-called language universals, the extraordinary capacity of children to develop language despite a poverty of stimulus, and the increasing evidence for a sudden emergence rather than a gradual invention of language all pose a substantial challenge to Darwinism.

Darwinian Explanations

Linguistic behaviorists—led by American linguist and folk hero Daniel Everett—offer the simplest naturalist explanation: Language is a human invention that was developed piece by piece out of existing forms of communication. The success of the behaviorist approach hinges on the plausibility of the notion that human communication is quantitatively but not qualitatively different, a supposition that has been repeatedly challenged.

All efforts to teach human language to nonhuman primates failed. Aspirations of teaching vocal language to primates were downgraded to teaching nonvocal ASL (American Sign Language) and eventually to accepting a simplified GSL (Gorilla Sign Language), which has shown such meager success that it arguably does more to affirm the gap between man and primate than to close it. The inadequacy of the continuality model is also evident in the opposite direction. There simply does not appear to be any animal model from which human speech could have developed. Songbirds and primates are often cited as possibilities, yet neither delivers on its initial promise. Although birds acquire songs in a process parallel to human language acquisition, the abilities themselves are comparable only in a superficial sense, as birds lack the flexibility of grammar and other aspects of meaning that are found in human speech.[5] Primate communication, such as the specialized vocal calls of the vervet monkeys, is also unlikely as a protolanguage. These primate calls share no parallel acquisition process, and they appear to be triggered instinctually and do not occur in the absence of a referent. In fact, infant apes raised

---

4. Szathmáry, "Origin of the Human Language Faculty," 42.
5. Doupe and Kuhl, "Birdsong and Human Speech," 620.

in isolation or among other species of ape will still essentially produce all the species-specific calls.[6]

Another obstacle is the circular dependence of language and reason. The invention of a complex language requires a highly functioning reason faculty, while the reason faculty itself seems dependent in some degree on language. Furthermore, the surface-level differences in human languages are underscored by seemingly inexplicable linguistic similarities at a deeper level—auxiliaries and inversion rules, nouns and verbs, subjects and objects, phrases and clauses, case and agreement, and so on.[7] These language universals suggest a biological explanation rather than merely a cultural one. This has led the *linguistic nativists*, championed by Noam Chomsky, to argue for a language organ or grammar gene.

While the nativist approach arguably makes better sense of known language facts, it has several fundamental problems. First, whereas behaviorists claim continuality despite the lack of a feasible animal proto-language, nativists claim a biological language faculty despite no certainty of what, where, or how such a faculty works. No language organ or grammar gene has been discovered. The *Broca's area* and the *Wernicke's area* of the brain and the FOXP2 gene have all been presented as possibilities, but each is related only indirectly to speech and language. Linguistic nativist Steven Pinker admits, "No one has yet located a language organ or a grammar gene, but the search is on."[8]

Even if the hypothetical language organ is accepted, a second difficulty is how such a function could have developed through Darwinian means. Language provides little to no benefit or adaptive value for an individual outside a larger community that shares the ability. An individual with the language mutation would not recognize the ability's power and would be unable to pass it on to nongifted peers. Chomsky acknowledges, "It is perfectly safe to attribute this development to 'natural selection,' so long as we realize that there is no substance to this assertion, that it amounts to nothing more than a belief that there is some naturalistic explanation for these phenomena."[9]

Despite linguistic nativists and behaviorist's Promethean efforts, the human language ability remains puzzling. In an article titled "The

6. Pika et al., "Gestural Communication," 42.

7. Pinker, *Language Instinct*, 32.

8. Pinker, *Language Instinct*, 34.

9. Chomsky, *Language and Mind*, 85.

Mystery of Language Evolution," eight neo-Darwinian power-players made a shocking admission: "The richness of ideas is accompanied by a poverty of evidence, with essentially no explanation of how and why our linguistic computations and representations evolved."[10] There is an almost poetic irony that one of the realms of human life about which Darwinists have the least to say is speech itself.

A Theistic Explanation

Linguist Derek Bickerton concedes that the known facts of language "pose no problem for those who believe, as many still do, that we result from a unique act of creation," but for those who reject a supernatural world-view, as he does, the problems raised by language "must remain puzzling indeed."[11] Human language is less mystifying from a theistic perspective.

The Bible reveals that God created the universe through the spoken word. Adam's speech and his comprehension of God's commands indicate that early in creation, man already possessed a language faculty (which is not to be confused with possessing a *language*). God named things during creation and let man name things in Eden (Gen 2:19–20). Language was not, therefore, bestowed on Adam as a fully formed entity. God seems to have started the process and then handed the reins to Adam and his descendants. In doing so, God established one of the defining qualities of human language: the need to name things. The naming mandate is a biblical precedent not found elsewhere in nature.

Critics of linguistic nativism assert that the theories are often more reflective of a divine origin than a Darwinian one and are merely "invoking a miracle."[12] By replacing Chomsky's loosely gripped Darwinism with a biblical explanation, the most problematic aspects of language become sensible. The fundamental flaw of the nativist approach is not that it fails to account for the known facts of the language phenomena, but that such facts cannot easily be explained through a traditional conception of Darwinism.

As the idiom says, "If it looks like a duck and walks like a duck, it is probably a duck." Yet, nativist linguists have continued to argue for a pig, a horse, a cow—seemingly *any* animal will do—just so long as that

10. Hauser et al., "Mystery of Language Evolution," 1.

11. Bickerton, *Language & Species*, 2.

12. Everett, *How Language Began*, 71.

animal is not a duck. Thus, they present a theory with the appearance and hallmarks of a divine origin account but label it Darwinian.

If the language faculty emerged at once—as it appears it must have—then a divine explanation is better equipped to account for a linguistic big bang than is a naturalistic theory built on the mechanism of slow and gradual development. Ultimately, the precise details of the human language ability are as mysterious to theists as they are to naturalists. But a divine theory of language suffers from none of the dilemmas of inconsistency that naturalist accounts do. A divine origin of language was man's first assumption. It also remains his best.

The Challenge of Aesthetics

An exquisite poem makes a mockery of any reductive notion of literature as merely transferring information or ideas. Language is communicative by definition, but the five stanzas of William Butler Yeats's "The Wild Swans at Coole" represent something more. Literature is composed of words, but it is far more than words. Literature is *art*. From the verbosity of Charles Dickens to the crisp prose of Ernest Hemingway, literature's aesthetic dimension must be taken into account.

Darwinian Explanations

Darwin toiled to fit the concept of beauty into his evolutionary paradigm. The difficulty that the aesthetic dimension of nature poses for a Darwinian worldview is formidable, but a more particular problem for an explanation of literature is the uniqueness of human-created art.

Scholars who argue for animal artistic sensibilities occasionally conflate all aesthetics with art, e.g., when Richard Prum speaks of the peacock's tail feathers: "These superbirds are artworks in themselves, rare and special, and can be compared to highly refined human genres of art."[13] But Leo Tolstoy did not possess an *Anna Karenina* gene; the masterpiece was a purposeful creation. Art necessitates an artist. Any legitimate argument for animal artistry must go beyond the aesthetic characteristics of the animal itself.

Perhaps the most sensational argument for animal artistry is the emergence of "elephant art," which ranges from the innocent doodles

13. Rothenberg, *Survival of the Beautiful,* 77.

of an Asian elephant named Siri to the "elephant art" academy at which elephants are taught to paint self-portraits. The art has been described as "the sudden release of a spirit that has been pent up for a long time, an animal in a cage."[14] While undoubtedly a remarkable feat, elephant self-portraits are the result of human influence on the elephant, not an authentic aesthetic sensibility. The elephants paint only one picture—the one they have been taught through positive reinforcement. In fact, recent studies have suggested that the experience has a negative impact on the animals' welfare.[15]

The simplicity of Siri's minimalist sketches presents a stronger case, but an unconvincing one. Art implies a degree of presentation, intent, awareness, and sensibility. The sketches "seem right out of the minimalist canon of twentieth century art,"[16] only because the trainer removed the canvas at the right moment, as the elephant would continue muddling up the painting until the minimalist lines blended into a messy splotch. The elephants' activity can be interpreted as the emergence of an artistic sensibility only in an anthropomorphic sense.

Both birds and whales—nature's two famous musicians—are also frequently cited as proof of animal artistry. Both species' songs, however, are primarily communicative. They are perceived as artistry because the sounds are more pleasing to human ears than bleating goats or braying donkeys. Like a child looking at the clouds and seeing enchanting shapes, the only examples of animal art found in nature are those humans imagine.

If animals do not naturally create art, then why do humans? Denis Dutton suggests that art developed due to its role in courtship. Yet, in order for aesthetic sensibilities to factor into courtship, they must already be valued. Dutton creates a circular relationship in which art is valuable because suitors desired it, and suitors desired art because it was valuable. To avoid this pitfall, Dutton charts a path akin to Alfred Russell Wallace's by linking sexual selection with natural selection and declaring that art served as a fitness signifier. He compares art to large biceps or physical beauty, whereby the creation of art signifies the fitness of the brain in the same way muscular arms demonstrate fitness of the body. The analogy is contrived, however, because physical strength has clear survival advantages, while artistic ability does not. The capacity to write a haiku

---

14. Rothenberg, *Survival of the Beautiful*, 220.

15. English et al., "Is Painting by Elephants?," 471.

16. Rothenberg, *Survival of the Beautiful*, 220.

is an undependable indication of a person's ability to survive in a violent Darwinian world.

Steven Pinker attempts to circumvent these problems by using three related metaphors—recreational drugs, strawberry cheesecake, and pornography—to argue that art is a manufactured pleasure high akin to the *soma* drug in Aldous Huxley's *Brave New World*. Pinker's framework is dubious as a whole, but it is particularly inadequate regarding literature, which cannot be reduced to sensory pleasure in the same way the auditory and visual arts might. As a result, Pinker is forced instead to offer the metaphor of "a chess manual,"[17] opting for a utilitarian rather than an aesthetic function.

A Theistic Explanation

Natural theology holds that God's existence is made known through the beauty and sublimity of nature—Edmund Burke's famous two aesthetic modes of experience. The Bible also indicates that the beauty of human artistry acts in a similar manner. Regarding the tabernacle, the temple, and the ark of the covenant—the three physical Old Testament structures symbolic of God's physical dwelling amongst men—the biblical text reveals that the design patterns came from God himself. God provided humans with the source of beauty, the perception of beauty, and the mandate to create art and works of aesthetic pleasure. Both man's innate creativity and desire for beauty find their natural origin in two profound biblical propositions: "God created," and "God saw that it was good." Where naturalism has failed to account for these desires, the Bible provides their source, value, and motivation. Harriet Beecher Stowe writes, "In all ranks of life the human heart yearns for the beautiful; and the beautiful things that God makes are his gift to all alike."[18] Beauty is not merely a concept the Christian worldview explains; it is a reality that stems from the heart of its theology.

The Challenge of Literary Meaning

Language and aesthetics—two of Darwin's oldest and most difficult problems—have continued to haunt Darwinists like Dickens's first two

17. Pinker, *How the Mind Works*, 542.
18. Stowe, quoted in Ballou, *Treasury of Thought*, 49.

Christmas ghosts. With the problem of *literary meaning*, Darwinists encounter the third specter. American poet Ezra Pound declared, "Literature is language charged with meaning. Great literature is simply charged with meaning to the utmost degree."[19] Literary meaning is the "why" of literature—the reasons for writing and reading it. Literary meaning takes a carefully fashioned architectural structure and purposes it as a house to be entered, explored, and lived in.

Darwinian Explanations

The transition away from the building blocks of language—the linguistic and aesthetic elements—and toward literature's meaning is a path Darwinists enthusiastically tread. Joseph Carroll, a founding father of Literary Darwinism, summarizes his approach to literary criticism: "Adaptationist literary scholars . . . are convinced that through adaptationist thinking they can more adequately understand what literature is, what its functions are, and how it works—what it represents, what causes people to produce it and consume it, and why it takes the form that it does."[20]

Literary Darwinists ascribe a pragmatic motivation to the origin of humanity's storytelling urges. Pinker writes: "Life is like chess, and plots are like those books of famous chess games that serious players study so they will be prepared if they ever find themselves in similar straits."[21] But this utilitarian motivation for storytelling has several shortcomings.

First, a chess manual offers clear and easy application for a person preparing to play chess, but the same synergy cannot always be found between literature and life. Second, literature is often an exceedingly poor guide for real life, as Don Quixote, in Miguel de Cervantes's classic novel, discovers. Third, accounts of prior chess matches are an objective and trustworthy guide, whereas the outcomes of various characters' decisions in literature stem from the author's imagination, which is informed by personal bias, ignorance, and subjectivity. If the origin of storytelling is reduced to conveying practical wisdom and instructional content, then ancient man, without modern luxuries, would presumably be better off using a more straightforward means of accomplishing this objective. For Literary Darwinists, the influence of literature must be overwhelmingly

19. Pound, *ABC of Reading*, 28.
20. Carroll, *Literary Darwinism*, vii.
21. Pinker, *How the Mind Works*, 542.

positive, but literature has often been used to influence society negatively. For example, the propaganda literature of Nazi Germany cannot be said to lean naturally toward a higher morality.

The content of great literature is also problematic when assuming a Darwinian origin. Literary Darwinism is "relentlessly *thematic*. At the extreme, the theme is a kind of microversion of the story of natural selection itself. The Darwinian saga somehow becomes the very story of most fictions."[22] As a result, *Pride and Prejudice* becomes a Darwinian fable about mate selection, the *Iliad* is about the competition for resources, and *Hamlet* is about a young man's dilemma between self-interest and

22. Kramnick, "Against Literary Darwinism," 334 (emphasis original).

genetic self-interest.[23] Literary Darwinists are guilty of judging a book by its cover; they draw conclusions on the thematic material that are consistent with their theory, while largely missing the actual story.

Joseph Campbell's monomyth is imperfect and reductive as a comprehensive interpretative theory, but his wider point on the frequency of many motifs and narratives is indisputable. Whatever the reason—whether mystical or merely from a shared cultural history—a select number of themes and motifs have pervaded literature from the earliest preserved manuscripts to today. Darwinian literary criticism does not stumble in explaining the existence of universals but rather in accounting for the content of those universals. One of the most striking aspects of the monomyth, or any other archetypal paradigm, is how starkly anti-Darwinian it is.

Altruism and the Christ-figure motif have no parallel in nature. Romance—literature's favorite theme—is equally awkward for Darwinian literary criticism. Jane Austen's *Pride and Prejudice* is a favorite of the literary Darwinists, with its famed opening line providing ample fodder for a Darwinian interpretation.[24] Such interpretation overlooks Austen's biting satire and the book's assault on pragmatic mating. Similarly, literature's enduring fascination with good versus evil confronts readers with a conception of morality that is tricky to pin to a naturalistic worldview.

A narrative birthed out of a Darwinian world presumably consists of rising tension but no denouement—a continuous narrative of struggle and conflict with no happily ever after. This is not the story man has told. If Darwinism is responsible for man's desire to tell stories and the primary muse for those stories' content, then man has been a most ungrateful benefactor. Man has taken the storytelling gift and used it as a ladder to climb higher and grasp for a reality far removed from Darwinism.

A Theistic Explanation

Literary Darwinist Jonathan Gottschall imagines a scenario involving two tribes—the Story People and the Practical People—who are similar in every way other than the activities that give them their names. Faced with the gauntlet of natural selection, he writes, "Wouldn't most of us

23. Max, "Literary Darwinists."

24. "It is a truth universally acknowledged, that a single man in possession of a good fortune, must be in want of a wife."

have bet on the Practical People outlasting those frivolous Story People? The fact that they didn't is the riddle of all fiction."[25] The answer to the riddle, according to the Bible, is that the Practical People in Gottschall's scenario never existed. The human race has always been a people of stories—pupils learning at the feet of a great storyteller.

Christian theology holds that the Bible is God's revelation to man, and that revelation discloses that God is a literary being. Moreover, when God took on flesh in the incarnation of Christ, his primary teaching method was story and metaphor. In this way, the human creation of literature is simply a continuation of a literary heritage established by God at the creation of the world and given further validity through the storytelling of Christ. Whereas a Darwinian world cannot provide enough inherent utility to justify the emergence of man's otherwise trivial storytelling instinct, the Christian Bible—being itself a work of sublime literature—provides literature the highest possible endorsement and vindication.

Conclusion

Literature contains a magic that resists reduction to the cold microscopes of philosophical or scientific scrutiny. Perhaps the most potent evidence for a divine explanation of literature is simply the joy of settling into a cozy chair with a good book and surrendering oneself wholly to the experience. Literature is a staggering reminder that there is more to the universe than can be seen with the naked eye. Poetically, it is through the existence of one of man's greatest creations that he is pointed back to the reality of his own creation, and ultimately to the God who created him.

Bibliography

Ballou, Maturin M., ed. *Treasury of Thought: Forming an Encyclopedia of Quotations from Ancient and Modern Authors.* Boston: Houghton Mifflin, 1881.

Bickerton, Derek. *Language & Species.* Chicago: University of Chicago Press, 1990.

Carroll, Joseph. *Literary Darwinism: Evolution, Human Nature, and Literature.* New York: Routledge, 2004.

Chomsky, Noam. *Language and Mind.* 3rd ed. New York: Cambridge University Press, 2006.

Darwin, Charles. *On the Origin of Species.* 1859. Reprint. London: D. Appleton, 1861.

Dawkins, Richard. *The God Delusion.* Boston: Mariner, 2008.

25. Gottschall, *Storytelling Animal*, 19–20.

Doupe, Allison J., and Patricia K. Kuhl. "Birdsong and Human Speech: Common Themes and Mechanisms." *Annual Review of Neuroscience* 22.1 (July 1999) 567–631.

English, Megan, et al. "Is Painting by Elephants in Zoos as Enriching as We Are Led to Believe?" *PeerJ* 2 (July 2014) e471. https://peerj.com/articles/471/.

Everett, Daniel. *How Language Began: The Story of Humanity's Greatest Invention*. New York: Liveright, 2012.

Gottschall, Jonathan. *The Storytelling Animal: How Stories Make Us Human*. New York: Houghton Mifflin Harcourt, 2012.

Hardy, Thomas. "The Problem." In *Thomas Hardy: The Complete Poems*, edited by James Gibson, 120. Basingstoke, UK: Palgrave Macmillan, 2001.

Hauser, Marc D., et al. "The Mystery of Language Evolution." *Frontiers In Psychology* 5 (May 7, 2014) 1–12.

Kramnick, Jonathan. "Against Literary Darwinism." *Critical Inquiry* 37.2 (January 1, 2011) 315–47.

Max, D. T. "The Literary Darwinists." *The New York Times,* November 6, 2005. www.nytimes.com/2005/11/06/magazine/the-literary-darwinists.html.

Pika, Simone, et al. "The Gestural Communication of Apes." In *Benjamins Current Topics*, edited by Simone Pika et al., 35–49. Amsterdam: John Benjamins, 2007.

Pinker, Steven. *How the Mind Works*. New York: Norton, 2009.

———. *The Language Instinct: How the Mind Creates Language*. New York: HarperCollins, 2007.

Pound, Ezra. *ABC of Reading*. 1934. Reprint. New York: New Directions, 2010.

Rothenberg, David. *Survival of the Beautiful: Art, Science, and Evolution*. New York: Bloomsbury, 2013.

Szathmáry, Eörs. "The Origin of the Human Language Faculty: The Language Amoeba Hypothesis." In *New Essays on the Origins of Language*, edited by Jürgen Trabant and Sean Ward, 41–54. Berlin: De Gruyter, 2001.

Weitz, Morris. "The Role of Theory in Aesthetics." *The Journal of Aesthetics and Art Criticism* 15.1 (September 1956) 27–35.

By grounding architecture in primitive man's supposed needs on the African savannah, Richard Neutra misconstrued the nature of man and found himself repeatedly at odds with the historical testimony of great architecture. By insisting that "form follows function" and construing function in the most basic terms of survival, he sidelined the creative and aesthetic capacities and tendencies of humanity, given by God for human flourishing.

False Facades

The Implausibility of Neutra's Evolutionary Architecture

Eric Williamson

In the second book of Samuel, David finds himself at peace and dwelling in his new house in Jerusalem. David now had a kingly palace. Solomon would later build a house for God. Both were steeped in meaning: David's house displayed the kingship and the prominence of the nation; the future house of the Lord illustrated the people's dedication to the One who had been dedicated to them. No longer dwelling in a tent, the Lord's house was to be impressive. The design was so important that it was divinely articulated to the artisans. Solomon's Temple was a building full of beauty and ornament, all of which signified the glory of the Lord.

Most architects would agree that buildings represent something other than themselves. Some architects will dispute the connection of beauty and ornament with architecture, but they will acknowledge that their design points to meaning.

Richard M. Neutra is an important figure in the world of architecture. And, from a Christian perspective, he is also worth considering, not only because of his influence, but also because of the meaning he attempted to imbue in his design. Having apprenticed under Frank Lloyd Wright, Neutra helped introduce the International Style to America. In 1932, the Modern Museum of Art stated that he was one of the principle architects of international modernism. His architecture is also notable because of the evolutionary assumptions incorporated into his style. Neutra believed that his design attracted people due to "psychophysiological"[1] reflexes for survival.

Neutra's Architecture, Anthropology, and the Aesthetic

The modernist movement freed itself from the frivolous ornamentation of the past. The most notable slogan of the movement came from Louis Sullivan: "Form follows function."[2] Neutra's architectural approach was an attempt to draw out design based on evolutionary psychology. His homes look the way they do because of humanity's supposed evolutionary heritage. Because our primitive ancestors lived on the African savannah for eons, we are most comfortable living in similar conditions. Adhering to the International Style, Neutra relied on the rectilinear, meaning that his homes were composed of straight lines. Harkening back to our origins, these horizontal lines refresh our collective memory of the plain. The excessive use of glass provides perpetual views of nature. The setting could be dangerous, requiring shelter, so his homes provided both the comfort of nature as well as protection from it. Based on these assumptions, his homes were popular because they met our evolutionary needs.[3]

1. Neutra, quoted in Lavin, "Open the Box," 18.

2. Sullivan influenced Frank Lloyd Wright, one of the most well-known architects of the twentieth century. Neutra had a strong desire to work with Sullivan, but only met him later in Sullivan's life. See Hines, *Richard Neutra*.

3. Neutra scholar Sylvia Lavin states, "Neutra conceived of the glass house as an attempt to satisfy a psychoevolutionary need inherited from large primates. Locked in a constant state of being prey and predator, observer and observed, human beings desired architecture to provide shelter and panoramic views simultaneously" (Lavin, "Richard Neutra," 48–49).

These ideas are detailed in his work, *Survival through Design*.[4] His method, called "biorealism,"[5] sought to apply biological and behavioral research. He contended that the principles of architecture were drawn out of science, with its interest in survival and social goods, rather than from aesthetic theory.[6] "Tangible observation rather than abstract speculation will have to be the proper guide,"[7] and architects should shoulder a moral imperative, designing for the species, not the individual.[8]

According to Neutra, beauty is a spandrel—an evolutionary holdover that serves no purpose, but which isn't harmful. Ornate symbolism is no longer required because it has no function. Instead, the function of architecture is to protect people. Columns, which were once necessary, have no function due to the development of steel frames. Mathematics dominates the form of the building. Everything is computed and arranged according to physical principles and safety ordinances.

4. Originally published in 1954, the book witnessed numerous reprints. In the foreword to the thirtieth anniversary edition, his son, Raymond Neutra, states that the book was intended to help architects and their clients by grounding design in a solid foundation. Furthermore, "*Survival through Design* was the attempt of the general practitioner to use the then-available scientific information and his own experience so as to present guidelines for a biologically sound environment" (Neutra, *Survival through Design*, ix). Thomas Hines states, "Of all twentieth-century architects, he was the one most interested in and most knowledgeable about the biological and behavioral sciences. He wrote and lectured extensively on the psychological, physiological, and ecological dimensions of architecture" (Hines, *Richard Neutra*, 6). Hines claims that Neutra's book was particularly influential for its time.

5. Neutra, *Survival through Design*, viii.

6. For instance, his "Palace of Justice" in Orange County, California used "psychosomatic" principles in order to foster justice and fairness for the building's internal proceedings.

7. Neutra, *Survival through Design*, 7.

8. "There seems really one thing left to do; that is to by-pass speculative issues quietly, take heart, organize the procedure, and confidently attack the stupendous ubiquitous problem of design, as far as feasible, with an eye on tried inductive method. And never must we lose a sincere, enlightened interest in the ultimate consumer— our species as a whole. Whatever those theoretical convictions may be in which we sometimes like to indulge, for all practical purposes we seem *born* and *built to make anticipations*. Equipped with brains, as we are, we must plan and design. We cannot leave our salvation up to the old-fashioned brand of *Kismet*, nor to a new-fashioned one either" (Neutra, *Survival through Design*, 15 [emphasis original]).

Against Neutra's Anthropology

Neutra's influence shouldn't be underestimated. As a leading figure in the International Style, his impression surrounds us. While his homes were constructed decades ago, their semblance can be seen in familiar places. McDonald's, Wendy's, and Burger King have replaced their dated facades with rectilinear shapes and more glass. Trendier places, such as Panera and Starbucks, had already set the pace. It made sense for these healthier eateries to adopt a design that focuses on health. A visit to a redesigned McDonald's has the look of a health spa. It has dropped the iconic mansard roof for straight lines. The new face of McDonald's says that it's current, never mind that customers didn't have an issue with the old mansard roof; billions had been served under it.

To the contrary, the late Philip Johnson, another celebrity architect, once stated, "You cannot not know history."[9] With this remark, Johnson abandoned modernism. Though he'd once worked under the modernist icon, Mies van der Rohe, he rejected the purely functional aim of modern architecture.[10] In this vein, Witold Rybczynski, architectural writer and professor of architecture at the University of Pennsylvania, argues that history is critical for architecture. Buildings might not be intentionally reflective of icons of the past, but they are inevitably reminiscent of past styles.[11] The styles in history demonstrate a high degree of continuity

9. Johnson, "Whither Away-Non-Miesian Directions," 227. As a notable public figure, Johnson's history is troubled by his past political views. At one time, a supporter of the Nazi movement, he was suspected to be a German spy. Later in his career, he attempted to justify his former political position by claiming that it was before the "Jewish problem." Unlike Martin Heidegger's sullied career, Johnson's connection with the Nazi party has remained unexamined for the most part. For more on Johnson's political views, see Varnelis, "We Cannot Not Know History," 92–104.

10. In a documentary on his work, Johnson claims that form comes first. He believed the concept of the form came first, and then the architect has to find a use for it. "You have a foundation and you invent the function. It's not the other way around. It has nothing to do with functionalism. Someday I will beat that into the heads of the architects but that will take another century or so" (Wolf, *Philip Johnson*, 35:38–35:52). This is said in reference to his Ghost House on his estate in New Canaan, Connecticut. He had the form of the house before he knew what to do with it. In the same vein, Johnson's final words in the documentary are remarks about the fluctuating trends of architecture. He states, "I think architecture is going to be changed. Maybe" (Wolf, *Philip Johnson*, 51:12–51:15).

11. Rybczynski, *How Architecture Works*. Similarly, Mark Torgerson, professor of worship arts at Judson College, also sees the historical influence in architecture: "Architecture does not develop in a vacuum. Like all of the arts, architectural designs emerge

even within the diversity of design. This fact not only goes against the International Style, but against Neutra's belief that architecture is informed by our evolutionary ancestors and their habitat. Architecture shows that humans are not only comforted by lengthy horizontal lines, but also by curves and elevated designs.

In his historical survey on architecture, Vincent Scully describes two different approaches to design. It either "echoes the shapes of the landscape or contrasts with them."[12] Either way, the focus lies up current settings, not the prehistoric environment. If we concede Neutra's evolutionary inclinations, Native Americans should have designed structures that mirrored the landscape of their supposed African heritage rather than wigwams and hogans.

In contrast with Native American architecture, and in contrast to Neutra's view, Greek architecture departed representation, dealing in contrast. Their design incorporated abstract forms.[13] The apsidal house, or temple, was the forerunner to the dome. Later Greek temples fully fleshed out the emphasis of abstract geometrical forms. Scully goes on to argue that Roman Classical architecture emphasized space rather than the physical building itself. Unlike Neutra's "near-nature" approach, Scully said that Roman architecture sought to "enclose, to keep nature

---

from a combination of historical precedents, cultural influences, and the individual choices of architects and clients. No architect begins with nothing. All architects are shaped by the existing buildings around them, by the values and ideas of their culture, and by their own interpretations of life experiences" (Torgerson, *Architecture of Immanence*, 43). The same has been said about Frank Lloyd Wright's style. Art historian Nikolaus Pevsner agrees that Wright's achievement was a new vision but that it fused together "practical precedents" in American domestic architecture (Pevsner, *Sources of Modern Architecture*, 181). Although he borrowed these concepts from other architectural schools, Wright achieved what no other architect had been able to do. This aspect helps explain his expansive influence.

12. Scully, *Architecture*, 5. Scully notes that it's a general claim, but these separate approaches can be seen in Greek and non-Greek settings. Greek architecture contrasted with the landscape, while all other architecture mirrored it.

13. Scully understands this to be their representation of the rise of man's abilities and victories. Greek culture also honored heroes and gave sepulcher to their memory. He writes that the vases were "big, architectural hollows themselves, abstract in form, looming over the graves as emblems of the paternal curl and introducing into the old landscape a new shout of human grief and defiance" (Scully, *Architecture*, 48).

out, to trust in the manmade environment as a total construction."[14] He finds this form of architecture to project a concept of the transcendent.[15]

In Scully's timeline, the popularity of architectural landscaping demonstrated the intentional turn back to nature. But this is different from Neutra's characterization. Instead, the classic garden shows humanity's authority over nature, reflecting the personality of its owner, e.g., the gardens at Versailles. On this model, order wasn't to be found in haphazard wilderness. Rather, gardens reflected design by a designer, imposing his transcendent ideals on nature. Scully claims that this sort of garden architecture connected the real with the ideal.

History shows that design runs contrary to Neutra's evolutionary comforts. While domestic buildings were typically small and closed, the more important structures in the community did not align with straight lines and pure functionality. Ziggurats and pyramids did not align with the horizon. Some of these were free from ornament, but this isn't true for all of them. Later in history, cathedrals erupted across the horizon. These massive buildings were clothed in ornamentation. Their styles were later adopted and adapted for secular buildings such as hospitals, bridges, guildhalls, and residential colleges.

During the Renaissance, Andrea Palladio gathered the Roman style into the facades of his Italian Villas.[16] When he visited Rome in 1541, he applauded its classical form. For Palladio, the ancient ruins proved the worth of the architecture. Not only did they physically endure, they also gave testament to the transcending value of their beauty. Where kingdoms and cultures ebb and flow, Palladio believed that Roman architecture passed the harshest tests of time.[17]

14. Scully, *Architecture*, 111.

15. "Roman architecture eventually came to enclose space entirely, to create perfectly controlled interiors, set off from the messy inconsistencies of the natural order. Therefore, the Pantheon was a planetarium and Hagia Sophia a perfect embodiment of Neoplatonic wisdom in its condensation of the ideal shapes of circle and square. All that was the foundation of medieval architecture in Western Europe, where the major preoccupation remained the creation of transcendent interior space" (Scully, *Architecture*, 110).

16. He was born Andrea di Pietro. As was common to the time, architects would often change their name. "Palladio" derives from the Latin for "wise."

17. In his third book on architecture, Palladio commented on his appraisal of Roman architecture: "And to every one, that is not altogether void of judgment, it may be very manifest, how good the method was, which the ancients observed in building, since after so much time, and after so many ruins and mutations of empires, there still remain both in Italy, and out of it, the vestiges of so many of their sumptuous edifices, by which we are

This appreciation for contrast has continued through the history of architecture, extending into modern times, with no less a personage than Le Corbusier (1887–1967). His most famous home, Villa Savoye, lifts the structure off the ground.[18] Finally, responding to the simplistic nature of modernism's less-is-more style, postmodern architect Robert Venturi proclaims, "less is a bore."[19] Rather than form's following function, Venturi argues that architecture necessarily contains contradictions. If there were multiple functions to the form, then architecture was no simple art form. He believed that modernists, such as Mies, overlooked architectural problems in order to promote simplicity. Similar to Palladio, Venturi looked to styles from the past. Unlike Palladio, Venturi irreverently transgressed architectural rules.[20] So diversity, even confusion, rules. As Rybczynski puts it plainly: "Stylistic consensus is unusual."[21]

This short glimpse into architecture's history presents a few problems for Neutra's evolutionary anthropology. If the human predilection desires evolutionary comforts, we should find a uniform style in architecture.[22]

---

able to get at a certain knowledge of the Roman virtue and grandeur, which perhaps had not otherwise been believed. (Palladio, *Four Books of Architecture*, 147).

18. This aspect is one of his five points of "new architecture." The Villa Savoye effectively showcases all five points (Le Corbusier, *Towards a New Architecture*).

19. Venturi, *Complexity and Contradiction*, 17.

20. Ada Louise Huxtable, architecture critic for *The New York Times*, once described his approach (along with his firm) as a "religious war." In turn, this explains why the architectural world initially rejected Venturi's approach. "Almost everything that the Venturis have to say is heresy, if you have been brought up as a true believer in modern architectural doctrine as formulated in the early part of this century. Everything Venturi and Rauch designs is a slap in the face of the true believers. And to use irony or wit in the pursuit of either theory or design—as a tool to shock awareness or as a comment on the cultural condition—is the original sin" (Huxtable, "Plastic Flowers Are Almost All Right," D22).

21. Rybczynski, *Look of Architecture*, 79.

22. In my own town of Asheville, North Carolina, neighborhoods illustrate styles threading history. The oldest neighborhoods represent Victorian and Queen Anne Victorian. Many of the homes were developed in the Barber-style from Knoxville architect, George Barber. Jack Thomson, executive director of Asheville's Preservation Society, sees these older neighborhoods as representations of the architectural development of the time. While the older neighborhoods have a Victorian basis, they also contain homes in a distinctive Arts & Crafts design that followed the older ones. Because of the outdoorsy backdrop of Asheville, Arts & Crafts burgeoned. A neighborhood's architecture reveals its age and its span of development. Thomson notes the diversity of expression in one Asheville neighborhood: "'[Albemarle Park] was developed in a very expressive way . . . so you'll have a Dutch Colonial house with a gambrel roof, a large Rustic Revival log-style house, a stucco-finish house that feels like you're

The diversity of style shows that there is no universal design fit for architecture. For one thing, architects sampled above discuss the inevitable influence of the client, whose demands alter the design plans. What's more, the architect himself has his stylistic inclinations. And these variations have shown themselves throughout history. If Neutra were correct, then we should witness an abundance of the rectilinear and unornamented buildings and homes throughout history. It is just the reverse. Besides, the savannah model is doubtful. Those living on the African plains would be in constant fear of predators and rival communities. In this case, the comforting design does not match up with a Neutra house, but rather with a man cave. A guarded, easily defended abode sounds more like it; indeed, an early realtor would have had a difficult sale trying to get a primate to settle into a glass box.

Argument against Neutra's Aesthetic

Neutra's reductive anthropology leads to a reductive aesthetic. He reduces human needs to basic physical needs, implying that humans are nothing more than matter and need nothing more than matter. While he does attempt to meet psychological needs, he misses our complexity. His modern style can be inhospitable and unlivable, indifferent to privacy and physical comfort. Both of these issues impact two icons of the International Style: Mies van der Rohe's Farnsworth House and Philip Johnson's Glass House. Their bucolic setting may save privacy, but it is largely impractical in urban settings or subdivisions. And they both have problems with energy efficiency and temperature control. It's implausible to think that this sort of house can be the paragon of domestic architecture. Indeed, Mies's biographers, Franz Schulze and Edward Windhorst, write that the Farnsworth House is more like a temple than an abode. "It rewards aesthetic contemplation before it fulfills domestic necessity."[23]

Reducing man to a simple biological organism makes health a main focus of modern domestic architecture. However, the health benefits are limited, particularly for Neutra's style. Studies in environmental

---

in Normandy, a Swiss chalet-type house and a Georgian Revival. The architectural vocabulary is very diverse and tied more to diversity of expression during a condensed timeline" (West, "Best Nests," para. 10).

23. Schulze and Windhorst, *Mies van der Rohe*, 256. They note that because Mies didn't want to forsake the openness of the house, he rejected any screens to shield the sun, turning the house into a "cooker."

psychology have found that excessive exposure to straight lines (the rectilinear) overstimulates and causes stress. In one study, neuroscientists found evidence that individuals have an improved emotional response to curvilinear forms.[24] Once again, Neutra's design doesn't fit his evolutionary assumptions or his dictum that any design hindering survival should be abandoned or augmented.[25]

Neutra believed that natural selection eliminated anything that had no purpose. Thus, he dispensed with ornament and beauty, convinced that they no longer had a function, analogous to the human appendix.[26] This belief tracks with the contemporary notion that most of our DNA is useless: junk DNA. However, the idea of junk DNA is currently facing counterevidence.[27] Francis Collins, a theistic evolutionist and former head of the Human Genome Project, has recently backed away from the junk argument.[28]

Aside from biological and psychological evidence, architecture has shown a resistance to Neutra's idea of beauty. Palladio's influence is pervasive. James Ackerman, professor of art at Harvard University, contends that Palladio is the most imitated architect of all time.[29] Much of his influence was due to his work, *The Four Books on Architecture*. Most architects

24. Vartanian et al., "Impact of Contour," 10446–53. The irony, especially for Neutra, is that this article resulted from a conference discussing evolution and neuroscience: "In the Light of Evolution VII: The Human Mental Machinery," in 2013, at the National Academies of Sciences and Engineering in Irvine, California.

25. "Any design that impairs and imposes excessive strain on the natural human equipment should be eliminated, or modified in accordance with the requirements of our nervous and, more generally, our total physiological functioning. This principle is our only operational criterion in judging design or any detail of man-made environment, regardless of how difficult it may seem to apply the principle in specific cases. We must keep in mind that in nature even minor deficiencies in adaptation have in the long run obliterated entire species. Obscure, seemingly insignificant elements of our man-made environment may produce disastrous effects" (Neutra, *Survival through Design*, 86).

26. Neutra, *Survival through Design*, 47.

27. The ENCODE (The Encyclopedia of DNA Elements) project claims their findings reveal 80 percent of DNA is functional. The ENCODE Consortium, "Integrated Encyclopedia of DNA Elements," 57–74.

28. "In terms of junk DNA, we don't use that term anymore because I think it was pretty much a case of hubris to imagine that we could dispense with any part of the genome, as if we knew enough to say it wasn't functional . . . Most of the genome that we used to think was there for spacer turns out to be doing stuff." Francis Collins, J. P. Morgan Healthcare Conference, 2015, quoted in Olasky, "Admission of Function."

29. Ackerman, *Palladio*.

who imitated Palladio had never actually visited his buildings. However, they embraced his approach to design, incorporating his style in buildings around the globe. In the United States, Palladio's touch is clearly seen in Thomas Jefferson's Monticello as well as his design of the University of Virginia. Much of the architecture in Washington, DC is considered to be in the Palladian school. Philosopher George Berkeley's home, Whitehall, in Rhode Island, is considered to be the first Palladian home in New England. Even the popular Georgian style is heavily Palladian.[30]

Palladio believed that architecture imitated nature and following its instruction leads to the "true, good and beautiful method of building."[31] In his work, he echoed the perspective of the Roman architect, Vitruvius, whose formula for *good* architecture aimed at three components: strength, function, and delight.[32] In order for a building to be a good building it must endure, it must be hospitable, and it must be visually pleasing.

Conclusion

Contrary to Neutra's architecture and aesthetic approach, the experience of beauty draws us beyond the material world. Ironically, Neutra's straight lines can't be found in nature. Indeed, as with Roman classicalism, geometrical forms are manifest in Neutra homes. In one way, I agree with Neutra: Our drives to build and design are informed by our ancestors. We want to build. We want to cultivate. But it's not because we've evolved; it's because we've been created in the image of God. He is the first designer, and his design is good. He also instructed our first ancestors to care for the garden and to oversee his creation, a directive which has worked out, in part, in depictions of nature in buildings. The instructions for Solomon's Temple included the representation of flora and fauna, looking back to Eden.[33]

---

30. Witold Rybzcynski states, "The Georgian style is basically Palladian" (*Perfect House*, 125). Palladio's influence is visible on many churches in the United States. James Gibbs was an English architect in the eighteenth century. His design for the church, St. Martin in the Fields, influenced numerous churches in England and in the United States. Similar to Palladio, Gibbs's book helped spread his designs to other architects (Gibbs, *Gibbs' Book of Architecture*).

31. Palladio, *Four Books of Architecture*, 47.

32. In the Latin, *firmitas, utilitas,* and *venustas.*

33. See 1 Kings 6. Also, see Beale, *Temple and the Church's Mission.*

Mark Robbins, the former dean of the School of Architecture at Syracuse University, claims that the home defines us.[34] Indeed, what we've built through the centuries reveals a good deal about us, and the signs don't point to an evolutionary mechanism. Rather, they indicate a fixed but creative nature, grounded in the *imago Dei*, a nature attuned to good sense and aesthetic sensibility, all of them gifts of God.

Bibliography

Ackerman, James S. *Palladio*. New York: Penguin, 1991.

Beale, G. K. *The Temple and the Church's Mission: A Biblical Theology of the Dwelling Place of God*. Downers Grove, IL: InterVarsity, 2004.

The ENCODE Consortium. "An Integrated Encyclopedia of DNA Elements In the Human Genome." *Nature* 489 (September 6, 2012) 57–74.

Gibbs, James. *Gibbs' Book of Architecture*. Mineola, NY: Dover, 2008.

Hines, Thomas S. *Richard Neutra and the Search for Modern Architecture: A Biography and History*. Los Angeles: University of California Press, 1994.

Huxtable, Ada Louise. "Plastic Flowers Are Almost All Right." *The New York Times*, October 10, 1971. https://www.nytimes.com/1971/10/10/archives/plastic-flowers-are-almost-all-right.html.

Johnson, Philip. "Whither Away-Non-Miesian Directions." In *Philip Johnson Writings*, edited by Peter Eisenman and Robert A. M. Stern, 227–38 . New York: Oxford University Press, 1979.

Kwan, Kai-man. *The Rainbow of Experiences, Critical Trust, and God: A Defense of Holistic Empiricism*. New York: Continuum, 2011.

Lamster, Mark. *The Man in the Glass House: Philip Johnson, Architect of the Century*. New York: Little, Brown, 2018.

Lavin, Sylvia. "Open the Box: Richard Neutra and the Psychology of the Domestic Environment." *Assemblage* 40 (December 1999) 6–25.

———. "Richard Neutra and the Psychology of the American Spectator." *Grey Room* 1 (Fall 2000) 42–63.

Le Corbusier. *Towards a New Architecture*. Translated by Frederick Etchells. Mineola, NY: Dover, 1986.

Lindeberg, H. T. *Domestic Architecture of H. T. Lindeberg*. New York: Acanthus, 2003.

Neutra, Richard. *Survival through Design*. New York: Institute for Survival, 1984.

Olasky, Marvin. "Admission of Function: Junking Slurs About 'Junk DNA.'" *World Magazine*, June 24, 2016. https://wng.org/articles/admission-of-function-1620609700.

Palladio, Andrea. *The Four Books of Architecture*. Translated by Adolf K. Placzek. Mineola, NY: Dover, 1965.

Pennoyer, Peter, and Anne Walker. *Harrie T. Lindeberg and the American Country House*. New York: Monacelli, 2017.

Pevsner, Nikolaus. *The Sources of Modern Architecture and Design*. London: Thames and Hudson, 1989.

34. Robbins, "Preface," 9.

Robbins, Mark. "Preface." In *Modern American Housing: High-Rise, Reuse, Infill*, edited by Peggy Tully, 8–12. New York: Princeton Architectural, 2013.

Rybczynski, Witold. *How Architecture Works: A Humanist's Toolkit*. New York: Farrar, Straus, and Giroux, 2013.

———. *The Look of Architecture*. New York: Oxford University Press, 2003.

———. *The Perfect House: A Journey with the Renaissance Master Andrea Palladio*. New York: Scribner, 2002.

Schulze, Franz, and Edward Windhorst. *Mies van der Rohe: A Critical Biography, New and Revised*. Chicago: University of Chicago Press, 1995.

Scully, Vincent. *Architecture: The Natural and the Manmade*. New York: St. Martins, 1991.

Swinburne, Richard. *The Existence of God*. New York: Oxford, 1979.

Torgerson, Mark. *An Architecture of Immanence: Architecture for Worship and Ministry Today*. Grand Rapids: Eerdmans, 2007.

Varnelis, Kazys. "'We Cannot Not Know History': Philip Johnson's Politics and Cynical Survival." *Journal of Architectural Education* 49.2 (November 1995) 92–104.

Vartanian, Oshin, et al. "Impact of Contour on Aesthetic Judgments and Approach-avoidance Decisions in Architecture." *Proceedings of the National Academy of Sciences* 110 (June 18, 2013) 10446–53.

Venturi, Robert. *Complexity and Contradiction in Architecture*. New York: Little, Brown, 1988.

West, Kay. "Best Nests: Finding a Home in Asheville's Distinctive Neighborhoods." *Mountain Xpress*, July 17–23, 2019. https://mountainx.com/news/finding-a-home-in-asheville/.

Wolf, Barbara, dir. *Philip Johnson: Diary of an Eccentric Architect*. New York: Checkerboard Film Foundation, 1996, DVD.

Atheist Denis Dutton did remarkable work in identifying artistic and aesthetic commonalities throughout the world, thus providing an antidote to the cultural relativism associated with these phenomena. Unfortunately, his commitment to a naturalistic, evolutionary account of things caused him to miss the more obvious and sustainable explanation that God is the author of the skill and delight in play when we create and receive works of imagination and craft.

Theism and Universal Signatures of the Arts

PAUL R. SHOCKLEY

"Human beings are born image-makers and image-enjoyers."

—DENIS DUTTON[1]

THE ARTS ARE CELEBRATED, cherished, and cultivated in *every* culture. The imagery. The colors. The movements. The sounds. The arts offer historical markers of a given generation. They disclose our communities' moral, political, and social conditions and promote human relationships that transcend cultural, ethnic, and religious boundaries. They have a predictive power not found in charts, polls, and statistics.[2] They reflect something of our souls, express longings for something greater within, and mirror conditions of our situational settings. They disclose who and what we are and what we live for, and they enable us to envision possibilities of what could be. The arts are powerful. They can affect dramatic personal and social change.[3] Undervalued as a critical source of scholarship, the arts are worthy of investment by academic institutions and programs.

Though the arts differ in time and clime, artists worldwide speak about a fire within, an impulse, a compulsion—a drive to create art,

1. Dutton, *Art Instinct,* 33.
2. Dewey, *Art as Experience*, 342.
3. Brooks, "How Artists Changed the World."

dance, and music in the communities in which they are embedded. This feature is an intrinsic part of their humanity, giftedness, and imagination. Using the power of a brush, musical notes, and movement, they cultivate aesthetic qualities that give us pause and relief from the mundane, from our daily grind, and from our various sufferings and problems in life.[4] While the arts are vast and varied, they are tied together by certain underlying features, known as aesthetic universals.

In what follows, I will summarize Denis Dutton's (1944–2010) rich contribution to philosophical aesthetics, wherein he makes an empirical case for aesthetic universals.[5] I'll offer an evaluation, in which I affirm the use of aesthetic universals as empirical evidence against cultural relativism. (However, Dutton's commitment to evolutionary naturalism is irrational for the basis of aesthetic universals; it is logically self-defeating.) Then I'll argue that a more probable source for aesthetic universals is found in theism. We can justify this conclusion by appealing to a cumulative case for God's existence, Judeo-Christianity, and the application of coherence.[6]

Dutton's Case for Aesthetic Universals

Underpinning art is something all too easily overlooked, neglected, and marginalized. Today, we focus on the diversity of the arts to the neglect of its universal features. The emphasis on relativism in popular culture contributes to the neglect of artistic universals, aesthetic signatures, and common notions of everyday beauty that transcend our cultural and social constructs.

As an evolutionist and naturalist, philosopher Denis Dutton argues that the arts are evolutionary adaptations.[7] Nevertheless, in his 2003 work, *Art Instinct: Beauty, Pleasure, and Human Evolution*, he offers an empirical case for twelve universal signatures of beauty, inclusive core items which "cross cultures and historical epochs."[8] He says, "It is time to look at the arts in the light of Charles Darwin's theory of evolution—to

---

4. Shockley, *Worship as Experience*, 25–26.

5. Dutton, *Art Instinct*; Dutton, "Aesthetic Universals," 203–14.

6. Shockley and Prezas, *Thinking with Excellence*, 48–56.

7. Dutton, *Art Instinct*, 4.

8. Dutton, *Art Instinct*, 51.

talk about instinct and art,"[9] and asserts that the arts and our desires for them involve "prehistoric tastes" shared across the world today.[10]

He begins by surveying the thought of Aristotle, Tolstoy, Hume, Kant, Schiller, and Bell, all of them arguing for universal standards, concluding,

> All such attempts to identify universal features of art share an element in common: they presuppose or posit the existence of a fundamental human nature, a set of characteristics, including interests and desires, uniformly and cross-culturally present in the constitutions of human persons.[11]

Dutton's Justification for Human Universalism Is Darwinian Evolution

Dutton's view of shared humanity is Darwinian evolutionary naturalism. In this vein, he contends that after we first look to the past to discover adaptations from our "ancestral environment," we can then examine culture and history to understand how "evolved adaptations, strictly conceived, are modified, extended, or ingeniously enhanced—or even repressed—in human life."[12] Thus, we discover the infusion of ancient evolutionary "interests, preferences, and capacities in our aesthetic appreciations, interests, practices, and values."[13] He goes on,

> The explanatory power of evolutionary psychology lies foremost in identifying adaptations . . . A Darwinian aesthetics will achieve explanatory power neither by proving that art forms are adaptations nor by dismissing them as a byproduct but by showing their existence and character are connected to Pleistocene interests, preferences, and capacities.[14]

And he continues,

> Evolutionary psychology postulates that human pleasures, such as the pleasures of sex or the enjoyment of sweet and fatty foods, have their genesis in evolutionary history: our ancestors

9. Dutton, *Art Instinct*, 3.

10. Dutton, *Art Instinct*, 3.

11. Dutton, "Aesthetic Universals," 204.

12. Dutton, "Aesthetic Universals," 98.

13. Dutton, "Aesthetic Universals," 91.

14. Dutton, "Aesthetic Universals," 96.

who actively enjoyed sex and consumed fats and carbohydrates survived and left more living offspring than those who did not. The same argument can be applied to countless other aspects of the emotional dispositions of human beings, including, for example, responses to human faces and comportment, or the threats and opportunities presented by the natural world and its flora and fauna. The argument can also be applied to art and its content.[15]

Along the way, he identifies a set of *cluster criteria*, "signal characteristics of art considered as a universal, cross-cultural category."[16] He says, "Some of the items single out features of works of arts; others, qualities of the experience of art."[17] He also acknowledges that he does not claim that these universal signatures are unique to art.[18] So here they are:

1. Direct pleasure. The arts are "valued as a source of immediate experiential pleasure in itself." In other words, stories, artifacts, or performances are a source of gratification, aside from practical, functional uses.

2. Skill and virtuosity. The arts require and demonstrate the "exercise of specialized skills." Artistic abilities, practices, and training are cherished, emphasized, and honored.

3. Style. According to "rules of form, composition, or expression," the arts we create are in recognizable genres.

4. Novelty and creativity. Original, unpredictable arts are valued and praised.

5. Criticism. The language of judgment and appreciation is evident in evaluating the arts, whether formally or straightforwardly.

6. Representation. In varying degrees, the arts "represent or imitate real and imaginary experiences of the world."

7. Special focus. The arts tend to be "bracketed off from ordinary life, made a separate and dramatic focus of the experience."

---

15. Dutton, "Aesthetic Universals," 207–8.
16. Dutton, "Aesthetic Universals," 210–11; Dutton, *Art Instinct*, 51–52.
17. Dutton, *Art Instinct*, 51.
18. Dutton, *Art Instinct*, 52.

8. Expressive individuality. "The potential to express individual personality is generally latent in art practices, whether or not it is fully achieved."

9. Emotional saturation. In differing degrees, works of art are "shot through with emotion." These emotions can be aroused by the art's content and/or prompted by artistic tone distinct from the represented content.

10. Intellectual challenge. Works of art are inclined to "utilize the combined variety of human perceptual and intellectual capacities to the full extent."

11. Art traditions and institutions. Works of art are designed according to (and, to a certain extent, given significance by) their position "in the history and traditions of their art."

12. Imaginative experience. Considered to perhaps be the most important feature among the twelve, art objects offer "an imaginative experience for both producers and audiences."[19]

Evaluating Dutton

In sizing up his account, we should look to the criteria of empirical adequacy, viability, explanatory power, pragmatic value, and existential relevance.[20] To make his case, he is generous with examples, as he speaks of soaring larks, jaw-dropping piano virtuosity, Russian icon painting, Pueblo pottery, the criticism of critics by critics, "lattice-crust cherry pie," a Chekhov story, and world-record track-and-field performances.

His aesthetic universals pull together values and practices we cultivate, celebrate, and memorialize in civic events, special gatherings, rituals, and sacred spaces.[21] We identify with these artistic signatures, and they with us.[22] One thinks of the Eiffel Tower, Stonehenge, Jerusalem's Temple Mount, the Roman Colosseum, and Japanese gardens. Even in rural areas, the celebration of, and competitions among, choice fruit and vegetables take on art forms and practices that involve these universals.

---

19. Dutton, *Art Instinct*, 51–58.

20. Shockley and Prezas, *Thinking with Excellence*, 48–56.

21. Shockley, *Worship as Experience*, 35–38.

22. Shockley, *Worship as Experience*, 19.

Wine competitions, livestock judging, and Fashion Week events in Paris are rich with these markers. Everywhere you turn, you find artful aspects in play, even in kung fu, whatever the class or social division. East and West, classically or currently, these universals manifest themselves as they are woven into the fabric of communities and societies.

And the benefits are manifold. They contribute to creating national masterpieces, setting apart or distinguishing one group of people from others and serving as cultural, social, and religious identifiers. And there are economic benefits. We create the arts, and the arts affect us.[23] They can contribute to temporal and enriching experiences of meaning, purpose, and significance, whether one is the artist or spectator, performer or audience, writer or reader.

I applaud Dutton's scholarship. His understanding of anthropology and aesthetic philosophy is excellent, and his work stands against relativism in these matters (a position holding that epistemic beliefs, moral virtues, duties, values, and aesthetic standards acquire their validity only through the approval of culture alone).[24] Nevertheless, his reliance on evolutionary naturalism is flawed and demonstratively inferior to the account offered by theists.

The mere fact that various arts emerge from different cultures does not imply that aesthetic universals do not exist. Proponents of objective values, whether moral or aesthetic, do not necessarily dismiss the importance of diversity, multiculturalism, and freedom of expression.[25]

Suppose a relativist contends that valid aesthetic values or judgments are exclusively a *product of culture* and that different cultures will have different standards. In that case, the relativist commits the fallacy of reductionism, for he does not adequately consider other competing sources such as the *human* powers of creative reasoning and capacities, existential drives within, felt needs, and biological and familial factors.

If relativism is true, then one cannot legitimately criticize the arts. Expert critics, participants, and patrons of the art world are only expressing their opinions, for they do not have an objective basis for evaluation. Any clear, accurate distinction between what is art and what isn't is ambiguous; prescriptive judgments about the instrumental use of the arts in the organized life of the community are viewed as mere power plays;

23. Shockley, *Worship as Experience*, 33.
24. Pojman and Fieser, *Ethics*, 253.
25. Wreen, "How Tolerant?" 329–39.

and the altruistic value of supporting the arts is dismissed. One cannot even use the arts to determine whether a particular community is getting worse or better, for there is no objective aesthetic standard to make such an evaluation. Consequently, all that remains is a cacophony of opinions from vested interests, vying for social clout.

So Dutton manages to avoid this relativism, but he runs into big problems of his own. For instance, he encounters distinguished philosopher Alvin Plantinga's epistemological critique of purely naturalistic reasoning.[26] Plantinga argues that evolution is not about logical argumentation, abstract reasoning, and accurate conclusions drawn from empirical data. Instead, evolution is about the survival of the fittest and the propagation of the genes. Combined with naturalism, whereby our neurology dictates our behavior and beliefs for the sake of adaptation, Dutton's position devalues itself.

26. Plantinga, *Where the Conflict Really Lies*, 344–45.

The Cumulative Case Approach Favoring Theism

Better to track with the observation of Roger Scruton: "Art, as we have known it, stands on the threshold of the transcendental. It points beyond this realm of accidental and disconnected things to another realm, in which human life is endowed with an emotional logic that makes suffering noble and love worthwhile."[27] And theism serves this conviction best. Not surprisingly, a broad range of philosophical, historical, religious, existential, and biblical data coalesce to affirm the probability of God's existence and his being the ultimate source for aesthetic universals. We have good reasons to make this claim by justifying this position with logical consistency, evidence, existential relevance, workability, and viability.[28]

Suppose we synthesize the cosmological, *Kalam* cosmological, ontological, teleological, and moral arguments for God's existence along with arguments based on desire, religious need, and innate ideas. Then we have a reasonable basis to believe that there is a divine order and design to reality and the nature of our humanity. The ordering and design of creation have evidential justification with discoveries made on biological levels (e.g., irreducible complexity, specified complexity, and DNA information) and cosmology (the anthropic principle). The evidence for objective moral values and duties is also confirmed in our reactions when we are the object of immoral or unjust actions and in the moral judgments we make when we observe horrific evils like genocide, human trafficking, and racism. Thus, the idea that we are the accidental byproduct of time, energy, and chance becomes unlikely. The claim that the universal aspects of our humanity are design-related is more probable—and that applies to our taste for beauty.

Analogues to the Moral Argument

Moral arguments for the existence of God begin with the assumption that we believe there is a moral law binding upon mankind, for why else

---

27. Scruton, *Beauty*, 156.

28. Though it is beyond the scope to unpack every argument, evidence, and existential proof, significant resources are available, such as Craig, *Reasonable Faith*; Geisler and Turek, *I Don't Have Enough Faith*; Habermas, *Historical Jesus*; Kaiser, *Tough Questions;* Kreeft and Tacellie, *Handbook of Christian Apologetics*; Lewis, *Mere Christianity*; Pearcey, *Finding Truth*; Plantinga, *God, Freedom, and Evil;* and Schaeffer, *God Who Is There.*

would we offer excuses to each other? And since we recognize a moral law, we should posit a transcendent lawgiver—God. Similarly, we could argue from shared recognition of such a thing as beauty, pressing the skeptic to account for such a thing.

To sketch this out, we can draw from three versions of the moral argument, those supplied by C. S. Lewis (1898–1963), Hastings Rashdall (1858–1924), and W. R. Sorley (1855–1935). Consider the following three:[29]

1. Beauty implies a mind of beauty;

2. There is objective beauty;

3. Therefore, there is an objective mind of beauty.[30]

Second:

1. An absolutely perfect ideal of beauty exists (at least psychologically in our minds);

2. An absolutely perfect idea of beauty can exist only if there is an absolutely perfect mind of beauty;

   a. Ideas can only exist if there are minds, for thoughts depend on thinkers;

   b. Absolute ideas depend on an Absolute Mind (not an individual mind like ours);

3. Hence, it is rationally necessary to postulate an Absolute Mind as the basis for the absolutely perfect idea of beauty.[31]

And third:

1. There must be objective beauty; otherwise,

   a. There would not be such significant agreement on its meaning;

   b. No fundamental disagreements of beauty would ever have occurred, each person being right from his own perspective.

   c. No value judgment of beauty would ever have been wrong, each being subjectively right.

29. Shockley, *Worship as Experience*, 199–202. These three aesthetic arguments were initially presented in PowerPoint, "Can Beauty Point Us to God?" at https://pr-shockley.com/aesthetics; cf. Geisler, *Baker's Encyclopedia*, 498–500.

30. Shockley, *Worship as Experience*, 199.

31. Shockley, *Worship as Experience*, 201.

d. No question of beauty could ever be discussed, there being no objective understanding of beauty;

e. Contradictory views would both be right, since opposites could be equally correct.

2. Objective beauty is beyond individual persons and beyond humanity as a whole:

a. It is beyond individual persons, since they often sense a conflict with beauty/ugliness;

b. It is beyond humanity as a whole, for they measure the progress of civilization by its art-products in terms of beauty.

3. Objective beauty must come from an objective Mind of beauty because:

a. Beauty has no meaning unless it comes from a mind; only minds emit meaning;

b. Beauty is meaningless unless it is a meeting of mind with mind, yet people inherently desire to experience beauty;

4. Hence, the discovery of, and desire for, beauty makes sense only if there is a Mind or Person behind it.

5. Therefore, God exists.[32]

Religious Experiences

Religious experiences complement this idea of divine ordering, and design for these structures is not accidental. Spiritual experiences include the witnesses of general revelation, such as creation, design, conscience, and Godward longings. Memorable encounters with God, changed lives, internal peace, bona fide miracles, answered prayer, and enduring meaning and significance all attest to the probable existence of God. Lastly, aesthetic experiences point us beyond ourselves to God. They can be transcultural, such as when a range of different people are looking upon a great work of art, listening to a song, or watching a dance performance. How do we best account for their existence and transcultural effect? Once again, it points us to a specific ordering of reality reflective of a Design Maker.

---

32. Shockley, *Worship as Experience*, 200–201.

The Historicity of Jesus Christ and the Scriptures

Of course, the philosophers don't have the last word. If we add the historical and evidential claims made by Judeo-Christianity, such as God's presence among his people; the incarnation, teachings, miracles, and bodily resurrection of Jesus Christ; and the plain, normative, and factual fulfillment of predictive prophecies, then we have additional grounding for aesthetic universals. Jesus Christ confirmed the reliability of Scripture. Given the embarrassment of riches from manuscript evidence (over 7,000 known New Testament manuscripts and portions thereof), the historical reliability of biblical Scripture, and the uniqueness of this Scripture compared with other religious texts, we have good reasons to believe in the historical claims of the Bible.

Existential Aspects of Our Personhood

We possess Godward longings—existential struggles that reveal our need for God and point us beyond ourselves, especially after discovering that nothing on earth can satisfy these aspects of our human condition. Some of these Godward longings include the quest for personal meaning, purpose, and significance. We are looking for someone we can believe in, the realization of hope, and a worthwhile existence. We long for genuine love—and for love in return—and forgiveness for wrongs committed. We yearn for restoration, wholeness, and peace. We hunger for sublime experiences, beauty, goodness, immortality, truth, and ultimate intelligibility. When our existential needs are unmet, we find ourselves afraid, angry, broken, cynical, despondent, fearful, or weary.

When our existential longings find no fulfillment, our emptiness remains, the achievement of our long-term goals is vacuous, the long-term goals we have achieved are vacuous, physical pleasures are vaporous, and we lack enduring satisfaction in the acquisition of the material objects, power, recognition, sensuality, and wealth we seek; one of two choices emerges: (1) there is nothing on earth that can satisfy our existential longings; thus, we have to learn how to live without fulfillment of these longings, or (2) a God may exist who can satisfy them.

Of course, one's longing doesn't prove the existence of the object of that longing, whether it be a potential spouse with a rich set of desired attributes, a slot on the Olympic team well-suited to one's skill set, or a rain cloud just over the horizon for a drought-afflicted farmer. But a general and persistent longing throughout humankind could well indicate essential wiring to connect with something of the sort. And it certainly doesn't suggest that common yearnings prove that it's all a fantasy, a mere projection of our wants. So, again, we find ourselves postulating a benevolent Creator who satisfies the heart needs he's placed within us.

Conclusion

"What about someone who believes in beautiful things, but doesn't believe in the beautiful itself and isn't able to follow anyone who could lead him to the knowledge of it? Don't you think he is living in a dream rather than a wakened state?"[33]

How much more reasonable it is that God is the author of these phenomena, these aesthetic universals. For he is the Author of the universe and all that is within it, including beauty and the cultural developments it prompts. Thus, using a cumulative case, the factual existence of aesthetic universals across cultural time and space finds greater logical, evidential, and existential justification from theism than Dutton's advocacy for, and philosophical pre-commitment to, evolutionary naturalism. Following Plantinga's critique, evolutionary naturalism is logically self-defeating. But if we follow these aesthetic universals along we will find they point us to him who is by his very nature the standard of what is true, good, and beautiful.

Bibliography

Brooks, David. "How Artists Changed the World." *New York Times*, August 2, 2016. https://www.nytimes.com/2016/08/02/opinion/how-artists-change-the-world.html.

Craig, William Lane. *Reasonable Faith.* Third ed. Wheaton, IL: Crossway, 2008.

Dewey, John. *Art as Experience.* New York: Penguin, 2005.

Dutton, Denis. "Aesthetic Universals." In *The Routledge Companion to Aesthetics*, edited by Berys Gaut and Dominic McIver Lopes, 203–14. New York: Routledge, 2001.

———. *The Art Instinct: Beauty, Pleasure, and Human Evolution.* New York: Bloomsbury, 2003.

Geisler, Norman. *Baker's Encyclopedia of Christian Apologetics.* Grand Rapids: Baker, 1999.

---

33. Plato, *Complete Works*, 1103.

Geisler, Norman L., and Frank Turek. *I Don't Have Enough Faith to Be an Atheist*. Wheaton, IL: Crossway, 2004.

Habermas, Gary. *The Historical Jesus: Ancient Evidence for the Life of Christ*. Joplin, MO: College Press, 1996.

Kaiser, Walt C. *Tough Questions about God and His Actions in the Old Testament*. Grand Rapids: Kregel, 2015.

Kreeft, Peter, and Ronald K. Tacellie. *Handbook of Christian Apologetics*. Downers Grove, IL: Intervarsity, 1994.

Lewis, C. S. *Mere Christianity*. New York: MacMillan, 1940.

Pearcey, Nancy. *Finding Truth*. Colorado Springs, CO: David C. Cook, 2015.

———. *Total Truth: Liberating Christianity from Its Cultural Captivity*. Wheaton, IL: Crossway, 2004.

Plantinga, Alvin C. *God, Freedom, and Evil*. Grand Rapids: Eerdmans, 1977.

———. *Where the Conflict Really Lies: Science, Religion, and Naturalism*. Oxford: Oxford University Press, 2011.

Plato. *Plato: Complete Works*. Edited by John M. Cooper. Indianapolis: Hackett, 1997.

Pojman, Louis P., and James Feiser. *Ethics: Discovering Right from Wrong*. 8th edition. Boston: Cengage Learning, 2016.

Schaeffer, Francis A. *The God Who Is There*. Downers Grove, IL: InterVarsity, 1973.

Scruton, Roger. *Beauty: A Very Short Introduction*. New York: Oxford University Press, 2011.

Shockley, Paul R. *Worship as Experience: An Inquiry into John Dewey's Aesthetics, the Community, and the Local Church*. Nacogdoches, TX: Stephen F. Austin State University Press, 2018.

Shockley, Paul R., and Raul F. Prezas. *Thinking with Excellence: Navigating the College Journey & Beyond*. New York: Two Creeks, 2019.

Wreen, Michael. "How Tolerant Must a Relativist Be?" *Public Affairs Quarterly* 15.4 (October 2001) 329–39.

The Testimony of Nature

Everywhere we look, things point to other things. An exclamation mark signals excitement. A frown warns of displeasure. Impressions on a creek bank announce the recent presence of wildlife. And, as the old maxim goes, "Red sky at night, sailor's delight." Writers ancient and modern, Christian and not, have addressed this phenomenon. But those who have limited their sign-reading to the material world have missed nature's notification that God is above it all, the creator of everything wondrous and beneficial.

Here's Your Sign

The Divine Semiotics of Beauty

William E. Elkins Jr.

"The heavens declare the glory of God, and the sky above proclaims his handiwork. Day to day pours out speech, and night
to night reveals knowledge. There is no speech, nor are there
words, whose voice is not heard. Their voice goes out through
all the earth, and their words to the end of the world."

—PSALM 19:1–4 (ESV)

"While insolent and foolish people concoct a false notion of beauty,
reducing it to the level of their senses, beauty comes from heaven
and will lead any sane spirit to the place from which it came."[1]

—MICHELANGELO

SEMIOTICS CAN BE DEFINED simply as "the study of signs." Subsequently,
a "sign" can be defined as anything that "stands for" something else.[2] C.
S. Peirce, founder of the American semiotic tradition, writes, "The entire
universe . . . is perfused with signs, if it is not composed exclusively of

---

1. As quoted in Hildebrand, *Beauty in the Light,* 71.
2. As quoted in Hildebrand, *Beauty in the Light,* 71.

signs."[3] Peirce was not known for being overtly religious, but in this case, he sounds much like the psalmist in Psalm 19:1. Nevertheless, the challenge of Peircian semiotics is identifying what these signs signify. (Both theists and atheists cite Peirce in support of their position). Even still, understanding nature as a sign or as divine communication is not only supported by Scripture (Ps 19:1–4; Rom 1), but the tools and categories of modern semiotics may also assist biblical theists in recovering the ancient idea that nature (including beauty) is proclaiming God's glory.

The term "semiotics" originated in John Locke's *Essay Concerning Human Understanding* (1690). In this essay, Locke suggested a science to study "signs the mind makes use of in acquiring knowledge."[4] The study of signs has been recognized as an important discipline dating back to the ancient Greeks, who studied "natural signs" primarily to diagnose medical ailments.[5] Later, Christian thinkers developed semiotic theories that (among other things) seek to assist us in acquiring a greater knowledge of God.[6]

Augustine

Some scholars consider Augustine, Bishop of Hippo (354–430), to be the father of semiotics.[7] However, Augustine was not the first philosopher to write about signs. Discussions of the meanings and uses of signs can be found in the writings of Aristotle, as well as the Epicurean and Stoic philosophers. It appears that Augustine was influenced by Plotinus and Cicero.[8] R. A. Markus suggests that Augustine learned the concept of "signification" from Plotinus.[9]

Augustine's theory of signs developed and matured throughout his works (i.e., *De Magistro* and *De Trinitate*), but it was in *De Doctrina Christiana* (*Teaching of Christianity*) that Augustine's theory of signs were refined. In *De Doctrina Christiana*, Augustine made a distinction between

---

3. Robinson and Southgate, "God and the World of Signs," 15.

4. Rattasepp and Kull, "Semiotics," 492.

5. Rattasepp and Kull, "Semiotics," 492.

6. See the discussion of Augustine, Berkeley, Edwards, and Reid below.

7. These scholars include Umberto Eco, Tzvetan Todorov, and Susan A. Handelman. See Markus, *Signs and Meanings*, 1.

8. These scholars include Umberto Eco, Tzvetan Todorov, and Susan A. Handelman.

9. Markus, *Signs and Meanings*, 78.

natural signs and conventional signs. To Augustine, all signs communicate. However, natural signs are signs that have no mind or intention behind them, even as they require a mind to understand their meaning. Smoke can be a natural sign of fire, just as an approaching cumulonimbus cloud can be a sign of a potential thunderstorm in the mind of the observer. On the other hand, conventional signs are signs that originate from a mind in order to transfer certain information or ideas to another mind. For instance, Augustine understood that Scripture through the sign of human language reveals the mind and will of God.[10]

Along with Scripture, Augustine also proposed that the creation itself is a sign through which God communicates to us. He understood God's creation in terms of "things" (*res*) and "signs" (*signum*).[11] He also made a distinction between things which were meant to be enjoyed (*frui*) and things which were meant to be "used" (*uti*) as pointers to something else.[12] Therefore, Augustine believed that all of creation was a sign that points us to God, who is the only thing (*res*) that can bring true enjoyment (*frui*).[13] When Augustine insisted that created signs, like people, are to be used, he did not mean that in a negative sense; signs are to be used for the sole purpose of enjoying God. In other words, all creation is a sign that points us to the ultimate enjoyment of our Creator. As Susannah Ticciati writes, "The equivalence can briefly be stated as follows: to use is to treat as a sign, while to enjoy is to treat as a thing. Augustine argues that the world is to be used for the end of the enjoyment of God. Translated into the language of signification . . . the world is [to be treated as] a sign of God; or that all creatures are signs of God."[14] Simply put, God is the only "supreme thing" of which all other objects are mere "signs."[15] In another article, Ticciati concludes, "What Augustine means is that God is the only self-sufficient reality which does not gain its meaning by virtue of its signification of something else . . . God is the context within which

---

10. Augustine, *Teaching Christianity*, 129–31.

11. Augustine, *Teaching Christianity*, 106–7.

12. Augustine, *Teaching Christianity*, 107.

13. Augustine, *Teaching Christianity*, 107.

14. Ticciati, "Human Being as Sign," 22.

15. Augustine, *Teaching Christianity*, 106–8, 129–31.

everything else makes sense."[16] Therefore, creation is to be understood as a sign and "a means to the end of the contemplation of God."[17]

In *De Doctrina Christiana*, Augustine does not specifically cite beauty as a sign pointing to God. However, in his *Confessions*, he does speak of beauty as a "voice" or a sign. Concerning the "things" of nature, Augustine states,

> I asked the earth; and it answered, "I am not He;" and whatsoever are therein made the same confession. I asked the sea and the deeps, and the creeping things that lived, and they replied, "We are not thy God, seek higher than we." I asked the breezy air, and the universal air with its inhabitants answered, "Anaximenes was deceived, I am not God." I asked the heavens, the sun, moon, and stars: "Neither," say they, "are we the God whom thou seekest." And I answered unto all things which stand about the door of my flesh, "Ye have told me concerning my God, that ye are not He; tell me something about Him." And with a loud voice they exclaimed, "He made us." My questioning was my observing of them; and their beauty was their reply . . . Is not this beauty visible to all whose senses are unimpaired? Why then doth it not speak the same things unto all? Animals, the very small and the great, see it, but they are unable to question it, because their senses are not endowed with reason to enable them to judge on what they report. But men can question it, so that "the invisible things of Him . . . are clearly seen, being understood by the things that are made."[18]

Augustine understood that the beauty of creation is a universal sign or language (voice) that directs us to the Creator. His semiotic understanding of the world had a profound influence on later thinkers, many of whom also understood beauty in nature as a particular type of divine language.

16. Ticciati, "Castration of Signs," 165–66.

17. Ticciati, "Castration of Signs," 167.

18. Augustine, *Confessions*, 144–45.

The Development of Modern Semiotics

George Berkeley

George Berkeley (1685–1753) believed that our perception of the world is directly connected to the mind of God. Because of this connection, he concluded that the physical world is a sign or divine language that proceeds from God in order to instruct us. Concerning Berkeley's understanding of communication, philosopher Kenneth Pearce writes, "The purpose of the language as a whole . . . is to communicate information to us about other minds, including God, which can inform our actions, thus creating a linguistic context for meaningful interaction among a community of minds."[19] In "Siris," Berkeley suggested that if we study and perceive the world correctly, God's message will be understood. However, if we perceive the world incorrectly (i.e., through the lens of naturalism), then nature will be unintelligible, as if speaking in a foreign language.[20]

If Berkeley is correct, then how do we read nature properly, and what is it saying? James Danaher suggests that one of the problems in seeing a direct correlation between the physical world and a written or spoken language is that different observers do not always agree on the meaning. He picks up on the comparison, likening "lights and colours" of

19. Pearce, "Semantics of Sense Perception," 250.
20. Berkeley, "Siris," 245.

the visible world to marks on a page signifying something beyond themselves.[21] But how are these "lights and colours" used to convey meaning? Danaher proposes that the language of creation would be better understood as poetry:[22]

> If meaning can sometimes be carried in the sound alone or in the larger visual image rather than in the atomic concepts, the visual world may be a language after all in spite of the fact that we are not aware of the concepts which the signifiers of the visual language signify . . . If the visual world is a visual, poetic language whose meaning is meant to communicate a mood or an attitude rather than a conceptual understanding, then some people may understand such communication while other people miss it because they are intent only upon a conceptual understanding.[23]

If Danaher is correct, then the language that God is speaking through the created order is aesthetic in nature. God, therefore, is communicating something about himself to us through the beauty and order of creation. This seems to be Berkeley's conclusion when he wrote,

> As in reading other books, a wise man will choose to fix his thoughts on the sense and apply it to use, rather than lay them out in grammatical remarks on the language; so in perusing the volume of Nature, it seems beneath the dignity of the mind to affect an exactness in reducing each particular phenomenon to general rules, or shewing how it follows from them. We should propose to our selves nobler views, such as to recreate and exalt the mind, with a prospect of the beauty, order, extent, and variety of natural things: hence, by proper inferences, to enlarge our notions of the grandeur, wisdom, and beneficence of the Creator: and lastly, to make the several parts of the Creation, so far as in us lies, subservient to the ends they were designed for, God's glory, and the sustentation and comfort of our selves and fellow-creatures.[24]

What we should learn from the "beauty, order, extent and variety of natural things" is that God is great, good, and wise; therefore we should glorify him as our Creator. As Danaher explains, "The visual language

---

21. Danaher, "Is Berkeley's World?," 362.

22. Danaher, "Is Berkeley's World?," 370.

23. Danaher, "Is Berkeley's World?," 370.

24. Berkeley, *Treatise Concerning the Principles of Human Knowledge*, 142–43.

may be able to express larger, nonconceptual images of things like God's goodness and majesty, and thus produce within us a sense of awe, reverence, and humility in a way that concepts cannot."[25] If this is true, then beauty is an important part of God's visual language. This would also imply that our aesthetic sense is essential in the proper perception of this divine language.

George Berkeley did not intend to develop a complex theory of semiotics, but his belief that all things in nature are signs anticipated the semiotic theory of C. S. Peirce by a couple hundred years. Peirce even cited Berkeley as a major influence of his philosophy. It is also important to note that Berkeley was not the only thinker in the eighteenth century who understood the world, particularly its beauty, as a sign from God. Jonathan Edwards and Thomas Reid had similar views.

Jonathan Edwards

Jonathan Edwards (1703–58) developed a philosophy of idealism very similar to that of George Berkeley.[26] One common agreement between the idealism of Edwards and Berkeley is that both understood creation as a divine language. In *Images or Shadows of Divine Things,* Edwards writes,

> It is very fit and becoming of God, who is infinitely wise, so to order things that there should be a voice of His in His works, instructing those that behold them and painting forth and shewing divine mysteries and things more immediately appertaining to Himself and His spiritual kingdom. The works of God are but a kind of voice or language of God to instruct intelligent beings in things pertaining to Himself. And why should we not think that He would teach and instruct by His works in this way as well as in others, viz., by representing divine things by His works and so painting them forth, especially since we know that God hath so much delighted in this way of instruction.[27]

---

25. Berkeley, *Treatise Concerning the Principles of Human Knowledge,* 371.

26. Edwards believed that all things have their existence in reality because they exist in the mind of God. Edwards's idealism is so similar to Berkeley's theory that some scholars claim that he must have borrowed from Berkeley. However, several journal articles from the late 1800s to the early 1900s discussed the origin of Edwards's idealism and concluded that Edwards was unaware of Berkeley's work. See Gardiner, "Early Idealism," 573–96; MacCracken, "Source of Jonathan Edwards's Idealism," 26–42.

27. Edwards, *Images or Shadows,* 61.

If creation is the result of God's mind, then nature can communicate to us important ideas about God, much like a work of art can communicate something about the mind and ability of an artist. Edwards also understood that God did not leave us on our own to interpret the "images or shadows of divine things"; he also gave us the Bible. Edwards explained,

> The book of Scripture is the interpreter of the book of nature two ways, viz., by declaring to us those spiritual mysteries that are indeed signified and typified in the constitution of the natural world; and secondly, in actually making application of the signs and types in the book of nature as representations of those spiritual mysteries in many instances.[28]

Here, as well as in his other works, Edwards adopted the medieval concept of God's communicating through two books: the book of nature and the book of Scripture. To Edwards, Scripture helps us to see that nature is God's great sign and that it can communicate spiritual mysteries to us about the character and nature of God. However, like Augustine, Edwards not only saw nature as divine communication; he also recognized beauty as an important quality of this communication. Edwards wrote, "For as God is infinitely the greatest Being, so he is allowed to be infinitely the most beautiful and excellent: and all the beauty to be found throughout the whole creation, is but the reflection of the diffused beams of that Being who hath an infinite fullness of brightness and glory."[29]

Edwards divided the concept of beauty between "primary beauty" and "secondary beauty."[30] God's beauty is primary, whereas secondary beauty is a mere reflection of God's beauty. Secondary beauty to Edwards is the perception of harmony (e.g., proportion and agreement), which can be observed in nature, music, art, math, science, logic, and many other human expressions.[31] Edwards understood secondary beauty as a sign or a form of communication that ultimately points us to the beauty (glory) of God. In "A Dissertation Concerning the End for Which God Created the World," Edwards suggested that God's beauty (glory) was infused in creation and became a form of communication from God to us. It is through this expression of beauty in nature (secondary beauty), that we can learn to see God's beauty (primary beauty) and love him as the

28. Edwards, *Images or Shadows*, 109.

29. Edwards, "Nature of True Virtue," 125.

30. Woodell, "Jonathan Edwards." 46.

31. Woodell, "Jonathan Edwards," 88.

highest good and ultimate end. However, Edwards was well aware that the human ability to see God's "excellency" in creation is greatly hampered by sin. Humanity often confuses secondary beauty with primary beauty and therefore worships the creation rather than the Creator. For this reason, Edwards believed that God's grace was necessary to open our ears and eyes (made deaf and blind by sin) in order to properly hear his voice and see his glory on display in creation.[32]

Thomas Reid

Thomas Reid's (1710–96) common-sense philosophy was in many ways a reaction to the philosophy of both David Hume and George Berkeley. In Hume and Berkeley's empiricism, what can be known of the external world can only be found in our internal perception. This conclusion is the source of Hume's skepticism and Berkeley's idealism. However, Reid suggested that we can avoid these radical conclusions by embracing a more common-sense solution. Reid proposed that the external world should be understood as a sign or as a language. For example, in English, the word "apple" has no resemblance to a physical apple on a table. However, when someone says, "Hand me that apple," the listener knows by the context that a physical apple is being referenced. Reid understood that our perception of the physical world functions in much the same way. Internal sensations are like words; when they are experienced through sight, sound, taste, touch, or smell, they do not point to themselves but to external objects. In this way, sensations function like a language communicating quantity and qualities of the external world. To Reid, if sensations are signs of external objects, then we can escape the skepticism of Hume or the supposed solipsism of Berkeley by allowing the external world to have a voice.

As Reid developed his theory of signs, he made a distinction between natural signs and artificial signs. He also distinguished between three types of natural signs: (1) sensation as a sign immediately understood to be the external quality of that which caused it (i.e., hardness); (2) causal effects in nature that need to be investigated in order to understand their meaning (i.e., natural science); and (3) a combination of (1) and (2), that is, a sign that is a causal effect external to ourselves in

32. Edwards, "Dissertation Concerning the End," 120.

which the meaning is immediately understood (i.e., a facial expression).[33] Surprisingly, unlike Berkeley or Edwards, Reid did not often refer to the sign of nature signifying a Creator. However, in his discussion on beauty, he did not hesitate to attribute the beauty of nature as a sign of God.

In "On the Intellectual Powers," in the two sub-sections "Of Grandeur" and "Of Beauty," Reid particularly saw the mark of the Creator. He lamented that, in the spirit of modern philosophy, which had been influenced by the likes of Descartes and Hume, "beauty, harmony, and grandeur, the objects of taste, as well as right and wrong, the objects of the moral faculty, are nothing but feelings of the mind."[34] Reid, however, argued that a real excellence in objects does not depend on our feelings. This is supported in the fact that people "uniformly ascribe excellence, grandeur, and beauty to the object, and not to the mind that perceives it."[35] True to his project, Reid adds, "I believe in this, as in most other things, we shall find the common judgment of mankind and true philosophy not to be at variance."[36] And, when entertaining the possibility that our perception of beauty could be delusory, he wrote, "But we have no ground to think so disrespectfully of the Author of our being; the faculties he hath given us are not fallacious; nor is that beauty which he has so liberally diffused over all the works of his hands, a mere fancy in us, but a real excellence in his works, which express the perfection of their Divine Author."[37]

Reid understood that beauty, wherever it is found, is the result of a mind. He insisted that in order to perceive the mind of others, we should look to the expression of the mind imprinted in material objects: "Thus, the beauties of mind, though invisible in themselves, are perceived in the objects of sense, on which their image is impressed."[38] However, not only is the relationship between mind and object true of us; Reid believed that it is particularly true of the mind of God expressed in creation: "The invisible Creator, the Fountain of all perfection, hath stamped upon all his works signatures of his divine wisdom, power, and benignity, which are visible to all men. If we consider, on the other hand, the qualities in

33. Wolterstorff, *Thomas Reid*, 166–67.
34. Reid, "Essays on the Intellectual Powers of Man," 495.
35. Reid, "Essays on the Intellectual Powers of Man," 495.
36. Reid, "Essays on the Intellectual Powers of Man," 495.
37. Reid, "Essays on the Intellectual Powers of Man," 500.
38. Reid, "Essays on the Intellectual Powers of Man," 503.

sensible objects to which we ascribe beauty, I apprehend we shall find in all of them some relation to mind, and the greatest in those that are most beautiful."[39] In other words, Reid considered beauty to be the signature of God on his creation.

In the later eighteenth and nineteenth centuries, the semiotic understanding of the world found in Augustine, Berkeley, Edwards, and Reid seemed to lie dormant among philosophers. However, in the late nineteenth and early twentieth centuries, the work of an American philosopher not only built upon these ideas, but also helped develop semiotics into its own unique branch of philosophical inquiry.

Charles Sanders Peirce

C. S. Peirce (1839–1914) was a brilliant thinker. He advanced practically every field of study on which he focused, from astronomy and physics to philosophy. However, his work in logic and philosophy has been his most enduring legacy. He was the founder of pragmatism and is credited, along with Ferdinand de Saussure, as the founder of modern semiotics. Along with Leibniz, Duns Scotus, Kant, and Hegel, Peirce named Berkeley and Reid as the most important influencers of his work.[40] In fact, he identified Reid as the primary source for the category of "Secondness" in his semiotic theory.[41]

Peirce's semiotic theory (as well as his theology and philosophy) became more difficult and complex over time. Based on Peirce's writings, it appears that he was both a philosophical theist and an evolutionist. Therefore, it should be no mystery why his semiotic theory is adopted by both theists and evolutionists. For instance, William L. Power understands that for Peirce,

> [At the] level of acritical thought, action, and feeling, the universe can be viewed as "vast representament" of God (6.459). The cosmos can be viewed as a system of interconnected signs which, if interpreted correctly, can signify the divine reality. For Peirce, the universe is God's symbol, with indexical and iconic features (6.459). The general features of the cosmos as a vast developing environmental or ecological system can be taken as a

39. Reid, "Essays on the Intellectual Powers of Man," 503.
40. Brent, *Charles Sanders Peirce*, 327.
41. Brent, *Charles Sanders Peirce*, 52.

symbol of God's purposes for the creatures; the emergence and movements of actual things and existents in the spatiotemporal order can be taken as indexical signs of the creative producer; and the objective and subjective qualities and relations manifest in experience can be taken as iconic signs of the divine nature and identity. For Peirce, the cosmos is God's "great poem" (5.119) which signifies the divine artist and artistry.[42]

In this respect, Peirce's system of semiotics led him to a conclusion similar to that of Augustine, Berkeley, Reid, and Edwards. However, in spite of his belief in God (which for most of his life seemed to be a mix between Christian theism and something akin to pantheism), Peirce believed that all things evolved by chance. He did affirm that God was the Creator of the universe(s), and that there is evidence in nature of God's creative power. As Gary Alexander points out,

> Peirce refers to God in aesthetic terms, arguing that "the very meaning of the word 'God' implies . . . aesthetic spiritual perfection" (6.510). The only evidence for "the existence of a governor of the universe" that he finds plausible is the lawful character of that universe. In particular, the "character of those laws themselves," which he describes as "benevolent, beautiful, economical, etc.," leads Peirce to assert the presence of God within the developing cosmos (6.395).[43]

Peirce did not seem to answer the apparent contradiction in how God could be the Creator of the universe while, at the same time, evolution was governed by chance. Nevertheless, it appears that Peirce believed God established the "benevolent, beautiful, economical" laws of the universe and then let chance work within the parameters of these laws to allow biological life to evolve. After all, theistic evolution, the belief that God and evolution are compatible, was not an uncommon position in Peirce's day. Darwin himself suggested such a solution in his second edition of On the Origin of Species.[44] To theists and atheists alike, Peirce's attempt at melding Moses and Darwin together is problematic. However, Peirce did write an important essay concerning God's existence that deserves special attention.

42. Power, "Peircean Semiotics," 222–23.

43. Alexander, "Hypothesized God," 313–14.

44. Darwin, On the Origin of Species, 484.

Peirce's "Neglected Argument" for God

In his essay "A Neglected Argument for the Reality of God," many important features of Peirce's philosophy are evident, including semiotics, pragmatism, abduction, and philosophy of religion. He began his essay by asserting his belief that God is the Creator of all "three Universes of Experience."[45] In Peirce's philosophy, the first Universe is *Ideas*, which are "those airy nothings to which the mind of poet, pure mathematician, or another might give local habitation and a name within that mind."[46] The second Universe "is that of the Brute Actuality of things and facts."[47] The third Universe, "comprises everything whose being consists in active power to establish connections between different objects, especially between objects in different Universes."[48]

In the rest of the essay, the crux of Peirce's argument is that our mind will readily accept God's existence if it is allowed a small portion of time during the day to engage in what he calls an exercise in "Pure Play of Musement."[49] This musement takes the form of meditation on one or all three Universes. Peirce writes,

> The particular occupation I mean—a *petite bouchée* [small bite] with the Universes—may take either the form of aesthetic contemplation, or that of distant castle-building (whether in Spain or within one's own moral training), or that of considering some wonder in one of the Universes, or some connection between two of the three, with speculation concerning its cause.[50]

What Peirce is getting at is that we should take in the wonderment of the world, and as we contemplate ideas or tangible objects in the world, we should allow our minds to freely consider the best explanation (abduction) of their ultimate source. A proper explanation must also include how we came to possess the cognitive ability to even consider these things. Peirce writes,

> Darwinians, with truly surprising ingenuity, have concocted, and with still more astonishing confidence have accepted as

---

45. Peirce, *Peirce on Signs*, 261.
46. Peirce, *Peirce on Signs*, 262.
47. Peirce, *Peirce on Signs*, 262.
48. Peirce, *Peirce on Signs*, 262.
49. Peirce, *Peirce on Signs*, 266.
50. Peirce, *Peirce on Signs*, 263.

proved, one explanation for the diverse and delicate beauties of flowers, and others for those of butterflies, and so on; but why is all nature—the forms of trees, the compositions of sunsets—suffused with such beauties throughout, and not nature only, but the other two Universes as well?[51]

Anticipating a response from the naturalistic determinists, Peirce explained,

> Tell me, upon sufficient authority, that all cerebration depends upon movements of neuritis that strictly obey certain physical laws, and that thus all expressions of thought, both external and internal, receive a physical explanation, and I shall be ready to believe you. But if you go on to say that this explodes the theory that my neighbour and myself are governed by reason, and are thinking beings, I must frankly say that it will not give me a high opinion of your intelligence. But however that may be, in the Pure Play of Musement the idea of God's Reality will be sure sooner or later to be found an attractive fancy, which the Muser will develop in various ways. The more he ponders it, the more it will find response in every part of his mind, for its beauty, for it supplying an ideal of life, and for its thoroughly satisfactory explanation of his whole threefold environment.[52]

And he continues, "There is a reason, an interpretation, a logic, in the course of scientific advance, and this indisputably proves to him who has perceptions of rational or significant relations, that man's mind must have been attuned to the truth of things in order to discover what he has discovered. It is the very bed-rock of logical truth."[53]

Peirce was no orthodox theologian, but, unlike many scientists today, he was not afraid to follow the evidence in order to formulate the best explanation, even if the evidence pointed to God. Peirce understood that if we would pay close attention to the world, we might just conclude that all of creation is a sign (including its beauty) that points us to our Creator, a notion he shared with the psalmist, Augustine, Berkeley, Edwards, and Reid.

51. Peirce, *Peirce on Signs*, 265.

52. Peirce, *Peirce on Signs*, 266–67.

53. Peirce, *Peirce on Signs*, 272.

A Modest, Common-Sense Proposal for Natural Signs

In *Natural Signs and the Knowledge of God*, philosopher C. Stephen Evans, influenced by Thomas Reid's "common sense" philosophy, suggests that certain natural signs could be a means by which "a person becomes aware of God."[54] While God may be the ultimate cause of all natural signs, not all natural signs immediately impress upon human perception the idea of God's existence. Concerning this distinction, Evans writes,

> To look at the hypothesis that there are natural signs for God, it is legitimate to employ the content of the hypothesis, which in this case includes the existence of God. If God exists, then God is the creator and sustainer of every finite reality, so the idea of a causal link between God and the sign is unproblematic. However, just because God is the creator of everything finite, such a causal connection seems insufficient. Presumably, natural signs for God will be distinctive in some way. There may be some sense in which everything in the natural world can serve as a natural sign for God. However, if everything is a natural sign for God, then there will be no theistic natural signs in any distinctive sense. What is needed, I think, is the idea not only that God is the cause of the existence of the sign, but that God created the sign to be a sign. The function of the sign needs to be part of the reason why the sign exists, and this function must be anchored in God's creative intentions.[55]

When considering these particular natural signs that God placed in creation, Evans proposes two hypotheses: The Wide Accessibility Principle and the Easy Resistibility Principle.[56] The concept of the Wide Accessibility Principle is that whatever sign(s) God uses to point us to himself should not be so complicated that only philosophers or scientists can understand it, but rather accessible to everyone with properly functioning faculties.

However, along with the Wide Accessibility Principle, Evans proposes the Easy Resistibility Principle, which suggests that even though the knowledge of God would be available to all through certain natural signs, they could be easily rejected or resisted. Evans writes,

54. Evans, *Natural Signs*, 35.

55. Evans, *Natural Signs*, 35.

56. Evans, *Natural Signs*, 14–15.

According to this principle, though the knowledge of God is widely available, it is not forced on humans. Those who would not wish to love and serve God if they were aware of God's reality find it relatively easy to reject the idea that there is a God. To allow such people this option, it is necessary for God to make the evidence he provides for himself to be less than fully compelling. It might, for instance, be the kind of evidence that requires interpretation, and include enough ambiguity that it can be interpreted in more than one way.[57]

Why would God not make the evidence of his existence so overwhelming that no one could possibly deny it? In anticipation of this question, Evans suggests that to make God's existence too obvious would force those who do not love God to serve him begrudgingly because "it would be foolish and irrational to oppose God and God's purposes."[58]

Evans readily acknowledges that his two principles can be found in a well-known passage in the *Pensées* by French mathematician and philosopher Blaise Pascal. Pascal writes,

If he had wished to overcome the obstinacy of the most hardened, he would have done so by revealing himself to them so plainly that they could not doubt the truth of his essence . . . It was therefore not right that he should appear in a manner manifestly divine and absolutely capable of convincing all men, but neither was it right that his coming should be so hidden that he could not be recognized by those who sincerely sought him. He wished to make himself perfectly recognizable to them. Thus wishing to appear openly to those who seek him with all their heart and hidden from those who shun him with all their heart, he has qualified our knowledge of him by giving signs which can be seen by those who seek him and not by those who do not. "There is enough light for those who desire only to see and enough darkness for those of a contrary disposition."[59]

What kind of sign(s) could point us to God's existence? To begin, Evans suggests that it is highly likely that a natural sign pointing to God has a corresponding hardwired human ability to perceive it:

On the one hand, to be a natural sign at all, there must be some in-built propensity, when the sign is encountered, to form some

57. Evans, *Natural Signs*, 15.
58. Evans, *Natural Signs*, 15.
59. Pascal, as quoted in Evans, *Natural Signs*, 16.

relevant judgment as a result of the encounter with the reality mediated by the sign. If there are such theistic natural signs, we would then expect belief in God to be widespread, found in reasonably young children and across many cultures, and we would expect that those beliefs would be typically occasioned by the same types of experiences.[60]

What kind of sign(s) would have both an external and internal connection? Evans describes several types that would qualify, including what he called "cosmic wonder" and "beneficial order." Cosmic wonder signs consist of experiences that are "mysterious" or "puzzling," that are "crying out for some explanation."[61] When certain marvelous aspects of the universe are encountered, it may very well be a "calling card" that reflects God's "creative work."[62] Evans writes,

> It would not only be the case that the sign naturally tends to produce belief in God; it would do this because God created a contingent universe and gave humans a natural sense of wonder when they encounter that universe. We do find it natural to see the universe as something whose existence is surprising, something that "cries out" for explanation and naturally suggests to us that behind the universe lies something—or someone—that exists in a deeper and less surprising way.[63]

The "beneficial order" signs are "orderly, complex structures" that seem to exist for the purpose of bringing about some good:[64] "It is no accident that people often find an encounter with the natural world to be in some way 'spiritual,' and that experiences of the natural world frequently seem to produce, in a perfectly spontaneous way, a belief that some kind of purposive intelligence lies behind the beauty and order we find in nature."[65] (In this, Evans resonates with Peirce as well as Pascal.)

On this model, beauty is widely assessable in that it exists everywhere and is recognized by everyone—and is more often than not recognized as originating from God. It is also easily resistible as a sign for God's existence in that it can be ignored or explained away with theories,

60. Evans, *Natural Signs*, 37.
61. Evans, *Natural Signs*, 60.
62. Evans, *Natural Signs*, 63.
63. Evans, *Natural Signs*, 63–64.
64. Evans, *Natural Signs*, 90.
65. Evans, *Natural Signs*, 98.

such as those of evolutionary aesthetics or biosemiotics. Beauty also has a corresponding hardwired human ability to perceive it, known as the aesthetic sense or aesthetic perception. Finally, beauty also qualifies as a cosmic wonder and a feature of God's beneficial order. If metaphysical naturalism is true, then the beauty found throughout the universe and the human ability to perceive it is an inexplicable, gratuitous accident. However, if God exists, then beauty is likely one of the many signs or voices designed to declare God's glory to the whole human race—or at least to those willing, by the grace of God, to pause long enough to look and listen.

Bibliography

Alexander, Gary. "The Hypothesized God of C. S. Peirce and William James." *The Journal of Religion* 67 (July 1987) 304–21.

Augustine. *The Confessions of St. Augustine.* In *Nicene and Post-Nicene Fathers,* vol. 1, edited by Philip Schaff, translated by J. G. Cunningham, 1:27–207. 14 vols. Peabody, MA: Hendrickson, 1995.

———. *Teaching Christianity (De Doctrina Christiana).* Edited by John E. Rotelle. Translated by Edmund Hill. Hyde Park, NY: New City, 2003.

Berkeley, George. "Siris." In *The Works of George Berkeley.* vol. 3, edited by Alexander Campbell Fraser, 115–299. 4 vols. Oxford: Clarendon, 1901.

———. *A Treatise Concerning the Principles of Human Knowledge.* Edited by Jonathan Dancy. New York: Oxford University Press, 1998.

Brent, Joseph. *Charles Sanders Peirce: A Life.* Bloomington: Indiana University Press, 1998.

Danaher, James P. "Is Berkeley's World a Divine Language?" *Modern Theology* 18.3 (July 2002) 361–73.

Darwin, Charles. *On the Origin of Species by Means of Natural Selection.* 2nd ed. London: John Murray, 1860.

Edwards, Jonathan. "A Dissertation Concerning the End for Which God Created the World." In *The Works of Jonathan Edwards,* vol. 1, edited by Edward Hickman, 94–121. 2 vols. Peabody, MA: Hendrickson, 1998.

———. *Images or Shadows of Divine Things.* Edited by Perry Miller. New Haven: Yale University Press, 1948.

———. "The Nature of True Virtue." In *The Works of Jonathan Edwards,* vol. 1, edited by Edward Hickman, 122–42. 2 vols. Peabody, MA: Hendrickson, 1998.

Evans, C. Stephen. *Natural Signs and Knowledge of God: A New Look at Theistic Arguments.* Oxford: Oxford University Press, 2010.

Gardiner, H. N. "The Early Idealism of Jonathan Edwards." *The Philosophical Review* 9.6 (January 1900) 573–96.

MacCracken, John H. "The Source of Jonathan Edwards's Idealism." *The Philosophical Review* 11.1 (1902) 26–42.

Markus, R. A. *Signs and Meanings: World and Text in Ancient Christianity.* Liverpool: Liverpool University Press, 1996.

Pearce, Kenneth L. "The Semantics of Sense Perception in Berkeley." *Religious Studies* 44 (August 2008) 249–68.

Peirce, Charles Sanders. *Peirce on Signs: Writings on Semiotic by Charles Sanders Peirce.* Edited by James Hoopes. Chapel Hill: The University of North Carolina Press, 1991.

Power, William L. "Peircean Semiotics, Religion, and Theological Realism." In *New Essays in Religious Naturalism,* edited by W. Creighton Peden and Larry E. Axel, 222–23. Macon, GA: Mercer University Press, 1994.

Rattasepp, Silver, and Kalevi Kull. "Semiotics." In *The Wiley Blackwell Encyclopedia of Consumption and Consumer Studies,* edited by Daniel Thomas Cook and J. Michael Ryan, 492. West Sussex, UK: Wiley & Sons, 2015.

Reid, Thomas. "Essays on the Intellectual Powers of Man." In *The Works of Thomas Reid,* edited by William Hamilton, 1:360–88. 2 vols. Edinburgh: Elibron Classics, 2005.

Robinson, Andrew, and Christopher Southgate. "God and the World of Signs: Semiotics and Theology." *Zygon* 45.3 (August 2010) 685–88.

Ticciati, Susannah. "The Castration of Signs: Conversing with Augustine on Creation, Language and Truth." *Modern Theology* 23 (April 2007) 161–79.

———. "The Human Being as Sign in Augustine's *De Doctrina Christiana*." *Neue Zeitschrift für Systematicsche Theologie Und Religionsphilosophie* 55 (February 2013) 20–32.

Von Hildebrand, Dietrich. *Beauty in the Light of the Redemption.* Steubenville, OH: Hildebrand, 2019.

Wolterstorff, Nicholas. *Thomas Reid and the Story of Epistemology.* Cambridge: Cambridge University Press, 2004.

Wooddell, Joseph D. "Jonathan Edwards, Beauty, and Apologetics." *Criswell Theological Review* 5.1 (2007) 81–95.

The Bible is replete with talk about God's gracious provision, whether in the form of manna for Israelites fleeing Egypt, the milk and honey of the promised land, the rain that falls "on the just and the unjust," (Matt 5:45), and "our daily bread" (Matt 6:11). We can miss his gift of colors, particularly green, which connotes flourishing, delights and rests the soul, and points us toward spiritual realities.

"Wondrous Greenness"

Jonathan Edwards's Reading of the Color Green

Michael A. G. Haykin

In his tract, *De tribus diebus*,[1] the Augustinian theologian Hugh of St. Victor (c.1096–1141) pursued an investigation firmly founded on the Pauline dictum of Romans 1:20 that the invisible Creator can be discerned to some degree through the visible things of his creation. The beauty of color, for instance, bespeaks a beautiful Creator: "the ruby-red roses, dazzlingly white lilies, the purple violets, in all of which not only their beauty but also their origin is marvellous—for how does God's wisdom produce such beauty from the dust of the earth?"[2] But, Hugh continued, "green is the most beautiful color of all (*super omne pulchrum viride*)" in the divine chromatic palette, for it represents both new life in nature and the resurrection of the dead.[3] Living in a world quite different from that of Hugh's twelfth-century Parisian Abbey of St. Victor, the New England divine of the long eighteenth century, Jonathan Edwards (1703–58), was nevertheless a kindred soul, for he too was entranced by the colorful beauty of the world. In the summer of 1726, for example, he penned a small paper in which he observed:

1. *Concerning Three Days*

2. Hugh of St.-Victor, *De tribus diebus*, 74–75. "Perceiving uncreated Beauty . . . within created things . . . is central to Hugh's theology" (Coolman, *"Pulchrum esse,"* 176). For another study of this theme in Hugh of St. Victor, see Palmén, "Experience of Beauty," 234–53.

3. Hugh of St.-Victor, *De tribus diebus*, 12, 821B.

There are beauties that are more palpable and explicable, and there are hidden and secret beauties. The former pleases and we can tell why: we can explain and particularly point forth agreements that render the thing pleasing . . . The latter sort are those beauties that delight us and we can't tell why. Thus we find ourselves pleased in beholding the color of the violets, but we know not what secret regularity or harmony it is that creates that pleasure in our minds. These hidden beauties are commonly by far the greatest, because the more complex a beauty is, the more hidden is it. In this latter sort consists principally the beauty of the world; and very much in light and colors . . . That mixture of all sorts of rays, which we call white, is a proportionate mixture that is harmonious (as Sir Isaac Newton has shewn) to each particular simple color and contains in it some harmony or other that is delightful. And each sort of ray plays a distinct tune to the soul, besides those lovely mixtures that are found in nature—those beauties, how lovely, in the green of the face of the earth, in all manner of colors in flowers, the color of the skies, and lovely tinctures of the morning and evening.[4]

And like Hugh of St. Victor, Edwards believed that these natural beauties were reflective of the Triune Creator's beauty. As he noted in 1724:

[W]hen we are delighted with flowery meadows and gentle breezes of wind, we may consider that we only see the emanations of the sweet benevolence of Jesus Christ; when we behold the fragrant rose and lily, we see his love and purity. So the green trees and fields, and singing of birds, are the emanations of his infinite joy and benignity; the easiness and naturalness of trees and vines [are] shadows of his [i.e. Christ's] infinite beauty and loveliness; the crystal rivers and murmuring streams have the footsteps of his sweet grace and bounty. When we behold the light and brightness of the sun, the golden edges of an evening cloud, or the beauteous bow, we behold the adumbrations of his glory and goodness; and the blue skies, of his mildness and gentleness. There are also many things wherein we may behold his awful majesty: in the sun in his strength, in comets, in thunder, in the towering thunder clouds, in ragged rocks and the brows of mountains. That beauteous light with which the world is filled

---

4. Edwards, *Scientific and Philosophical Writings*, 6:306. For the date of this text, see the comments of Anderson, in Edwards, *Scientific and Philosophical Writings*, 6:297. And for Edwards's knowledge and reading of Isaac Newton's *Opticks,* see Loewinsohn, "Jonathan Edwards' Opticks," 26–31.

in a clear day is a lively shadow of his spotless holiness and happiness, and delight in communicating himself.[5]

This text bears eloquent witness to the intense attention that Edwards paid to the multifarious phenomena of the natural world as he walked in or rode through the fields and forests of America.[6] But we also see here his deep-seated conviction that the entire cosmos is replete with signs and emblems that are shadows of profound spiritual realities. "Typology," George Marsden has averred, "was central to Edwards'

5. Edwards, *Miscellanies*, 13:278–79. This text was probably written in February 1724. See Edwards, *Miscellanies*, 13:94.

6. On Edwards's habit in this regard, see Whitney, *Finding God in Solitude*, 97–101.

conception of the universe."[7] And as Edwards himself once asserted with unabashed confidence: "I am not ashamed to own that I believe that the whole universe, heaven and earth, air and seas, and the divine constitution and history of the holy Scriptures, be full of images of divine things, as full as a language is of words."[8] Reflecting then on the divine beauty that can be seen in one specific color, namely green, and its typological significance would not at all be frivolous for the American divine. [9]

"A Pleasant Green"

Like Hugh of St. Victor, Edwards was certain that the color green was the most pleasant and loveliest of colors. In a comment on Revelation 4:3, which was penned in the mid-1720s, Edwards observed that "green [is] the most pleasing color, and above all others easy and healthful to the eye."[10] Nearly twenty years later, commenting on the predominance of the color green in the rainbow of Revelation 4:3, Edwards noted:

> This rainbow was "in sight like unto an emerald," which is a precious stone of an exceeding lovely green color, so green that this color appears in nothing else so lively and lovely. This color is a most fit emblem of divine grace; it is a very lively color, not so dull as blue or purple, and yet most easy to the sight, more easy than the more fiery colors of yellow and red. It is the color of all the grass, herbs, and trees, and growth of the earth, and therefore fitly denotes life, flourishing, prosperity, and happiness, which are often in Scripture compared to the green and flourishing growth of the earth. As the benign influence of the sun on the face of the earth is shown by this color above all others, so is the grace, and benign influence, and communication of God fitly represented by this color. This color is the color of joy and

7. Marsden, *Jonathan Edwards*, 77.

8. Edwards, *Typological Writings*, 11:152. I am indebted to Sweeney, *Jonathan Edwards*, 104–5 for this quotation. For Edwards, "there is only one order of reality; God's revealed law and the law of nature agree" (Loewinsohn, "Jonathan Edwards' Opticks," 31).

On Edwards's typological reading of nature and Scripture, see especially Lowance, Jr., "Images or Shadows," 141–81; Wainwright, "Jonathan Edwards," 519–30; Knight, "Learning the Language," 531–51; Hunt, "Refiguring an Angry God," 21–35; Knight, "Typology," 190–209; Fabiny, "Edwards and Biblical Typology," 91–108; McClymond and McDermott, *Theology of Jonathan Edwards*, 116–29.

9. Stein, "Jonathan Edwards and the Rainbow," 440.

10. Edwards, *Apocalyptic Writings*, 5:99.

gladness. The fields are said to shout for joy, and also to sing, by their appearing in a cheerful green. As the color red is made use of to signify God's revenging justice, in Zechariah 1:8 and elsewhere, so is green the emblem of divine grace. As Dr. Doddridge observes, this don't imply that the rainbow had no other color, "but that the proportion of green was greater than ordinary."[11]

Two of the works that Edwards read specifically in his reflections on Revelation remarked on green having a pleasant nature. The commentary of Matthew Henry (1662–1714), a conduit of Puritan thought to the eighteenth century, had observed that the reason why the rainbow in Revelation 4 looked like an emerald was that this "most prevailing color was a pleasant green, to shew the reviving and refreshing nature of the new covenant."[12] Then, as the evangelical commentator Philip Doddridge (1702–51), whom Edwards referenced at the close of the above quote, pointed out, the "bright green" of the emerald was "vivid, though soft and agreeable" to the eyes.[13] Edwards's contemporary, the Particular Baptist John Gill (1697–1771), echoed this take on the emerald in Revelation 4 when he stated that the hue of this gemstone "is of an exceeding fine green, very delightful to the eye, and gives pleasure to the mind to look upon it."[14]

Edwards's discussion of green in the text cited above began with a color spectrum that ranged from dull to bright. At one end of this spectrum were "dull" colors such as blue and purple, and at the other end the "fiery colors of yellow and red." Green, Edwards implied, was in the middle of this spectrum. This median location of green is intriguing, for it points to both medieval and ancient convictions. Lothar of Segni (1161–1216), the future Pope Innocent III, stated that "green is a middle color (*viridis color medius est*) between white and black and red" in a treatise that he wrote on the mass prior to his papal election in 1198.[15] White,

11. Edwards, *Notes on Scripture*, 15:225. For the date, see Stein, "Jonathan Edwards and the Rainbow," 442–44. According to Stein, the final sentence was added after 1756 (Edwards, *Notes on Scripture*, 15:225n2).

12. Henry, *Exposition of the Several Epistles*, 693. On Edwards's reading of Henry's commentary, see Stein, "Jonathan Edwards and the Rainbow," 442–43.

13. Doddridge, *Family Expositor*, 6:466.

14. Gill, *Exposition of the New Testament*, 718 (commentary on Revelation 4:3). Cf. Hervey, *Collection of Sermons and Tracts*, 178: "a spacious field, arrayed in green, relieves and re-invigorates the eye, that has fatigued itself by poring upon some minute, or gazing upon some glaring object."

15. Innocent III, *De sacri sancti*, 1.65, 802C.

black, and red, of course, were major liturgical colors in the medieval sanctification of time: white, the color of purity, was used for holidays; red, linked to the Holy Spirit, at Pentecost; and black, associated with penitence, on Good Friday and throughout Advent. Green would now be employed for the remainder of the liturgical year, so-called ordinary time. Michel Pastoureau, the preeminent historian of color, sees this chromatic judgment about green by the future Innocent as fraught with significance: "green became a liturgical color in a large portion of Roman Christendom and thus acquired a certain prestige."[16] Further back, in antiquity, Aristotle (384–22 BC) also seemed to have thought of green as a middle color, and in *De coloribus*, a treatise in the Aristotelian canon that was wrongly attributed to him by medieval scholars, green is placed midway on the spectrum from white to black.[17]

Of course, green was also at the very center of the Newtonian chromatic spectrum.[18] Isaac Newton's (1642–1727) prism experiments between 1666 and 1672 had demonstrated that green was the central color in the rainbow's range from red to violet. This spectrum might be different from that of the medieval era, but green was still central and, from Edwards's vantage point, it was further proof of green being most pleasant to the sight. In Edwards's words:

> Red is the highest, strongest, harshest color, because it is caused by the densest and most rapid rays; blue is more gentle and weak. Red gives the most light because the rays have more of vivacity, and more strongly affect the organ [of sight]; blue is the nearest approaching to darkness. Red, long beheld, is painful to the eyes. Green and blue are pleasing, easy, gentle and inoffensive, and healthful to the organ [of sight].[19]

---

16. Pastoureau, *Green*, 40–42.

17. See Pastoureau, *Green*, 42–44.

18. Cf. the remark of Gill that the color green is "the prevailing one in the rainbow" (*Exposition of the New Testament*, 3:718).

19. Edwards, *Scientific and Philosophical Writings*, 6:241. It is noteworthy that this perspective has persisted in certain circles down to the present day. Christopher Hitchens tells the story of one of his primary school teachers in England, a Mrs. Jean Watts, who used to tell the children in her class, "So you see, children, how powerful and generous God is. He has made all the trees and grass to be green, which is exactly the color that is most restful to our eyes. Imagine if instead, the vegetation was all purple, or orange, how awful that would be" (*God Is Not Great*, 2). I am indebted to Dr. Mark Coppenger for this story by Hitchens.

Ultimately, this view of the pleasing view of green also went back to antiquity.[20] Pliny the Elder (23/24–79), for instance, was assured that "the mellow green" of emeralds, the greenest of all greens, was so soothing to the eyes that it removed fatigue.[21] Basil of Caesarea (*c*.329–79) similarly observed that a person's "eyes, after looking intently at glistening objects (*ta lampra*), obtain some relief by turning back to blues and greens."[22] After one's eyes have looked at a brilliant object—and here Basil probably had in mind the sun since *lampros* and its cognates were used to describe its brilliance—it was difficult to focus, and it was a relief to look at the blue sea and green vegetation of this world.

However, in Edwards's thinking, there were other considerations, weightier ones, for the identification of greenness as "a most fit emblem of divine grace."[23]

"A Cheerful Green"

Green was "the color of joy and gladness,"[24] Edwards asserted and other eighteenth-century authors concurred. Green was a "chearing [sic] color," according to Philip Doddridge.[25] Doddridge's fellow Congregationalist, the hymnwriter Isaac Watts (1674–1748), similarly brought joy and greenness together in "Sing to the Lord, Ye Distant Lands," his version of Psalm 96:11–12:

> Let heav'n proclaim the joyful day.
> Joy thro' the earth be seen;
> Let cities shine in bright array,
> And fields in chearful green.[26]

In their hymnic rendition of one of Watts's poems, "Eternal Wisdom, Thee We Praise," John (1703–91) and Charles Wesley (1707–88) altered

---

20. As Bruce R. Smith has noted, a good number of the associative ideas about color in the sixteenth and seventeenth centuries (and one could add the long eighteenth century despite the Newtonian revolution regarding color), went back to antiquity. (*Key of Green*, 4–5).

21. Pliny the Elder, *Natural History* 37.16.62–64.

22. Basil of Caesarea, *Saint Basil*, 1:34.

23. Edwards, *Notes on Scripture*, 15:225.

24. Edwards, *Notes on Scripture*, 15:225.

25. Doddridge, *Family Expositor*, 466 (commentary on Revelation 4:3).

26. Watts, *Works*, 4:89.

Watts's lines about the divine handiwork evident in British fields—"How did his wondrous skill array/Your fields in charming green"—to "Lo! here thy wondrous skill arrays/The earth in chearful green!"[27] And James Hervey (1714–58), a one-time member of the Wesley brothers' Holy Club in Oxford, noted "little boughs clad with a chearing green" when he catalogued aspects of a country scene not far from Dummer in Hampshire, where he was the parish minister in the late 1730s.[28] Again, this view of green had deep historical roots. The medieval theologian Bonaventure (1221–74), for instance, regarded green as a *color ridens* ("laughing color").[29]

In his reflection upon Revelation 4:3 that was cited above, Edwards supported his assertion that green was a joyous color by the following sentence: "The fields are said to shout for joy, and also to sing, by their appearing in a cheerful green."[30] This statement appears to be an echo of Watts's hymn noted above, which, in turn is based upon Psalm 96:12 (KJV): "Let the field be joyful." But other biblical passages confirmed Edwards in this chromatic reflection. Commenting on the phrase "our bed is green" in Song of Songs 1:16, Edwards observed in the *Blank Bible* that this was quite appropriate since green was "the emblem of love and joy."[31] And in another commentary on the emerald of Revelation 4:3, this one dating from the 1720s, Edwards detailed why greenness is the ideal color for conveying joy:

> Green is a symbol of joy and prosperity. The trees and fields, when they prosper and flourish, are most green, and are said to rejoice and sing and clap their hands; hereby therefore is signified the joyful and glorious nature of the gospel. As greenness is caused on the face of the earth, by the kind influences of the sun, so the joy and happiness of the gospel, is caused by the kind influences or grace and love of the Sun of Righteousness.[32]

Isaiah 55:12 specifically stated that "all the trees of the field shall clap their hands" for joy following the impact of the word of God (Isa

27. Watts, "Song to Creating Wisdom," in *Works*, 4:352; Wesley and Wesley, *Collection of Hymns*, 219.

28. Hervey, *Collection of the Letters*, 1:14.

29. Pastoureau, *Green*, 57.

30. Edwards, *Notes on Scripture*, 15:225.

31. Edwards, *"Blank Bible,"* 24:612.

32. Edwards, *Apocalyptic Writings*, 5:99.

55:10–11), while Isaiah 44:23 called upon the "forest and every tree therein" (KJV) to "break forth into singing" in response to the Lord's activity in history. Such texts provided Edwards with specific biblical links between greenness, the color of the "trees and fields," and the phenomenon of joy. And when one observed that this greenness and flourishing was the result of being bathed in sunlight, this was yet further proof that greenness was the best color to express joy, for the joyous clapping of the green world of vegetation typified "the joy and happiness of the gospel" that came from the "Sun of Righteousness." As Edwards noted in relation to Song of Solomon 5:14, green is representative of "divine grace and beauty, giving life and joy, as the beams of the sun in the spring, covering the earth with a vivid joyful green."[33]

A "*Wondrous Greenness*"

Edwards's early interest in the rainbow was evident in a number of scientific papers that he drew up in the 1720s.[34] At the same time, he was clearly fascinated by the typological significance of the rainbow in Revelation 4.[35] The rainbow, Edwards had noted at the same time as his scientific papers, "signified the gospel or covenant of grace, for the rainbow was the token of God's covenant to Noah."[36] In Genesis 9:8–17, God had established the rainbow as a covenantal sign of his grace and mercy to terrestrial life after Noah, his family, and a multitude of animals were saved from the flood. In Revelation 4:3, another rainbow appears, this time surrounding God's "throne, in sight like unto an emerald" (KJV). Given that the rainbow was indicative of divine mercy and grace, as was evident to Edwards from the Genesis account, it was natural for him to ask, "Why is it depicted as being green in this final book of the Bible?" Glenn Kreider has noted that it is "unclear whether Edwards interprets Revelation 4:3 to mean that the rainbow is multicoloured with green the primary hue, or if he interprets the rainbow as being purely green."[37] Ei-

---

33. Edwards, "*Blank Bible*," 24:623.

34. See, for example, Edwards, *Scientific and Philosophical Writings*, 6:298–301. See also Stein, "Jonathan Edwards and the Rainbow," 440–56.

35. For a full discussion of Edwards's reflections on the rainbow, see Kreider, "Jonathan Edwards's Interpretation," 107–25.

36. Edwards, *Apocalyptic Writings*, 5:99.

37. Kreider, "Jonathan Edwards's Interpretation," 110.

ther way, Edwards's conviction that green was the most pleasant of colors and his interpretation of greenness as typifying joy and life—both of which have been demonstrated above—meant that this "color is a most fit emblem of divine grace."[38]

This last remark was penned in the early 1740s, but Edwards had held this conviction about the emerald-green rainbow of Revelation 4 for over two decades. In the 1720s he was certain that the rainbow in Revelation 4 was "a fit symbol of grace and mercy" and by "its being so exceedingly green, even like an emerald, is held forth the transcendent greatness and glory of the grace of God in the gospel."[39] Three years after the Northampton revival of 1734–35, when Edwards had witnessed such a remarkable display of God's benignity and grace, he preached a series of sermons on 1 Corinthians 13, Paul's paean to God's love. In his first sermon, Edwards referenced Revelation 4:3 as an illustration of his assertion that God's throne is surrounded by love:

> Love is the principal thing which the gospel reveals in God and Christ . . . God as he sat on his throne was encompassed round with a circle of exceeding sweet and pleasant light, pleasant like the beautiful colors of the rainbow, like an emerald. An emerald is a precious stone of exceeding pleasant and beautiful color. This represents that the light and glory with which God appears surrounded in the gospel is especially the glory of his love and covenant grace.[40]

And in Edwards's eyes, no other color could have expressed this divine love at the heart of the gospel as well as the "wondrous greenness of the emerald."[41]

Bibliography

Basil of Caesarea. *Saint Basil: The Letters.* Translated by Roy J. Deferrari. 4 vols. Loeb Classical Library. Cambridge, MA: Harvard University Press, 1926–34.
Coolman, Boyd Taylor. "*Pulchrum esse*: The Beauty of Scripture, the Beauty of the Soul, and the Art of Exegesis in Hugh of St. Victor." *Traditio* 58 (2003) 175–200.

38. Edwards, *Notes on Scripture*, 15:225.

39. Edwards, *Apocalyptic Writings*, 5:99.

40. Edwards, *Ethical Writings*, 8:143, 145. I am indebted to Kreider, "Jonathan Edwards's Interpretation," 115–17, for drawing my attention to this text.

41. Edwards, *Apocalyptic Writings*, 5:99.

Doddridge, Philip. *The Family Expositor.* 6 vols. London: Waugh and Fenner, and Buckland, 1756.

Edwards, Jonathan. *Apocalyptic Writings.* Edited by Stephen J. Stein. *The Works of Jonathan Edwards,* vol. 5. 26 vols. New Haven: Yale University Press, 1977.

———. *The "Blank Bible," Part 1.* Edited by Stephen J. Stein. *The Works of Jonathan Edwards,* vol. 24. 26 vols. New Haven: Yale University Press, 2006.

———. *Ethical Writings.* Edited by Paul Ramsey. *The Works of Jonathan Edwards,* vol. 8. 26 vols. New Haven: Yale University Press, 1989.

———. *The Miscellanies (Entry Nos. a–z, aa–zz, 1–500).* Edited by Thomas A. Schafer. *The Works of Jonathan Edwards,* vol. 13. 26 vols. New Haven: Yale University Press, 1994.

———. *Notes on Scripture.* Edited by Stephen J. Stein. *The Works of Jonathan Edwards,* vol. 15. 26 vols. New Haven: Yale University Press, 1998.

———. *Scientific and Philosophical Writings.* Edited by Wallace E. Anderson. *The Works of Jonathan Edwards,* vol. 6. 26 vols. New Haven: Yale University Press, 1980.

———. *Typological Writings.* Edited by Wallace E. Anderson and Mason I. Lowance, Jr. with David Watters. *The Works of Jonathan Edwards,* vol. 11. 26 vols. New Haven: Yale University Press, 1993.

Fabiny, Tibor. "Edwards and Biblical Typology." In *Understanding Jonathan Edwards: An Introduction to America's Theologian,* edited by Gerald R. McDermott, 91–108. Oxford: Oxford University Press, 2009.

Gill, John. *An Exposition of the New Testament.* 3 vols. London: Matthew and Leigh, 1809.

Henry, Matthew. *An Exposition of the Several Epistles Contained in the New Testament, . . . And the Revelation.* London: 1721.

Hervey, James. *A Collection of Sermons and Tracts.* Hervey, James. London: n.p., 1761.

———. *A Collection of the Letters of the Late Reverend James Hervey, A.M.* 2 vols. Dublin: Faulkner and Wilson, 1760.

Hitchens, Christopher. *God Is Not Great: How Religion Poisons Everything.* Toronto: McClelland & Stewart, 2007.

Hugh of St.-Victor. *De tribus diebus. Patrologiae cursus completus … Series Latina* 176. 811C–838D. Paris: J.-P. Migne, 1854.

Hunt, Richard. "Refiguring an Angry God: The Nature of Jonathan Edwards." *Interdisciplinary Literary Studies* 4.2 (Spring 2003) 21–35.

Innocent III. *De sacri sancti altari mysterio Patrologiae cursus completus … Series Latina* 217. 774B–916A. Paris: Garnier Bros. and J.-P. Migne, 1890.

Knight, Janice. "Learning the Language of God: Jonathan Edwards and the Typology of Nature." *The William and Mary Quarterly* 48.4 (October 1991) 531–51.

———. "Typology." In *The Princeton Companion to Jonathan Edwards,* edited by Sang Hyun Lee, 190–209. Princeton: Princeton University Press, 2005.

Kreider, Glenn Richard. "Jonathan Edwards's Interpretation of Revelation 4:1—8:1." PhD diss, Dallas Theological Seminary, 2001.

Loewinsohn, Ron. "Jonathan Edwards' Opticks: Images and Metaphors of Light in Some of His Major Works." *Early American Literature* 8.1 (Spring 1973) 26–31.

Lowance, Mason I. Jr. "Images or Shadows of Divine Things: The Typology of Jonathan Edwards." *Early American Literature* 5.1 (Spring 1970) 141–81.

Marsden, George M. *Jonathan Edwards: A Life.* New Haven: Yale University Press, 2003.

McClymond, Michael J., and Gerald R. McDermott. *The Theology of Jonathan Edwards*. Oxford: Oxford University Press, 2012.

McDermott, Gerald R. *Understanding Jonathan Edwards: An Introduction to America's Theologian*. Oxford: Oxford University Press, 2009.

Palmén, Ritva. "The Experience of Beauty: Hugh and Richard of St. Victor on Natural Theology." *Journal of Analytic Theology* 4 (May 2016) 234–53.

Pastoureau, Michael. *Green: The History of a Color*. Translated by Jody Gladding. Princeton: Princeton University Press, 2014.

Smith, Bruce R. *The Key of Green: Passion and Perception in Renaissance Culture*. Chicago: The University of Chicago Press, 2009.

Stein, Stephen. "Jonathan Edwards and the Rainbow: Biblical Exegesis and Poetic Imagination." *The New England Quarterly* 47.3 (September 1974) 440–56.

Sweeney, Douglas A. *Jonathan Edwards and the Ministry of the Word: A Model of Faith and Thought*. Downers Grove, IL: InterVarsity, 2009.

Wainwright, William J. "Jonathan Edwards and the Language of God." *Journal of the American Academy of Religion* 48.4 (December 1980) 519–30.

Watts, Isaac. *The Works of the Late Reverend and Learned Isaac Watts*. 6 vols. London: Longman, Longman, Buckland, Oswald, Waugh, and Ward, 1753.

Wesley, John, and Charles Wesley. *A Collection of Hymns, for the Use of the People Called Methodists*. London: Paramore, 1780.

Whitney, Donald S. *Finding God in Solitude: The Personal Piety of Jonathan Edwards (1703–1758) and Its Influence on His Pastoral Ministry*. American University Studies. Series VII, Theology and Religion, vol. 340. New York: Lang, 2014.

It may strike us as odd that our omnipotent God would take a day off for rest at the end of creation week. But his pause was not due to exhaustion, but rather to his desire to contemplate the wondrous work he had accomplished. As we are made in his image, we should honor the complementary structures of work and leisure, the pragmatic and the reflective, toil and holiday (from the expression, "holy day")—a Sabbath rhythm constitutive of human flourishing, mirrored in and nurtured by the arts.

Beauty Rest

The Correspondence of Aesthetic Experience to a Sabbatical Understanding of Reality

RICHARD H. STARK III

IN HIS NOVEL, *LUKE Baldwin's Vow*, Canadian author Morley Callaghan tells the story of an orphaned boy named Luke who must now live with his aunt and pragmatic Uncle Henry, a country sawmill manager. Luke befriends an aged and decrepit dog, finding in his new companion a safe confidant for his unfiltered thoughts, fears, and emotions. However, while Luke sees in his dog a valuable comrade, his uncle plays the realist, informing Luke that the "sensible thing" would be to put the dog down. After all, it is only taking up space and eating their food, offering no contribution to the household in return. Understandably, Luke is horrified and determined to prevent his uncle from ever carrying out such a plot. When the uncle arranges to have the dog tied to a rock and drowned in a river, Luke rushes to the animal's rescue, diving into the water to cut him free, swimming him to shore, and resuscitating him. At that moment, Luke promises himself one thing—that he would spend his life "protect[ing] all that was truly valuable from the practical people in the world."[1]

As the West has increasingly succumbed to naturalism and secularism, it has consequently emphasized the practical over the transcendent. After all, if the material world and this life are all that exist, then personal survival is paramount. If something gets in the way of one's survival or

1. Callaghan, *Luke Baldwin's Vow*, 147, 187.

happiness, the rational thing may just be to dispense with it. If one is in an unfulfilling marriage, he should walk away. If experiencing an inconvenient pregnancy, she should end it. If an invalid grandmother's hospital bills are piling up, the family should pull the plug. If people are just animals—animate matter alone—little reason exists to mull over morals, bog down in sentiment, and waste valuable resources and time. One must be practical about such things. Of course, a naturalist need not take such a position, but this approach would be the consistent outworking of a purely materialist worldview.

Moreover, in a more secularized society, anything peripheral to material needs (perceived or actual) might well be discarded. Perhaps for this reason, many schools emphasize studies in math and science—practical subjects for understanding and manipulating the material universe—to the reduction and, at times, elimination of the humanities in the curriculum.[2] To be sure, employment opportunities for philosophy majors do not seem very promising. And when productivity and efficiency matter most, little time exists for seemingly worthless pursuits, which may be why, when schools make budget cuts, the first area to go is often the arts. There is little time to sing, dance, play, or paint when one is simply trying to survive.

And yet, throughout human history, mankind has made time for these pursuits, even at the most inconvenient times—in Jewish concentration camps, in enslavement, in prison, on the brink of martyrdom, and in the throes of fatal illness. Even within a secularized age, while some schools have pushed the arts to the side, they remain a crucial part of many lives and of society as a whole. Indeed, for some, the arts have become a surrogate spirituality—a final vestige of transcendence in a universe seemingly devoid of the supernatural.[3]

Clearly, the arts are a significant aspect of existence, but if, as naturalism purports, the world is only matter, one must wonder why the arts play such a significant role and have such an emotive impact within the human experience.[4] In his landmark book, *A Secular Age*, philosopher Charles Taylor asserts that since the "power [of the arts] seems inseparable from their epiphanic, transcendent reference," the burden of proof rests on the "unbeliever, to find a non-theistic register in which to

2. Of course, some humanities departments are guilty of propagating problematic ideologies, but the issue at this point is the value of the humanities *per se.*

3. Ryken, *Liberated Imagination*, 70.

4. Keller, *Making Sense of God*, 17.

respond to [the arts] without impoverishment."[5] After all, the practical course of action would be to follow Uncle Henry and put the dog down, but something inside the human heart knows the dog has value beyond its productivity—and the arts have value even if that value cannot be quantified. Yet those who deny the existence of God must grapple with why the arts are such a fundamental part of humankind's existence when they do not seem necessary for physical survival.[6]

In contradistinction, the Christian worldview makes room not only for the efficient but also for the meaningful. Even when the pessimistic, atheist philosopher Arthur Schopenhauer sought to grapple in his philosophical system with the power of the arts, he found himself having to borrow from a Judeo-Christian concept to explain the significance of an aesthetic experience. He argued that within an evil, hostile universe, which is the physical representation of a "striving" will and an "impulse to self-preservation," the experience of beauty is comparable to the experience of Sabbath rest.[7] In so doing, perhaps Schopenhauer unintentionally pointed to a framework in which the arts can make sense and correspond to reality. In other words, while music, painting, and poetry seem foreign

5. Taylor, *Secular Age*, 607.

6. Keller, *Making Sense of God*, 17.

7. Schopenhauer, *World as Will and Representation*, 2:299, 2:583, 1:196; Foster, "Ideas and Imagination," 227. See also Janaway, *Schopenhauer*, 40–41; Young, *Schopenhauer*, 86. Asserting that behind all reality is an impersonal and evil "blind urge" or will, Schopenhauer held that the material universe is the physical representation of this will and that mankind is the will's "conscious" manifestation even though man too is "blindly" driven by the will's urges (Schopenhauer, *World as Will and Representation*, 1:110, 1:150, 1:308–9, 2:579, 2:484–85). The will is "never satisfied" and is further manifested in man's will-to-live, which parallels Charles Darwin's concept of survival of the fittest and perpetuates universal suffering (2:299, 1:87–88, 1:309. See also Janaway, *Schopenhauer*, 40–41; Young, *Schopenhauer*, 86). Therefore, Schopenhauer concluded, "So long as our consciousness is filled by our will, so long as we are given up to the throng of desires with its constant hopes and fears, so long as we are the subject of willing, we never obtain lasting happiness or peace" (Schopenhauer, *World as Will and Representation*, 1:196). However, Schopenhauer suggested that one could find a "temporary respite" from the "striving of [the] will" through an aesthetic experience, which allows one to momentarily become "will-less" and thereby "painless" (1:178–79, 1:184–86; Foster, "Ideas and Imagination," 218, 227). Schopenhauer referred to such an experience as *Sabbath*, claiming, "It is the painless state, prized by Epicurus as the highest good and as the state of the gods; for that moment we are delivered from the miserable pressure of the will. *We celebrate the Sabbath* of the penal servitude of willing; the wheel of Ixion stands still" (Schopenhauer, *World as Will and Representation*, 1:196 [emphasis mine]).

to the carnage of a "survival of the fittest" universe, they seem perfectly at home in a cosmos created by the Lord of the Sabbath.[8]

After all, the God of the Bible is not just concerned with practicality. As Leland Ryken and others have noted, God did not just make a "functional" universe but a "beautiful" one.[9] Moreover, when he inspired Scripture, God did not communicate solely in prose and syllogisms; he called out in poetry and song. And when he ordained the "rhythm" of time, he did not merely mandate a workweek; he ordered a day of refreshment and revelry.[10] Such a worldview not only makes space for the arts; it views them as crucial to the existence of humankind, who bears the image of such a God. Whereas the only logical explanation naturalism can offer for the presence of the arts in evolutionary history is that of an interesting anomaly or a survival mechanism, a Christian sabbatical perspective views the arts as not only integral to survival but also to human flourishing. Hence, perhaps like Luke with his dog, Christianity can save the arts from the narrowly practical people of the world. Indeed, the creational, redemptive, and eschatological aspects of Sabbath seem to demonstrate that the phenomena of art make more sense in a Christian and sabbatical understanding of reality than in a naturalistic framework.

Sabbath and Creation

When most people consider the Sabbath, they think of the divine directive to keep one day a week free of labor: "Six days you shall labor, and do all your work, but the seventh day is a Sabbath to the Lord your God" (Exod 20:9–10a). However, the principle of Sabbath runs much deeper than a mandatory day-off policy. Indeed, the commandment from God finds its foundation in the creation account of Genesis 1–2: "For in six days the Lord made heaven and earth, the sea, and all that is in them, and rested on the seventh day. Therefore the Lord blessed the Sabbath day and made it holy" (Exod 20:11). Hardly arbitrary, then, according to a biblical worldview, the Sabbath is inherent to "the very structure of reality" and "is based on a cosmic foundation, the universal need for regular rest"—and as such, it also serves as a covenantal sign between God and

8. For a more extensive response to Schopenhauer and a treatment of art and Sabbath, see Stark, "Art and Sabbath."

9. Ryken, *Liberated Imagination*, 70.

10. Ryken, *Liberated Imagination*, 90; Dawn, *Keeping the Sabbath Wholly*, xi.

Israel (Exod 31:13, 16–17) and demonstrates Israel's allegiance to God (Lev 19:30; 26:2; Isa 56:4–7; 58:13–14).[11]

Even before the command to keep the Sabbath was given with the law at Sinai, resting on the seventh day was already an established practice among the Hebrews. In Exodus 16, the Israelites gathered enough manna on the sixth day in order to have something to eat on the seventh day because "tomorrow is a day of solemn rest, a holy Sabbath to the Lord" (Exod 16:23). In fact, just as God rested from his work in creation, so too would he now participate in the rest cycle of his people; therefore, "on the seventh day, which is a Sabbath, there will be" no manna (Exod 16:26). Thus, in light of the creation and the wilderness narratives, Sabbath for the Israelites was about more than just a command to keep—it was a way of life. Indeed, as Marva J. Dawn suggested, it was the point around which all of life revolved, establishing a "rhythm" of labor and respite and infusing the cosmos with purpose.[12]

As one returns to the creation account of Genesis 1–2, the fascinating component is not that dependent creatures require rest but rather that a God who is self-sufficient and who "neither slumbers nor sleeps" (Ps 121:4) participated himself in the Sabbath rest of creation. Genesis 2:2 states, "On the seventh day God finished His work that He had done, and He rested on the seventh day from all His work that He had done." Even more fascinating is that according to Exodus 31:17, he was "refreshed." Such a statement is perhaps jarring to a framework that asserts the existence of an omnipotent God. However, rather than suggesting that God was somehow deficient, requiring periodic recuperation, these passages convey that God was satisfied with his work, calling it "very good" and signifying that his work was accomplished.[13] Moreover, the world he had created was in perfect order; it was in a state of *shalom*, reflecting his peace and wholeness.[14] In other words, mankind and all of creation were in perfect relationship with the Godhead, and the fact that God was "refreshed" demonstrates that God did not simply rest because

11. Weiss, "*Sabbatismos*," 688; Barack, *History of the Sabbath*, 30; Lincoln, "From Sabbath to Lord's Day," 345.

12. Dawn, *Keeping the Sabbath Wholly*, xi, 49. See also Ryken, *Liberated Imagination*, 90.

13. Pipa, "Christian Sabbath," 121; Lincoln, "Sabbath, Rest, and Eschatology," 198; Lincoln, "From Sabbath to Lord's Day," 348.

14. Dawn, *Keeping the Sabbath Wholly*, 146; Brueggemann, *Sabbath as Resistance*, 57.

his work was done; instead, he took special interest in his creation, savoring the world he had made.[15] Thus, contra those who associate talk of the Sabbath with legalistic Pharisaism, when God formally issued the fourth of the Ten Commandments to "remember the Sabbath day, to keep it holy" (Exod 20:8), he was not playing the role of killjoy; instead, he was inviting mankind to participate in a joyful, pleasure-filled respite with him and his creation, taking time not only to labor but also to enjoy the fruit of one's labor.[16]

Hence, one sees that inherent to the doctrine of creation is a beautiful universe that displays the glory of its Creator (Rom 1:20)—a universe designed to be enjoyed both by the Creator and by his image-bearers.[17] And carved into the very structure of that universe is a recurring day of rest specifically designed for the enjoyment of God and his creation.[18] Dawn therefore seemed to understand the spirit of the Sabbath well when she said, "Observing the Sabbath gives us the opportunity to be as careful as we can to fill our lives with beauty and to share beauty with the world around us."[19] Indeed, she added, "When we observe a day especially set apart for beauty, all the rest of life is made more beautiful."[20]

With this call to perceive and appreciate the goodness of life and of God, one finds a welcoming home for the cultivation and appreciation of the arts. For starters, as an outlet for the creative component of the divine image, artmaking mimics the "sabbatical structure" God established when he created the universe.[21] For instance, Karl Barth noted that the "first [full] day" of man's existence, after his creation on the sixth day, was the primordial Sabbath; thus, before beginning the inaugural workweek, man first rested in communion with the Creator and the cosmos.[22] Therefore, the cycle of work and rest begins with the centering of who one is in relationship to God and the created order, resulting in an invigoration

---

15. Arand, "Responses to Skip MacCarty," 94; Pipa, "Christian Sabbath," 121.

16. Pipa, "Christian Sabbath," 121.

17. Hasel, "Sabbath in the Pentateuch," 24–25; Dressler, "Sabbath in the Old Testament," 30.

18. Hasel, "Sabbath in the Pentateuch," 24–25; Dressler, "Sabbath in the Old Testament," 30; Guthrie, *Creator Spirit*, 207–8; Dawn, *Keeping the Sabbath Wholly*, 174.

19. Dawn, *Keeping the Sabbath Wholly*, 174.

20. Dawn, *Keeping the Sabbath Wholly*, 174.

21. Lincoln, "From Sabbath to Lord's Day," 345.

22. Barth, *Church Dogmatics*, 3.4.52. See also Lee, *Religion and Leisure in America*, 188.

for the work ahead. Likewise, while the stereotype of an artist may be that of an aloof, elite type who is struck with a flash of genius, many artists testify that the process of creativity first requires time for reflection.[23] Anglican bishop and musician/poet Andrew Rumsey, for instance, argues, "The poet's first response to the world is stillness and wonder, passive reflection before active exposition. Poetry 'takes in' before it 'gives out,' and considers itself addressed by creation, called to attention."[24] For German luthier Martin Schleske, the crafting of stringed instruments involves taking the time to "understand differently and anew the inner and outer elements of [one's] life," allowing one to "slow down" long enough to "pay attention."[25] This slowing down, he notes, allows one to "be more conscious, more concentrated, more passionate, and more sustainable."[26] Acclaimed artist Makoto Fujimura likewise views artistry as "a discipline of awareness, prayer, and praise."[27] Thus, many artists testify that, before they can create, they must first carve out time to engage in the observation, contemplation, and cultivation of ideas through their artistic form, calling their audience likewise to take notice. Such experiences with art make good sense within a sabbatical understanding of reality, encouraging a tension and "interpenetration of work and leisure" and cultivating what Barth called an "attitude of rest."[28]

This restful demeanor can even inspire playfulness—experimentation with words, lines, notes, and colors—which provides its own sort of refreshment.[29] Consider for instance the "playfulness of [the] poet," who does not limit himself to exacting propositions, standard paragraphs, and literal descriptors, but also speaks in couplets, rhymes, metaphors, and meters, delving into the delight that results from the discipline of one's

23. Crouch, *Culture Making*, 97.

24. Rumsey, "Through Poetry," 52.

25. Schleske, *Sound of Life's Unspeakable Beauty*, xiii, 12; Glaspey, *Discovering God*, 59.

26. Schleske, *Sound of Life's Unspeakable Beauty*, 12.

27. Fujimura, *Art and Faith*, 3.

28. Lee, *Religion and Leisure in America*, 29; Barth, *Church Dogmatics*, 3.4.563. Barth asserted that "there must be contemplation because, in order to attain to rest, man must be in the attitude of rest. And he achieves this attitude only when he takes a step away from himself and obtains a detached survey of himself, not proceeding at once to forget himself in a new active affirmation of life, but remaining fixed as it were, and attaining knowledge of himself in complete detachment" (3.4.563). See also Begbie, *Voicing Creation's Praise*, 206.

29. Huizinga, *Homo Ludens*, 122, 129, 134.

craft.[30] Moreover, the attitude of rest that began the creative process sustains the artist throughout and leads to another period of rest when his or her work is done. In other words, like the "sabbatical structure of time," which begins and ends with rest, the creative process proceeds out of rest and culminates with satisfaction in a completed project, at which point, as an image-bearer, the artist mimics his Maker in delightfully looking at his creation and declaring it "very good."[31]

This same work-Sabbath rhythm is evident in the enjoyment of art. One cannot fully absorb a work of art if one is in a hurry. As Terry Glaspey has pointed out, "Learning to appreciate great art often takes time."[32] And just as artists must slow down and observe in order to create, the art they produce calls viewers to do the same. In the words of Thomas Dubay, the arts call one to "notice, linger, appreciate, wonder."[33] Thus, Glaspey argues that the arts "teach us how to open our eyes and our ears. They retrain us about what is worth attending to. They re-sensitize us when life has desensitized us. They bring to the foreground the things that we might otherwise miss."[34] In this way, the sabbatical value of periodic pausing creates space for aesthetic enjoyment within the Christian worldview.

Moreover, the artist's use of ambiguity can further "draw us forward," serving as an "invitation [to] come and see."[35] Should one accept the invitation, one must get to work, engaging a text or painting; contemplating symbols and motifs; and combing the depths of metaphors and meanings, sound and silence, and light and shadow. Nevertheless, the viewer who is willing to do so will—like the artist behind the work—find refreshment both in the process itself and in the satisfaction of resolution. Therefore, contra a naturalistic framework, the primordial Sabbath of the Judeo-Christian tradition provides a plausible structure for the human

30. Huizinga, *Homo Ludens*, 134.

31. Lincoln, "Sabbath, Rest, and Eschatology," 198; Pipa, "Christian Sabbath," 121; Ryken, *Liberated Imagination*, 91. See also Dressler, "Sabbath in the Old Testament," 29; Pieper, *In Tune with the World*, 47; Lincoln, "From Sabbath to Lord's Day," 348; Ryken, *Liberated Imagination*, 89–90.

32. Glaspey, *Discovering God*, 27.

33. Dubay, *Evidential Power of Beauty*, 178.

34. Glaspey, *Discovering God*, 35; Veith likewise noted, "Art is powerful because it heightens perception . . . by lifting an object or experience out of its normal context so that it can be apprehended freshly and more fully" (*State of the Arts*, 206).

35. Guthrie, *Creator Spirit*, 18. See also Ryken, *Liberated Imagination*, 227.

experience of art as one shares in the divine rhythm of productivity and pleasure both in the creation and appreciation of art.

Sabbath and Redemption

The redemptive elements of Sabbath likewise correspond to the human experience of art. With the disruption of the *shalom* of the created order due to the fall of mankind, the Sabbath of the perfect creation was broken. Nevertheless, the sabbatical structure of time would be reinforced after the exodus with the Mosaic law and would highlight salvific themes. Deuteronomy 5:15 says, "You shall remember that you were a slave in the land of Egypt, and the Lord your God brought you out from there with a mighty hand and an outstretched arm. Therefore the Lord your God commanded you to keep the Sabbath day."[36] Hence, tied to the commandment of Sabbath-keeping is a call to remember divine deliverance out of slavery and into the promised land.[37] But this aspect of the Sabbath command pointed to an even higher reality. Part of the Jewish tradition of Sabbath observance involves singing the *Zemirot*, which express a "longing for the appearance of the prophet Elijah," who would announce the Messiah's arrival.[38] "According to tradition, the prophet Elijah, messenger of the good tidings of the Messiah's coming, will not arrive on Friday when everyone is busy preparing for the Sabbath, nor on Saturday when Jews are at rest. Consequently he is expected immediately after the Sabbath," at which point he will "bring the good tidings of redemption for Israel and humanity."[39]

Unsurprisingly, then, in the New Testament, Christ is portrayed as the fulfillment of the Sabbath. Jesus himself said that he fulfilled Isaiah 61:1–2, which describes the Year of Jubilee, an aspect of sabbatical law (Luke 4:16–21). Furthermore, though accused by religious leaders of breaking the Sabbath, Jesus promised, "Come to me, all who labor and are heavy laden, and I will give you rest" (Matt 11:28).[40] Even his resurrection, which immediately followed the Sabbath, heralds the

---

36. See also Deut 7:18; 8:18; 16:3, 12; 24:18, 22.

37. The redemptive aspect of Sabbath is also evident in Israel's Sabbath years and in the Year of Jubilee, in which indentured workers were released from their servitude.

38. Millgram, *Sabbath*, 13–14. See also Goldman, *Guide to the Sabbath*, 44–45.

39. Millgram, *Sabbath*, 21.

40. Lincoln, "Sabbath, Rest, and Eschatology," 201–2.

"accomplishment of the work of salvation" and begins the process of making all things new, thereby restoring the *shalom* that had been disrupted.[41] Thus, as Samuele Bacchiocchi indicated, "The coming of Christ is seen as the actualization, the realization of the redemptive typology of the Sabbath."[42] As such, whether in regard to rescue from Egypt or from sin, the Sabbath in the Judeo-Christian tradition provides an outlet for remembering God's faithfulness in saving his people.[43] In this way, Sabbath invites one to pause and to ponder the meaning of existence and the God behind that existence.

Because the arts naturally invite contemplation, they seem to parallel the redemptive component of Sabbath, potentially facilitating reflection, remembrance, and even repentance. Indeed, an aesthetic encounter can often feel religious in nature. In *The Idea of the Holy*, Rudolf Otto suggested that "in great art the point is reached at which we . . . are confronted with the numinous itself, with all its impelling motive power," leaving one in silent awe.[44] From a Christian perspective, one might say that mankind is wired for such a response because God has revealed his glory in the created order (Rom 1:20), and as such, the experience of beauty in the world is an opportunity to taste the glory of the One who made all things good. Thus, as Roger Lipsey asserted, the experience of "the spiritual in art confronts us with what we have forgotten."[45] C. S. Lewis called these confrontations "signposts" that point to the longing for "what [mankind] really wants," namely the "Joy" of the original creation.[46] Indeed, Lewis argued,

> Apparently, then, our lifelong nostalgia, our longing to be reunited with something in the universe from which we now feel

41. Lincoln, "Sabbath, Rest, and Eschatology," 205.

42. Bacchiocchi, *Sabbath in the New Testament*, 77; see also 58–59.

43. See Dederen, "Reflections on a Theology," 299; Heb 3–4.

44. Otto, *Idea of the Holy*, 69, 71.

45. Lipsey, *Spiritual in Twentieth-Century Art*, 14.

46. Lewis, *Surprised by Joy*, 130; Lewis, "Weight of Glory," 39. Lewis argued, "The books or the music in which we thought the beauty was located will betray us if we trust to them; it was not *in* them, it only came *through* them, and what came through them was longing. These things—the beauty, the memory of our own past—are good images of what we really desire; but if they are mistaken for the thing itself, they turn into dumb idols, breaking the hearts of their worshippers. For they are not the thing itself; they are only the scent of a flower we have not found, the echo of a tune we have not heard, news from a country we have never yet visited" (Lewis, "Weight of Glory," 30–31). See also Lewis, "On Stories," 105.

cut off, to be on the inside of some door which we have always seen from the outside, is no mere neurotic fancy, but the truest index of our real situation. And to be at last summoned inside would be both glory and honour beyond all our merits and also the *healing of that old ache*.[47]

In the spirit of the Sabbath, the practice of which cultivates reflection and remembrance, the arts can also serve a palliative function, supplying a momentary repose from the suffering of a fallen world. As previously mentioned, individuals have long turned to the arts to cope with great sorrow and trauma. Whether enduring oppression or facing illness or even death, people have produced and taken comfort in art.[48] Even today, art and music therapy provide outlets for people to process trauma, navigate dementia and Alzheimer's, and manage emotional and physical pain. Art can thus offer a brief diversion and prepare one to once again "return . . . to the chaotic world in which [he] live[s]" after a period of refreshment.[49]

Furthermore, the capacity of the arts to facilitate memory and spiritual longing can serve a "moral function," encouraging behavioral change or repentance.[50] In a biblical example, when Nathan confronted David regarding David's sexual immorality and abuse of power, the prophet did so in story form, which allowed David enough disassociation from his own situation to see clearly the evil he had committed and to experience the proper disdain toward his actions, culminating with his cry for a "clean heart," a "right spirit," and forgiveness (Ps 51:10). The novel *Uncle Tom's Cabin* notably opened the eyes of many people in Antebellum America to the horror of slavery and the need to live up to the ideal that "all men are created equal." In this regard, Margaret R. Miles contends, "We need images [and music and literature] that express—that help us to 'see'— what we are about, and . . . that represent—that make present—aspects of human possibility."[51] With their capacity to give an individual another perspective and to allow one to empathize with another's situation, the arts can facilitate a change in attitude and behavior, reminding one of

47. Lewis, "Weight of Glory," 42 (emphasis mine).

48. See Klein et al., *Terezín*. See also Wolterstorff, "Thinking about Church Music," 4; De Grazia, *Of Time, Work and Leisure*, 338.

49. Hans, *Play of the World*, 3. See also Cosper, *Stories We Tell*, 57–58; Begbie, "Through Music," 153.

50. Veith, *State of the Arts*, 208.

51. Miles, *Image as Insight*, 149.

what is good and what is true.[52] Therefore, while seemingly out of place in naturalism, within a Christian worldview, the arts seem perfectly consistent with the redemptive aspect of the Sabbath and its call to reflect and remember; within this system, the value of art can be highlighted as a good gift that provides an outlet for one to long for a connection to the divine, to experience relief from the fallenness of the present world, and to be reminded of what is truly important in life.

Sabbath and the Eschaton

The sabbatical structure of time within the Christian tradition also points to the eternal rest of the eschaton in which creation's *shalom* will be restored.[53] Even though they would say this reality has not yet fully arrived, Christians believe that, as God's redeemed people, they experience the first fruits of this coming kingdom even now.[54] Thus, when believers practice Sabbath, they "anticipate . . . the future, eternal consummation of Joy" in heaven.[55]

Far from being a nonmaterial, incorporeal environment, the new creation outlined in the Bible will be "a new heaven *and* a new earth" (Rev 21:1)—a beautiful restored order. The coming kingdom will also be full of artistry: streets of gold that are "like transparent glass" (Rev 21:21), walls "built of jasper" (Rev 21:18), gates "made of a single pearl" (Rev 21:21), and much musical expression (Rev 4:8–9; 5:8–14). Theologian Anthony A. Hoekema even suggests that based on Revelation 21:24–26, "the best contributions of each nation . . . in this present life will . . . be retained and enriched in the life to come."[56]

In line with this theological understanding, one might say that the arts can point to the culminating rest of the eschatological Sabbath, particularly in their ability to embody rhythms of tension and release within a span of time.[57] For instance, musician and theologian Jeremy S.

52. See Plato, *Republic*, Book III, 401–2; Avila, "From Film Emotion to Normative Criticism," 236.

53. Lincoln, "From Sabbath to Lord's Day," 345; Lincoln, "Sabbath, Rest, and Eschatology," 204, 213. See also Wolterstorff, *Art in Action*, 84; Guthrie, *Creator Spirit*, 179.

54. Lincoln, "Sabbath, Rest, and Eschatology," 205. See Heb 3–4.

55. Dawn, *Keeping the Sabbath Wholly*, 151.

56. Hoekema, *Created in God's Image*, 94.

57. Sherry, *Spirit and Beauty*, 142. See also Borthwick et al., "Musical Time and Eschatology," 271–94.

Begbie says that, as tension builds in music, it demonstrates that the music is "going somewhere" and "asks for my patience, my trust that there is something worth waiting for."[58] Begbie argues, "Each fulfillment constitutes an increase in the demand for fulfillment at a higher level. Every return closes *and* opens, completes *and* extends, resolves *and* intensifies"; Begbie notes that this "pattern of tension and [release]" provides a "sense of the incompleteness of the present, that not all is now given" even as one awaits the "final resolution."[59]

Begbie continues that one sees a similar pattern in literary works. He perceives that while music is the "coming into being and dying of tones" over a period of time, literature is the "coming into being and dying of words."[60] With its "beginning, middle, and end" structure consisting of exposition, rising action, climax, falling action, and resolution, a good story takes one on a journey that culminates in a suitable ending to the story.[61] One might argue that such a structure follows that of the revealed narrative of Scripture and exhibits the human longing for the final resolution of the eschaton. J. R. R. Tolkien contended that this longing is especially evident in the human proclivity for a happy ending:

> The consolation of fairy-stories, the joy of the happy ending: or more correctly of the good catastrophe [which Tolkien also called *eucatastrophe*], the sudden joyous "turn . . ." is one of the things which fairy stories can produce supremely well, [and it] is not essentially "escapist," nor "fugitive . . ." [I]t is a sudden and miraculous grace . . . giving a fleeting glimpse of Joy, Joy beyond the walls of the world.[62]

Thus, the rhythm of tension and release and the longing for resolution in the viewer or listener fit well within an eschatological Sabbath framework. Conceivably, these aspects of the arts might shed light on the human desire for transcendence and eternal rest. Perhaps, as Patrick Sherry claimed, the arts "have a prophetic function" in that "in their highest achievements, [they] glimpse eternal beauty, and anticipate and give a foretaste of the reality beyond, which is to come."[63] Indeed, perhaps

---

58. Begbie, *Theology, Music and Time*, 38, 87, 92.

59. Begbie, *Theology, Music and Time*, 99, 107 (emphasis original).

60. Begbie, *Theology, Music and Time*, 92.

61. Thompson, *Storytelling in the New Hollywood*, 21.

62. Tolkien, "Consolation of the Happy Ending," 365.

63. Sherry, *Spirit and Beauty*, 144. See also Hart, *Beauty of the Infinite*, 4, 411.

they can even stir a desire not just to enjoy temporal beauty but also to "gaze upon the beauty of the Lord" (Ps 27:4).[64] Hence, the enjoyment of the arts, while anomalous within a naturalistic understanding of reality, seems quite consistent within a sabbatical rhythm of life.

Conclusion

Thus, the creational, redemptive, and eschatological aspects of the Sabbath seem to provide a welcoming home for the cultivation and appreciation of the arts. Indeed, one might argue that such a theistic framework even appears foundational for understanding the role of art in the human experience. Meanwhile, from a purely pragmatic perspective, one cannot think of a more uneconomical enterprise. Participation in the arts is not efficient and takes time and resources away from "valuable" contributions to society. For every minute one's head is "lost in the clouds," precious time is squandered away from productivity. Moreover, from a purely survivalist standpoint, such contemplation would not appear beneficial toward a species's propagation, as those who stop to ponder over the why behind the universe or the significance of a random item would be the first to be eaten in the wild.

The Christian worldview, on the other hand, makes room not only for the resourceful use of time but also for the "wasteful." Certainly, the fit between aesthetic experiences and a sabbatical understanding of reality does not necessarily demand that Christianity is true. But apologetics does not just deal with proofs and classical argumentation. Another vital aspect of apologetics involves stepping into a worldview and seeing how ably it corresponds to reality and makes sense of human experience—or as apologists Joshua D. Chatraw and Mark D. Allen have put it, "try[ing] it on for size."[65]

Engagement with the arts provides such an opportunity, for in the words of pastor Tim Keller, "Art will continue to provoke in people the inescapable intuition that there is more to life than scientific secularism can account for."[66] One must grapple with the question of why, from the beginning, human beings have not only concerned themselves with the necessities for survival but also with grandeur, desiring not just

64. See Harries, *Art and the Beauty of God*, 132.

65. Chatraw and Allen, *Apologetics at the Cross*, 121–22.

66. Keller, *Making Sense of God*, 17.

functionality but also beauty and pleasure. They will settle for bland meals to survive, but they will also crave *delicious* food. They do not simply construct shelter; they *decorate* dwelling places. And when they communicate, they articulate not only the literal but also the figurative and melodic. They will even "waste" time and resources to do so—because the bare necessities may sustain physical bodies, but the restfulness of the arts cultivates the mind and soul, pointing to meaning and providing spiritual tranquility. Intuitively, humans know that the good things in life are not merely what can be consumed. Humans crave connection, meaning, and purpose; the arts, like the Sabbath, help men and women wrestle with the nature of reality and why they exist, demonstrating the significance of life. For this reason, Fujimura (alluding to poet Lewis Hyde) suggests that "art must be treated as a gift, not merely a commodity."[67]

Many people would agree with such a sentiment, but that outlook makes little sense in a purely material universe in which human beings are just more highly evolved animals. Animals do not stand in

67. Fujimura, *Art and Faith*, 66.

amazement at a sunset, compose sonnets to their beloved, or weep at swelling music; they have no register for such transcendence and know not the difference between a priceless artifact and a chew toy. As Glaspey aptly noted, "I marvel at the delicate beauty of the rose. My dog relieves himself on the rose bush."[68] The fact that humans marvel at objects like roses, ceasing momentarily from productivity to ponder and enjoy, suggests that a solely material explanation of roses is insufficient and that a purely survivalist approach to existence is incongruent with human experience. A "survival of the fittest" universe, with its emphasis on functionality, productivity, and viability, has little concern for the distraction of beauty. But in a world imbued with the spirit of the Sabbath, man not only has dominion to grow the roses; he has been charged to literally stop and smell them.

Bibliography

Arand, Charles P. "Responses to Skip MacCarty: Response by Charles P. Arand." In *Perspectives on the Sabbath: Four Views*, edited by Christopher John Donato, 90–99. Nashville: B & H Academic, 2011.

Avila, Mitch. "From Film Emotion to Normative Criticism." In *Reframing Theology and Film: New Focus for an Emerging Discipline*, edited by Robert K. Johnston, 219–37. Grand Rapids: Baker Academic, 2007.

Bacchiocchi, Samuele. *The Sabbath in the New Testament: Answers to Questions*. Berrien Springs, MI: Biblical Perspectives, 1985.

Barack, Nathan A. *A History of the Sabbath*. New York: Jonathan David, 1965.

Barth, Karl. *Church Dogmatics*. Edited by G. W. Bromiley and T. F. Torrance. 4 vols. in 14 parts. New York: T. & T. Clark, 1955–69.

Begbie, Jeremy S. *Theology, Music and Time*. New York: Cambridge University Press, 2000.

———. "Through Music: Sound Mix." In *Beholding the Glory: Incarnation through the Arts*, edited by Jeremy Begbie, 138–54. Grand Rapids: Baker Academic, 2001.

———. *Voicing Creation's Praise: Towards a Theology of the Arts*. New York: T. & T. Clark, 1991.

Borthwick, Alastair et al. "Musical Time and Eschatology." In *Resonant Witness: Conversations between Music and Theology*, edited by Jeremy S. Begbie and Steven R. Guthrie, 271–94. Grand Rapids: Eerdmans, 2011.

Brueggemann, Walter. *Sabbath as Resistance: Saying No to the Culture of Now*. Louisville: Westminster John Knox, 2014.

Callaghan, Morley. *Luke Baldwin's Vow*. Philadelphia: John C. Winston, 1948.

Chatraw, Joshua D., and Mark D. Allen. *Apologetics at the Cross: An Introduction for Christian Witness*. Grand Rapids: Zondervan Academic, 2018.

Cosper, Mike. *The Stories We Tell: How TV and Movies Long for and Echo the Truth*. Wheaton, IL: Crossway, 2014.

68. Glaspey, *Discovering God*, 48.

Crouch, Andy. *Culture Making: Recovering Our Creative Calling*. Downers Grove, IL: IVP, 2008.

Dawn, Marva J. *Keeping the Sabbath Wholly: Ceasing, Resting, Embracing, Feasting*. Grand Rapids: Eerdmans, 1989.

Dederen, Raoul. "Reflections on a Theology of the Sabbath." In *The Sabbath in Scripture and History*, edited by Kenneth A. Strand, 295–306. Washington, DC: Review & Herald, 1982.

De Grazia, Sebastian. *Of Time, Work and Leisure*. New York: Vintage, 1994.

Dressler, Harold H. P. "The Sabbath in the Old Testament." In *From Sabbath to Lord's Day: A Biblical, Historical, and Theological Investigation*, edited by D. A. Carson, 21–41. Eugene, OR: Wipf & Stock, 1999.

Dubay, Thomas. *The Evidential Power of Beauty: Science and Theology Meet*. San Francisco: Ignatius, 1999.

Foster, Cheryl. "Ideas and Imagination: Schopenhauer on the Proper Foundation of Art." In *The Cambridge Companion to Schopenhauer*, edited by Christopher Janaway, 213–51. New York: Cambridge University Press, 1999.

Fujimura, Makoto. *Art and Faith: A Theology of Making*. New Haven: Yale University Press, 2020.

Glaspey, Terry. *Discovering God through the Arts: How We Can Grow Closer to God by Appreciating Beauty and Creativity*. Chicago: Moody, 2021.

Goldman, Solomon. *A Guide to the Sabbath*. London: Jewish Chronicle, 1961.

Guthrie, Steven R. *Creator Spirit: The Holy Spirit and the Art of Becoming Human*. Grand Rapids: Baker Academic, 2011.

Hans, James S. *The Play of the World*. Amherst: The University of Massachusetts Press, 1981.

Harries, Richard. *Art and the Beauty of God: A Christian Understanding*. New York: Mowbray, 1993.

Hart, David Bentley. *The Beauty of the Infinite: The Aesthetics of Christian Truth*. Grand Rapids: Eerdmans, 2003.

Hasel, Gerhard F. "The Sabbath in the Pentateuch." In *The Sabbath in Scripture and History*, edited by Kenneth A. Strand, 21–43. Washington, DC: Review & Herald, 1982.

Hoekema, Anthony A. *Created in God's Image*. Grand Rapids: Eerdmans, 1986.

Huizinga, Johan. *Homo Ludens: A Study of the Play-Element in Culture*. Mansfield Centre, CT: Martino, 2014.

Janaway, Christopher. *Schopenhauer: A Very Short Introduction*. New York: Oxford University Press, 2002.

Keller, Tim. *Making Sense of God: An Invitation to the Skeptical*. New York: Viking, 2016.

Klein, Gideon et al. *Terezín: The Music 1941–44* (CD), 1991.

Lee, Robert. *Religion and Leisure in America: A Study in Four Dimensions*. Nashville: Abingdon, 1964.

Lewis, C. S. "On Stories." In *Essays Presented to Charles Williams*, edited by C. S. Lewis, 90–105. Grand Rapids: Eerdmans, 1974.

———. *Surprised by Joy: The Shape of My Early Life*. In *The Beloved Works of C. S. Lewis*, 1–130. New York: Inspirational, 1986.

———. "The Weight of Glory." In *The Weight of Glory and Other Addresses*, edited by Walter Hooper, 25–46. New York: HarperOne, 1980.

Lincoln, A. T. "From Sabbath to Lord's Day: A Biblical and Theological Perspective." In *From Sabbath to Lord's Day: A Biblical, Historical, and Theological Investigation*, edited by D. A. Carson, 343–412. Eugene, OR: Wipf & Stock, 1999.

———. "Sabbath, Rest, and Eschatology in the New Testament." In *From Sabbath to Lord's Day: A Biblical, Historical, and Theological Investigation*, edited by D. A. Carson, 197–220. Eugene, OR: Wipf & Stock, 1999.

Lipsey, Roger. *The Spiritual in Twentieth-Century Art*. Mineola, NY: Dover, 1988.

Miles, Margaret R. *Image as Insight: Visual Understanding in Western Christianity and Secular Culture*. 1985. Reprint, Eugene, OR: Wipf & Stock, 2006.

Millgram, Abraham E. *Sabbath: The Day of Delight*. Philadelphia: The Jewish Publication Society of America, 1944.

Otto, Rudolf. *The Idea of the Holy: An Inquiry into the Non-Rational Factor in the Idea of the Divine and Its Relation to the Rational*. Translated by John W. Harvey. New York: Oxford University Press, 1926.

Pieper, Josef. *In Tune with the World: A Theory of Festivity*. Translated by Richard Winston and Clara Winston. South Bend, IN: St. Augustine's, 1999.

Pipa, Joseph A. "The Christian Sabbath." In *Perspectives on the Sabbath: Four Views*, edited by Christopher John Donato, 119–71. Nashville: B & H Academic, 2011.

Plato. *Republic*. Edited by C. D. C. Reeve. Translated by G. M. A. Grube. Indianapolis: Hackett, 1992.

Rumsey, Andrew. "Through Poetry: Particularity and the Call to Attention." In *Beholding the Glory: Incarnation through the Arts*, edited by Jeremy Begbie, 47–63. Grand Rapids: Baker Academic, 2001.

Ryken, Leland. *The Liberated Imagination: Thinking Christianly about the Arts*. 1989. Reprint, Eugene, OR: Wipf & Stock, 2005.

Schleske, Martin. *The Sound of Life's Unspeakable Beauty*. Translated by Janet Gesme. Grand Rapids: Eerdmans, 2020.

Schopenhauer, Arthur. *The World as Will and Representation*. 2 vols. Translated by E. F. J. Payne. New York: Dover, 1969.

Sherry, Patrick. *Spirit and Beauty: An Introduction to Theological Aesthetics*, 2nd ed. London: SCM, 2002.

Stark, Richard H III. "Art and Sabbath: A Christian Response to Arthur Schopenhauer's Palliative Aesthetic." PhD diss., The Southern Baptist Theological Seminary, 2015.

Taylor, Charles. *A Secular Age*. Cambridge, MA: Belknap, 2007.

Thompson, Kristin. *Storytelling in the New Hollywood: Understanding Classical Narrative Technique*. Cambridge, MA: Harvard University Press, 1999.

Tolkien, J. R. R. "The Consolation of the Happy Ending." In *The Christian Imagination: The Practice of Faith in Literature and Writing*, edited by Leland Ryken, 365–66. Colorado Springs, CO: Shaw, 2002.

Veith, Gene Edward, Jr. *State of the Arts: From Bezalel to Mapplethorpe*. Wheaton, IL: Crossway, 1991.

Weiss, Herold. "*Sabbatismos* in the Epistle to the Hebrews." *The Catholic Biblical Quarterly* 58 (1996) 674–89.

Wolterstorff, Nicholas P. *Art in Action: Toward a Christian Aesthetic*. Grand Rapids: Eerdmans, 1980.

———. "Thinking about Church Music." In *Music in Christian Worship: At the Service of the Liturgy*, edited by Charlotte Kroeker, 3–16. Collegeville, MN: Liturgical, 2005.

Young, Julian. *Schopenhauer*. New York: Routledge, 2005.

The Lived Aesthetic Testimony
of Christ and Christians

As useful as logical demonstrations for the reasonableness of the faith may be, the affective case is likely more powerful in this day when feelings reign. In this connection, the sacrificial, saving work of Christ on the cross is particularly compelling. So too are Christian acts, indeed all human acts, of self-forgetful loss for the sake of others, even unto death. These phenomena point beyond the spirit of the age and the explanatory fumblings of evolutionists to the Lord who modeled fatal altruism, and who indeed equips our souls for it.

The Beautiful Altruism of Jesus

MARK WARNOCK

Introduction

KRISTIN RENWICK MONROE, IN her book *The Heart of Altruism*, tells the story of Otto Springer, a German living in Czechoslovakia during World War II, who saved over a hundred Jews from the predations of the Nazis. Monroe found herself overwhelmed at the emotional immensity of his story, all he had seen and been through, and his unflagging generosity of spirit throughout.[1] "I knew I was in the presence of something extraordinary, something I had never before witnessed in such intensity and purity. I thought it was altruism. I knew it was real. I did not know if I could understand it myself, let alone explain it satisfactorily to others."[2]

When first responders entered the burning towers of the World Trade Center on September 11 to rescue trapped citizens, they did so at conscious risk to themselves. Many lost their lives in the towers' collapse. Their altruism, risking their lives for the benefit of others, produced in American culture a surge of gratitude and honor towards police, firefighters, and EMTs that persists to this day. The US cultural mood has also shifted towards those serving in the military. The Vietnam era was rife with contempt towards soldiers and Marines for being implementers of what was considered evil foreign policy. In the wake of 9/11, however,

1. Monroe, *Heart of Altruism*, xv.
2. Monroe, *Heart of Altruism*, xv.

113

servicemen and women have risked life and limb in the Middle East to protect the homeland from terrorist incursions. In addition, they have paid the price of extended absence from their families during these long tours of duty. A sense of reverence accompanies each "Thank you for your service," an expression now regarded as almost obligatory.

Literature, too, is replete with characters who willingly give their lives for the benefit of others, often for others who are unaware of the danger coming their way or who are powerless to resist it. In *A Tale of Two Cities*, Sydney Carton willingly goes to the guillotine in place of another, and his final thoughts capture the nobility of altruism: "It is a far, far better thing that I do, than I have ever done; it is a far, far better rest that I go to, than I have ever known."[3] Frodo, in *The Lord of the Rings*, willingly assumes the burden of the one ring and risks death to rid the world of

3. Dickens, *Tale of Two Cities*, 282.

its corrupting evil, despite the fact that the ring came into his possession only by chance.[4] We call these characters "Christ-figures," acknowledging Jesus as the paragon of altruistic sacrifice. Altruistic sacrifices resonate deeply with our moral sensibilities, which in part explains their frequent occurrence in literature.[5] Whenever this narrative appears—in literature, in film, or when lived out and reported in real-life stories—it nearly always produces a strong emotional response.

At the heart of the Christian story is a worthy, innocent man laying down his life for undeserving people. The story of Jesus has enduring appeal, in part because of the power of his altruistic, self-giving sacrifice. In this chapter, I will show how Jesus's sacrifice of himself for sinful humanity is an act of altruism in the strong sense. I will explore the aesthetic appeal that altruistic sacrifices have, and why they are so provocative. I will consider how Christian and secular worldviews might account for this phenomenon. This chapter will further argue that Jesus's altruistic offer of himself on behalf of sinful humanity is a significant apologetic for Christianity, making a compelling appeal rooted in its aesthetic beauty. I'll conclude with some suggestions for framing an apologetic that draws on this appeal.

Altruism at the Heart of the Christian Faith

What is altruism, exactly? A standard definition says that altruistic behavior "is motivated by a desire to benefit someone other than oneself for that person's sake." More colloquially, altruistic acts might be called benevolent or charitable. These terms capture the sense that altruistic actions aim toward the good of others.[6] A more fine-grained understanding differentiates strong and weak senses of altruism. Acts are altruistic in the weak sense when they are motivated by the prospect of benefitting someone else, or not injuring them.[7] An act is altruistic in a strong sense

4. Tolkien, *Lord of the Rings*.

5. The novelist Toni Morrison, in a lecture at Harvard, observed that nineteenth-century novels invariably end with the triumph of goodness. After World War I, that optimism receded, replaced by increasing attention to evil. Goodness and altruism, she observed, often remain muted or in the background in contemporary writing (Morrison, "Toni Morrison").

6. Kraut, "Altruism," para. 1.

7. Kraut, "Altruism," sec 1.2, para. 3.

when, in addition to expressing a benevolent aim, it is done despite a risk of "loss to one's well-being."[8]

Strong altruism is at the heart of the Christian gospel and is central to what makes Christianity distinct from other religions. In Christianity, God's demands are appeased not by human worshipers who obey laws, perform sacrifices, or satisfy divine conditions, but by the divine Son of God, who intercedes on behalf of sinners incapable of meeting the demands of God's righteousness. Jesus stands between sinful humanity and the wrath of God, and bears in his body the wrath due us, in an act of conscious, deliberate self-sacrifice.

Those who believe respond with grateful submission, repentance, and faith. God the Father also responds by accepting the sacrifice. He accepts, along with Jesus, all who come to him in Jesus' name. The Father also bestows on Jesus his Son "the name that is above every name, so that at the name of Jesus, every knee should bow . . . and every tongue confess that Jesus Christ is Lord, to the glory of God the Father."[9] In the Revelation to John, Jesus is described as worthy to open the scroll because he was slain and purchased people for God by his blood. The honor due to Jesus is, at least in part, merited not by his being and divine status, but by the sacrificial actions he performed for the good of sinners, despite the great cost of those actions.[10]

Jesus and Altruism

To set the stage for an apologetic of altruism, let me first make a biblical argument that Jesus' sacrifice meets the criteria for strong altruistic action.[11] First, it was *deliberate and considered*. Jesus predicted his sacrifice

---

8. Kraut, "Altruism," sec 1.2, para. 3.

9. Phil 2:9–11.

10. Heb 5:8–9.

11. There are Trinitarian considerations that complicate the demonstration of altruism. These considerations are not unimportant, and a lengthier treatment might take them into account. For instance, how is the intention of God the Father to save sinners shared by God the Son? Is Jesus' altruistic action in sacrificing himself the same kind of altruism as that of God the Father? If God the Father sacrifices his Son, and the Son sacrifices himself, is the Son's action more strongly altruistic than the Father's? Is God the Father's intent to save sinners altruistic independently from the sacrifice of the Son, or does their agreement and cooperation amount to a shared altruism?

many times,[12] and just before he took the final steps toward the cross, he contemplated it deeply at Gethsemane, asking for another way to be found if possible. In the end, he yielded to the will of God: "Not my will but yours be done."[13] There was a price to pay, and Jesus was aware of it and considered it carefully and deeply.

Jesus' sacrifice was *undertaken willingly*. Perhaps the most powerful statement of Jesus' intention is found in John 10: "I am the good shepherd. The good shepherd lays down his life for the sheep . . . No one takes it from me, but I lay it down of my own accord. I have authority to lay it down, and I have authority to take it up again."[14] Isaiah forecasts that willing intention: "Surely he has borne our griefs and carried our sorrows . . . He was oppressed and he was afflicted, yet he opened not his mouth."[15] In Philippians, Paul reverently reports that Jesus became "obedient to the point of death, even death on a cross."[16]

Jesus' sacrifice was *motivated by the prospect of the well-being of others*. Jesus' statement of his own purpose is that he came "to seek and save the lost."[17] Paul writes that the saying is "deserving of full acceptance" that Christ "came into the world to save sinners."[18] The culmination of that mission was his enduring the cross. Paul goes on to say in a moving passage that Christ, who died for sinners and was raised, now continues the extension of his good will towards sinners by interceding for us before the Father and assuring us that nothing can separate us from his love.[19] John, in his first epistle, likewise calls Jesus our advocate before the Father, the one whose sacrifice is offered to God for our sins.[20]

Finally, Jesus' sacrifice was *undertaken at great cost to his own personal well-being*. The sacrifice was holistic: he endured the stress and

12. Matt 16:21–23; 17:22–23; 20:17–19; Mark 8:31–32; 9:30–32; 10:32–34; Luke 9:21–22, 43–45; 18:31–34.

13. Luke 22:42.

14. John 10:11, 18.

15. Isa 53:4, 7.

16. Phil 2:8; Heb 5:8–9.

17. Luke 19:10. It is true that part of Jesus' motivation was obeying the Father and seeking his glory, but that motivation does not blunt Jesus' intention to do good toward sinners. No altruism is performed from unmixed motives, and having a mixture of motivations does not disqualify behaviors as altruistic (Kraut, "Altruism," sec. 1.1).

18. 1 Tim 1:15.

19. Rom 8:31–39.

20. 1 John 2:1–2.

anxiety of anticipating his ordeal; felt the sting of betrayal by Judas and abandonment by most of his followers; suffered the indignity of a kangaroo court trial and a brutal flogging; and faced the most painful and shameful execution that Roman brutality could conceive.

Jesus' offering of himself, moreover, was deliberate, conscious, directed toward the good of others, achieved at great cost to himself, and effective in producing the intended outcome.

Altruism and Aesthetics

Altruism is, first of all, a moral characteristic of behavior. In addition to this moral quality, however, altruism has an aesthetic dimension. Acts of self-sacrifice invariably evoke an emotional response from ordinary observers, sometimes a surprisingly strong one. Such acts can occasion awe, admiration, gratitude, and humility, and/or they can be seen as beautiful, noble, or worthy of imitation.

The aesthetic quality of altruism defies easy expression. The word used in the chapter title calls Jesus' sacrifice "beautiful," but that may not be the most apt term. "Beautiful," taken in its basic sense, means "pleasing to look upon." The cross, by contrast, is horrific to consider and only takes on more positive emotional tones once its theological meaning is considered. The other difficulty with the term "beautiful" is that it easily reduces to "pretty."

There are three aesthetic features of altruistic sacrifices that seem most salient. First, they are *attractive*, by which I mean that we are drawn to (and not repulsed from) altruistic acts and people who perform them. There are reporters whose primary beat is to find someone in the community doing good and tell their story. These altruistic stories are commonly used to close local TV newscasts. News editors tease the closing story during the newscast to keep people watching to the end, and it works. Even if the rest of the newscast was full of negative news, if they close with a fourth-grader's lemonade stand raising money for cancer research, viewers will leave happy.

Second, altruism is *moving*. It does not have a superficial or ephemeral effect, like a quick laugh to a clever joke soon forgotten. Altruism usually makes us feel more deeply and often provokes reflective thinking. Why is the fourth-grader raising money for cancer?

Finally, altruism is *praiseworthy*. This characteristic may be the one that best links the moral and aesthetic qualities of altruism: because the action is morally good, it properly evokes an emotionally positive response. Acts of altruism are routinely recognized, honored, pointed to, and glorified, and there is an easy consensus that they ought to be treated in this way.

There are common categories of emotional experiences that can help frame a proper understanding of altruism. Aesthetic experience is the broadest category, which encompasses any encounter that provokes a "judgment of taste,"[21] to use Kant's language, whether seeing the morning sky upon rising, entering a well-appointed office, or contemplating a painting in a gallery. A subset of aesthetic experience is religious experience, which entails a range of moving encounters prompted or framed by religious ideas. The final category is the sublime experience, which some writers have seen as sharing similarities with religious experience.[22]

The response to altruism does not seem to fit the pattern of the sublime experience, which is prompted by perceptions of immensity in time or space. Contemplating eternity, for instance, strains the ability of the mind to comprehend it, and the sense of being overwhelmed fills the space that cognition cannot. Similarly, contemplating vast reaches of space, like trying to grasp the size of the universe strains the limits of comprehension. The aesthetic response to altruism, however, is not ineffable or inexpressible. In the case of Jesus, a believer might describe his response as "gratitude"—no mystery there—and explain, "Jesus died for my sins." Further, the aesthetic response to altruism admits of degrees. It may provoke greater and greater levels of humility, devotion, gratitude, or love.[23]

Kant thought that judgments of taste carry in themselves an implication of universality. If one person thinks a painting is beautiful, that judgment carries an expectation that others would join in that judgment. C. S. Lewis, commenting on the injunction in the Psalms to praise the Lord,

21. Kant, *Critique of Judgment*, 37.

22. See for instance Warnock, "Imagination," 403–9. I leave aside mystical experiences, which are too distantly connected to altruism to bear consideration.

23. These emotional factors explain in part why Christians can stand in worship—in some contexts, for hours—with upraised arms, singing with emotional abandon of the worthiness of Jesus. Though it is beyond the scope of this chapter to explore, the glad-hearted worship of sincere Christians is another exhibit of aesthetic evidence to the truth of Christianity.

struck a similar note when he observed that all enjoyment overflows in praise. Praise, of course, is expressed communally, inviting others to join and affirm it.[24] This universalizing impulse is more an inclination than a law. Aesthetics have a kind of gravity that incline toward the good and the true, which is one reason the true, good, and beautiful have been classically connected in philosophy. This inclination is what makes altruism a possible apologetic for the Christian faith. When we are moved by the sacrifice of Jesus, it stirs us to find an explanation, one that could be shared by others.

Explaining Altruism

Altruistic acts demand explanation. It is counterintuitive for a person to act for the good of others, especially when at great cost to himself. Selfish action is the easiest to explain, either in terms of flawed human nature or evolution's selfish genes. Selflessness and generosity aren't quite as easy to explain, but it can be done. Strong altruism, however, where your own good is exchanged for that of others, is a particular puzzle for worldviews that do not include a God of self-donating love.

Evolutionary theorists, for instance, attempt to explain how altruism confers evolutionary advantage, but a strong consensus has not yet emerged from the extensive literature on the subject.[25] Selection for altruism seems not to work at the individual level, for an individual who sacrifices himself for others is less likely to reproduce. If that is the case, how could altruism ever have emerged? At the group level, there is a stronger case for altruism. Groups with high levels of altruistic behavior may be more likely to thrive than comparable groups without it. One might postulate that the reason altruistic behavior produces humility and admiration in humans is that we evolved that emotional response as a way of reinforcing the benefit of group protection that redounds to the advantage of all the individuals in a tribe or group. This idea was first broached by Darwin himself, but has proved controversial in the history of evolutionary theory.[26] Richard Dawkins, for instance, was one of many who pointed out that among a group of altruists, one opportunistic individual

---

24. Lewis, *Reflections on the Psalms*, 93–95.

25. A good summary of recent literature on evolution and altruism can be found in Harman, "Evolution of Altruism."

26. Darwin, *Descent of Man*, 157.

could take advantage of the group's altruism to the benefit of his own reproductive potential; thus, altruistic traits would be vulnerable to being comprised by one or a few comparatively selfish group members.[27] Yet altruism exists and must be explained. David Sloan Wilson summarizes altruism in evolution this way: "Selfishness beats altruism within groups. Altruistic groups beat selfish groups. All else is commentary."[28] Exactly how group altruism is to have evolved when it is vulnerable at the individual level of selection, however, remains mysterious.

More straightforward explanations come from Christian theology. Humans are made in the image of a God of self-donating love. Jack Mahoney suggests that if we apply a social model of Trinity, in which the persons of the Godhead relate to one another through other-centered love, human altruism is explainable as a manifestation of one dimension of the *imago Dei*. He summarizes: "Whenever and wherever it is to be found, human altruism or generosity, the breakout from any evolutionary self-obsession, can be seen as a reflection of, and participation in, the creative altruism and *agape* of God himself."[29] One could easily go further and explain that, where human selfishness undercuts altruism, it is a result of the fall. The Christian worldview here, as in many other places, expresses both the ideal and the reality, the beauty and the brokenness of human life.

One thread, then, of the altruism apologetic is that it is better explained by Christian theology than by other worldviews. This is not entirely satisfying, however. Jesus' altruism only carries the meaning it does in a Christian worldview. Secularists would consider Jesus just one more spiritual reformer who got on the bad side of the ruling powers of his day. The power of the apologetic is not that the logical answers Christianity provides are the best, but in that altruism demands an explanation in the first place.

The *moral* dimension of altruism is the part that most transparently demands explanation. What motivated her altruistic action? Why did she behave that way? The *aesthetic* dimension is another matter, more complex and intriguing. Why do we respond to altruism the way we do? What might our deep surge of emotion indicate? A psychologist would tell us to pay attention to our emotions, that they are saying something important.

27. Dawkins, *Selfish Gene*.

28. Wilson, *Does Altruism Exist?*, 23.

29. See for instance Mahoney, "Evolution, Altruism, and the Image of God," 677.

If a simple question in therapy provoked an angry, defensive response, a counselor would want to explore it. Similarly, when we respond aesthetically and emotionally to the altruism of Jesus, we should pay attention to it. It seems to be telling us something important about the world.

Some Objections

The story of Jesus is moving, but what does that prove? Skeptics might argue that the similarity between readers' response to fictional altruism and believers' response to Jesus' altruism just demonstrates the power of stories but says nothing about the truth of Christianity. Feuerbach might have said that Jesus' sacrifice is a story we tell to extol certain cultural values. Perhaps Frodo and Sydney Carton are called Christ-figures simply because the gospel is an older story. Moving stories in literary traditions aren't indicators of truth.

Research in the mental architecture of the imagination, however, prevents us from jumping too quickly to that conclusion. Single-code theory explains that we process imaginative ideas and beliefs about the real world using the same mental faculties. Shaun Nichols explains that imagination and belief share a common code, which allows cognitive structures to treat their contents similarly.[30] Nichols's sketch of mental architecture has belief and imagining in separate boxes, situated side by side in a parallel relationship to both the inferential, reasoning function of the mind and to its emotion-processing function.[31] Thus, ideas may be either imagined or believed, and the inferences drawn from them or emotions provoked by them may be similar, regardless of whether imagined or believed.[32] For instance, if I believe my wife is cheating on me, it will upset me, but even imagining it can be upsetting also.[33] This cogni-

---

30. Single-code theory has been the most productive in explaining a range of philosophical puzzles (Nichols, "Imagining and Believing," 129).

31. Nichols and Stich, "Cognitive Theory of Pretense," 125, 128. Nichols, "Imagining and Believing," 130, 132.

32. Nichols, "Imagining and Believing," 131–32. See also Meskin and Weinberg, "Emotions, Fiction," 18–34.

33. Emotional responses to beliefs tend to be stronger and more enduring than responses to imagination, of course, but single-code theory can allow for this also. For example, since imagining is more directly volitional than believing. I can choose to stop imagining, which will choke the emotional response (Nichols, "Just the Imagination," 464).

tive structure explains why, for instance, a reader can feel anger at Iago's treachery or sorrow over Desdemona's victimization in *Othello*, even though he knows they are not real.[34] A believer and an atheist, therefore, can both find themselves emotionally moved in a worship service because both believing and imagining can produce similar affective responses.

The key difference is that imagined ideas are quarantined from the rest of a person's beliefs and do not influence their actions in the same way that beliefs do. We don't hold annual memorials for Sydney Carton or file suit against Iago for slander and wrongful death. Fiction is imagined and quarantined. Beliefs, on the other hand, do influence our morals, actions, and general view of the world. Christians are not simply emotionally moved by the story of Jesus' sacrifice, but are moved to repent of sins, live in obedience to Christ's commands, and live for his glory. The etymology of belief is "by live"; that is, we live by what we believe.

Few would dispute that a person's aesthetic response to fictional altruism would not be as great as her response to real altruism in the world, especially when she benefits from it. A woman might be emotionally stirred by her evening reading of *A Tale of Two Cities*, but it pales next to the response she would have attending the memorial service for the firefighter who pulled her from the World Trade Center, only to perish minutes later in the collapse of the towers. The second response is deeper, more lasting, and more profound than the first. The aesthetic response, therefore, is greater when the altruistic sacrifice is taken to be true.

The truth of Jesus' sacrifice is what makes it so great and powerful. As a fiction, it is moving. As an event of history disconnected from its theological meaning, it is instructive or interesting. But as the true, real-in-the-world action of a loving God rescuing me by suffering and dying in my place, the aesthetical and emotional force is all the more powerful.

Which comes first, recognizing the truth of the meaning of Jesus' sacrifice or the emotional response to it? The answer, of course, is that they are connected. The aesthetic dimension shows that the truth of the matter is important to discover. The New Testament insists that Christianity is unimportant if it is false. "If Christ has not been raised, your faith is worthless" (1 Cor 15:17 CSB). If true, however, it is of utmost importance. The aesthetic dimension of the story of Jesus alerts us to that fact.

The argument I wish to make is that the beautiful altruism of Jesus is not a proof for the truth of Christianity, but a sign that points to it. It

34. Nichols, "Imagining and Believing," 133.

provides ample reason to consider deeply whether Christianity might be true. The aesthetic appeal does not make a statement, it raises a question. Something like, "Why is this so moving? Could it be true?"

Suggestions for Apologists

The theme of altruism stands out in our current culture because it is at odds with the way we have deified the self. Increasingly in the decadent West, the self is the highest authority and treasure. One sign of the ascent of the self (and the decay of our culture) is the disappearance of altruism. Long ago, people would make altruistic sacrifices to ensure the survival of their tribe or kin. A generation or two ago, parents frequently would make sacrifices to see that their children would be better off. Today the reverse is the case. The modern West is producing anti-altruists. They sacrifice everything else for themselves: their money, their marriages, their children, and even their bodies. Families and legislatures sacrifice future financial prosperity for present enjoyment by running up debt on credit cards or through reckless government spending laid onto the backs of future taxpayers. Men and women sacrifice decades-long marriages to relive the adolescent thrill of sexual adventure. Legal abortion enables people to literally sacrifice their children so as not to endanger their current lifestyle. Transgender people maim their own bodies to make them conform with the incorrigible dictates of an authoritarian self. No challenge to the authority of self can be tolerated.[35] The self functions as god for decadent Western man, and as in classical paganism, the gods must receive sacrifices. Gods don't make sacrifices. And, even more, the gods don't sacrifice themselves.

The inversion of the pagan pattern of sacrifice is the truly astonishing thing about Jesus. The divine Son offers himself as a sacrifice for others. It's incredibly counterintuitive and unexpectedly moving. It is good news, unbelievably good, to people who thought they had to earn their goodness. Those who believe the burden of sacrifice was entirely upon them are astonished to discover that God has taken upon himself the unbelievable burden, at great cost to himself, to the benefit of their own unworthy souls. When the story is told in a way that highlights this inversion, the aesthetic appeal of the story can provoke consideration of whether it might be true.

---

35. See Trueman, *Rise and Triumph*.

The best way to tap the magnetic power of altruism in Christian evangelism is simply to tell the story of Jesus. This suggestion may seem obvious, but many Christian apologists gravitate to the intellectual and abstract. Only a few years ago, the greatest apologetic challenge to Christianity was the New Atheism, with its arid intellectualism and demands of logic and evidence. Today, however, the hyperintellectual skeptic has largely been replaced by the present-focused emotivist. *The New York Times* recently reported how TikTok videos of a teenage girl crying over book endings are driving tens of thousands of book sales.[36] The rising post-Christian generations are dialed in to "the feels," which tend not to be stirred by logical syllogisms or theological propositions. Narrative and image are the native media for emotional engagement. The worldwide impact of projects that simply tell and show the story of Jesus, like *The Jesus Film*, *The Passion of the Christ*, and *The Chosen*, are a sign of this effect.[37]

Inviting people to enter empathetically into the experience of Jesus can be an effective apologetic. Frame the story so they can feel the sting of Judas's betrayal, the hostility of the Sanhedrin, Pilate's disinterested political calculus, the brutality of the scourging, the physical effects of crucifixion, the shame and humiliation, the helplessness and confusion of Jesus' followers, the seeming finality of his burial, and the unexpected joy of his resurrection.

Another opportunity to use the story of Jesus is in answer to the problem of suffering. Emotionally sensitive people are especially attuned to this problem, and intellectually framed apologetics often miss the heart of these questioners. Evil and suffering are more fitly addressed today by narrative. The entire Bible is God's narrative answer to the problem of evil and suffering. It explains the origins of suffering, its effects, and God's plan throughout history to solve the problem of evil, which culminates in the voluntary, altruistic suffering of his Son.

The Limits of This Approach

The emotional appeal of Jesus' altruism may be blunted if other apologetic concerns are pressing or unaddressed. The aesthetic appeal of the story will be compelling only to a person who believes key premises of the Christian worldview: that Jesus was a real historical figure, that his

36. Harris, "How Crying on TikTok Sells Books," para. 8.
37. Eshleman, "'Jesus' Film," 68–70.

sacrifice on the cross is effective for the removal of sin, that sin is a moral and existential problem of the highest order, that reconciliation with God is the highest human good, etc. For the narrative of sacrifice to have fullest impact, intellectual objections to these tenets of faith might need to be addressed first. This apologetic strategy, if it can be called that, might be considered a closing strategy. Once a person's questions about more foundational issues of Christian truth are settled, the nobility of the sacrifice of Jesus on their behalf may soften their resistance to repentance and conversion.

Having said that, it is entirely possible, as when reading fiction or watching a movie, that a person hearing the story of Jesus could suspend her disbelief and allow herself to experience the story from within the assumptions of the Christian worldview, which perhaps she might initially reject or question. If moved by the aesthetic power of the story, she might reconsider her skepticism about different tenets of Christian truth. This might especially be the case if she finds herself in a community of Christians who express the love and care and commitment to truth that you might expect to find if Christianity and all its claims were true.

Nevertheless, a renewed focus on the story and altruistic actions of Jesus may grant fresh power to Christian evangelism. In the current emotive mood of the West, the power of Jesus' costly intention to do good may prove the strongest indicator of truth and motivator of belief that can be found.

Bibliography

Darwin, Charles. *The Descent of Man and Selection in Relation to Sex*, vol. 1. 2 vols. New York: Appleton, 1872.

Dawkins, Richard. *The Selfish Gene*. Oxford: Oxford University Press, 1976.

Dickens, Charles. *A Tale of Two Cities*. New York: Arlington House, 1982.

Eshleman, Paul A. "The 'Jesus' Film: A Contribution to World Evangelism." *The International Bulletin of Missionary Research* (April 2002) 68–72. https://journals.sagepub.com/doi/pdf/10.1177/239693930202600202.

Harman, Oren. "The Evolution of Altruism." *The Chronicle of Higher Education*, February 9, 2015. https://www.chronicle.com/article/the-evolution-of-altruism/.

Harris, Elizabeth A. "How Crying on TikTok Sells Books." *The New York Times*, March 20, 2021. https://www.nytimes.com/2021/03/20/books/booktok-tiktok-video.html.

"Jesus Film Project® Study Confirms Billions Have Heard the Gospel Around the World." *Religion News Service*, March 13, 2017. https://religionnews.com/2017/03/13/jesus-film-project-study-confirms-billions-have-heard-the-gospel-around-the-world/.

Kant, Immanuel. *Critique of Judgment*. Translated by J. H. Bernard. New York: MacMillan, 1951.

Kraut, Richard. "Altruism." *The Stanford Encyclopedia of Philosophy* (Fall 2020 Edition), edited by Edward N. Zalta. https://plato.stanford.edu/archives/fall2020/entries/altruism/.

Lewis, C. S. *Reflections on the Psalms*. New York: Harcourt, 1958.

Mahoney, Jack. "Evolution, Altruism, and the Image of God." *Theological Studies* 71.3 (2010) 677–701.

Meskin, Aaron, and Jonathan Weinberg. "Emotions, Fiction, and Cognitive Architecture." *The British Journal of Aesthetics* 1 (2003) 18–34.

Monroe, Kristen R. *The Heart of Altruism: Perceptions of a Common Humanity*. Princeton: Princeton University Press, 1996.

Morrison, Toni. "Toni Morrison: 'Goodness: Altruism and the Literary Imagination.'" *The New York Times*, August 7, 2019. https://www.nytimes.com/2019/08/07/books/toni-morrison-goodness-altruism-literary-imagination.html.

Nichols, Shaun. "Imagining and Believing: The Promise of a Single Code." *The Journal of Aesthetics and Art Criticism* 62.2 (2014) 129–39.

———. "Just the Imagination: Why Imagining Doesn't Behave Like Believing." *Mind & Language* 21.4 (2006) 459–74.

Nichols, Shaun, and Stephen Stich. "A Cognitive Theory of Pretense." *Cognition* 74 (2000) 115–47.

Tolkien, J. R. R. *The Lord of the Rings: One Volume*. New York: Houghton Mifflin, 2005.

Trueman, Carl. *The Rise and Triumph of the Modern Self*. Wheaton, IL: Crossway, 2020.

Warnock, Mary. "Imagination—Aesthetic and Religious." *Theology* 83 (1980) 403–9.

Wilson, David Sloan. *Does Altruism Exist? Culture, Genes, and the Welfare of Others*. New Haven: Yale University Press, 2015.

Though we more typically speak of physical beauty or ugliness—of sunsets or a Quasimodo—moral beauty and ugliness are present all around us, arresting our attention. We're gratified, even astonished, at the sight of those who go the second mile in love toward their enemies and are repulsed by reports of child abuse and fraud. The Christian faith, with its understanding of God and man, explains these deeds and discernments in a way that naturalism cannot.

Christian Character as
Aesthetic Apologetics

MATT CRAWFORD

IN HIS ARTICLE, "AESTHETIC Arguments for the Existence of God," Peter
S. Williams outlines two categories of apologetic arguments using aesthetics. Epistemological arguments primarily focus on the human ability
to know that something is beautiful. Ontological arguments, on the other
hand, leverage the very existence of beauty for apologetic use.[1] This essay fits primarily in the former category, as it will focus on the apologetic
value of Christian character from an aesthetic perspective.

It is difficult for a naturalist to ground the concept of beauty, since
he has no objective reference point in a universe formed by accidents
and chaos. This means that the naturalist cannot properly explain ex-
emplifications of beauty which are widely recognized as aesthetically
pleasing, even across cultural and worldview boundaries. Christianity,
however, presents a coherent explanation of widely shared experiences
of beauty—whether in sensory or virtuous forms. Humanity's experience
of beauty points both to the existence of God and to the truthfulness of
the Christian worldview. Williams puts it this way: "Naturalism also fails
to account for the existence of human experience, including aesthetic experience . . . Therefore naturalism should not look like a good candidate

---

1. Williams, "Aesthetic Arguments."

for a world-view to anyone who wants to retain a reasonable belief in aesthetic value, and this gives one reason to prefer theism."[2]

The Beauty of Virtue

William Edgar introduces the virtuous aspect of the apologetic value of beauty: "If we contemplate beautiful things we eventually develop a greater awareness of the world and its problems . . . The beautiful bursts the bubble of our own autonomy, makes us attuned to the needs of the world around us."[3] Here Edgar points out a connection between our perception of beauty and a selfless view of the world. Beauty helps us realize that there is more to be valued than just ourselves and our own petty agendas, and aesthetic appreciation opens our eyes to a larger world in need around us. Because of the power of God, who is the Source of this beauty, this new perspective has the power to change our lives and our character.

Edgar is not the only one who sees this connection between beauty and virtuous character. Hans Urs von Balthasar, the Catholic theologian whose seven-volume *The Glory of the Lord* is one of the definitive works on Christian aesthetics, saw the beauty of human holiness as extending from God himself. He artfully states,

> For whatever else is true, the beautiful requires the reaction of the whole man, even though it is initially perceived by means of only one or more sense-faculties. In the end, however, all our senses are engaged when the interior space of a beautiful musical composition or painting opens itself to us and captivates us: the whole person then enters into a state of vibration and becomes responsive space, the "sounding box" of the event of beauty occurring within him . . . And it becomes clear at once that faith in the full Christian sense can be nothing other than this: to make the whole man a space that responds to the divine content. Faith attunes man to this sound; it confers on man the ability to react precisely to this divine experiment, preparing him to be a violin that receives just this touch of the bow, to serve as material for just this house to be built, to provide the rhyme for just this verse being composed. This was the reaction

2. Williams, "Aesthetic Arguments," 12–13.
3. Edgar, "Aesthetics," 109.

already envisaged when the Covenant was made on Sinai: "Be holy, because I am holy."[4]

So, the same God who infused the universe with beauty and gave us the arts to enjoy composes beautifully with the instruments or palettes of our lives. And this beauty in human beings is not primarily manifested in attractive physical forms, but in holy lives. God manifests his character and beauty through the changed lives of those who follow him.

Jonathan Edwards agrees with this understanding of righteous character as beautiful. William Danaher summarizes his view: "Edwards defined the moral life not in terms of making the right decisions, or cultivating the character through habituation, but in terms of the change of affections through the reception of a 'new sense' of the love of God. Edwards conceived of the love born of this change as a participation in the 'beauty' or 'excellency' that flows from God."[5] And this makes further sense if we subscribe to a Platonic connection between truth, beauty, and goodness. Virtue is inextricably united with beauty.

Herein lies an often-overlooked apologetic value of beauty. There is an aesthetically pleasing aspect to the virtue of those whose lives have been changed by an experience with the God of beauty. In fact, Von Balthasar saw aesthetics as absolutely essential to the task of Christian apologetics: "The saint is the apology for the Christian religion. He is holy, however, because he allows Christ to live in him, and it is in Christ that he 'glories.'"[6] This idea resonates with common sense, especially when we consider the alternative: People who claim the name of Christ yet live reprehensible lives are deemed hypocrites by the secular world. In fact, many who reject the gospel claim to do so on the basis of Christians whose lives are morally ugly. Apologetic arguments separated from a life of integrity are empty, yet the beauty of a virtuous Christian life will attract people to Christ. Again, Jonathan Edwards agrees:

> They who see the beauty of true virtue do not perceive it by argumentation on its connections and consequences, but by the frame of their own minds, or a certain spiritual sense given them of God—whereby they immediately perceive pleasure in

---

4. Von Balthasar, *Seeing the Form*, 220.

5. Danaher Jr., "Beauty, Benevolence, and Virtue," 394.

6. Danaher Jr., "Beauty, Benevolence, and Virtue," 229.

the presence of the idea of true virtue in their minds, or are directly gratified in the view or contemplation of this object.[7]

Of course, the attractiveness of reformed moral character in the lives of Christians is a thoroughly biblical idea. Jesus stated in John 13:34–35, "A new commandment I give to you, that you love one another: just as I have loved you, you also are to love one another. By this all people will know that you are my disciples, if you have love for one another." The hallmark of Christian discipleship is the love that Christians share with one another; the beauty of this love will stand out in contrast with the violence and hate in the rest of the world.

The apostle Paul's life stands out as a powerful example of the beauty of reformed character that brings glory to the beautiful God who does the work of reforming. Prior to his conversion, Paul was on a rampage against Christians wherever he could find them, chasing them down, sending them to jail, and even participating in their murders. He spoke against the name of Christ and had the blood of Christians on his hands. Paul shares this testimony and the change that took place in his life in 1 Timothy 1:12–17:

> I thank him who has given me strength, Christ Jesus our Lord, because he judged me faithful, appointing me to his service, though formerly I was a blasphemer, persecutor, and insolent opponent. But I received mercy because I had acted ignorantly in unbelief, and the grace of our Lord overflowed for me with the faith and love that are in Christ Jesus. This saying is trustworthy and deserving of full acceptance, that Christ Jesus came into the world to save sinners, of whom I am the foremost. But I received mercy for this reason, that in me, as the foremost, Jesus Christ might display his perfect patience as an example to those who were to believe in him for eternal life. To the King of ages, immortal, invisible, the only God, be honor and glory forever and ever. Amen.

Especially important for our discussion is Paul's note that God's purpose in changing Paul's life was to put God's own patience on display, both to bring him glory forever and to fulfill the *apologetic* purpose of leading others to believe in Christ "for eternal life."

---

7. Edwards, *Nature of True Virtue*, 99. Joseph D. Woodell actually finds four different apologetic implications in Edwards's *The Nature of True Virtue*, which is not expressly an apologetic work. See Wooddell, "Jonathan Edwards, Beauty, and Apologetics," 81–95.

Here we return to the *imago Dei* as an essential part of our understanding of beauty. The beauty of virtue is found in people as they continue to reflect the virtuous character of the God whose image is upon them. The image of God becomes even more apparent upon Christians as the work of the Holy Spirit within them conforms them to Christ. In addition, the image of God which remains upon unbelievers is what allows them to recognize the beauty of righteous living and to value it in other people. Even the hardened atheist, who publicly touts the lack of objective standards of morality, wants to be treated with respect and kindness by others and would object to violence directed his way. The unremovable image of God in all of us causes us to value the beauty of virtue. Naturalism will be hard pressed to explain our shared appreciation of conformity to at least some minimal standards of morality.[8]

Apologetic arguments from the attractiveness of the personal character of Christians are not new; they have a long and distinguished history within the faith. In fact, they appear in the earliest examples of apologetic writings found outside of Scripture. The moral character of believers in Christ was frequently used by early church fathers in apologetic defenses, especially when directed at the Roman Empire as a persecutor of Christians. There were frequent misunderstandings (deliberate or not) of certain Christian practices, such as the taking of the Lord's Supper. This practice was wrongly perceived by non-Christians in the early days of the Church to include elements of cannibalism through the misinterpretation of the symbolism of consuming Christ's body and blood. The Roman Empire used this misinformation as one basis upon which to cause Christians great suffering, even to the point of death.[9]

In response to this oppression, Christian apologists tried to clarify the misunderstandings of their practices and consistently pointed to the selfless love of Christians, even for those who persecuted them. They also reminded the governing authorities of their faithfulness as loyal subjects and their honorable contributions to their surrounding communities. Aristides, whom Avery Cardinal Dulles calls "the most important apologist prior to Justin," wrote to this end, "placing primary emphasis on the

---

8. This is why it does not make logical sense for Richard Dawkins and other atheists to deny the Christian worldview and then to denigrate the God of the Bible because he is "unjust . . . vindictive, bloodthirsty . . . racist . . . megalomaniacal," etc. (Dawkins, *God Delusion*, 31). As a naturalist, Dawkins has no way to ground his judgment of these characteristics as wrong, even if they *could* be attributed to God.

9. Edgar and Oliphint, *Christian Apologetics*, 27.

good moral lives of Christians, including their purity and charity . . . [thereby establishing] the basis for some of the most successful apologetics of the next few centuries."[10] Justin Martyr argued along the same lines, pleading his case before the Roman emperor Antoninus Pius: "And more than all other men are we your helpers and allies in promoting peace, seeing that we hold this view, that it is alike impossible for the wicked, the covetous, the conspirator, and for the virtuous, to escape the notice of God, and that each man goes to everlasting punishment or salvation according to the value of his actions."[11] These and other apologists pointed to the beauty of Christian virtue as evidence of the truthfulness of the Christian faith, making the point that the Christian community should be encouraged and nurtured rather than persecuted.

One particularly powerful and arresting aspect of Christian virtue is the ideal of forgiveness, as demonstrated and mandated by Christ himself. As Jesus was being placed on the cross, he prayed for those who were murdering him, "Father, forgive them, for they know not what they do" (Luke 23:34). Not only that, but Jesus' death was an atoning sacrifice offered to God *for* the very people who crucified him. He was explicit about his command to forgive: "For if you forgive others their trespasses, your heavenly Father will also forgive you, but if you do not forgive others their trespasses, neither will your Father forgive your trespasses" (Matt 6:14–15). He was revolutionary in his prescribed treatment of enemies: "You have heard that it was said, 'You shall love your neighbor and hate your enemy.' But I say to you, love your enemies and pray for those who persecute you" (Matt 5:43–44). Naturalism is not the only worldview lacking the beauty of this virtue—what other major worldview has as its leader One who gave up his life for those who hated him and then told his followers to act the same way? What other religion stresses the beautiful act of forgiveness like Christianity does?

Chuck Colson and Ellen Vaughn share a remarkable example of the virtue of Christian forgiveness in their book *Being the Body*. They tell the true story of Rusty Woomer, rightly convicted of murder and on Death Row in South Carolina, who came to know Jesus Christ as Savior while in state prison. Following his conversion, Rusty sent letters to the families of those whom he had killed, genuinely apologizing and asking for forgiveness. After a long delay, Lee Hewitt, the brother of a woman whom Rusty

10. Dulles, *History of Apologetics*, 31.

11. Martyr, *First Apology of Justin*, 62–63.

had murdered, wrote back and explained how he had hated and wanted to kill Rusty himself. But through his own journey in and out of prison, he had also become a Christian. Lee confessed to Rusty that Christ had worked a miracle of forgiveness in his own heart, and that he not only forgave Rusty, but he loved him. Rusty wrote his reply, "overwhelmed by the absolute joy Lee's gift of forgiveness sealed in [his] heart."[12] The rest of the account details Rusty's peaceful walk towards his eventual death by the electric chair and the massive impact he had on many people, even while behind bars. The forgiveness of Christ set both Lee and Rusty free, regardless of their physical location and circumstances, and led to moving reconciliation between the two men. The beauty of the virtues of forgiveness and love in spite of unimaginable personal injury is unmistakable, and it points to the beauty of the God, who changed the lives of both men. How could the emotional power of such a selfless and life-giving act of forgiveness be explained by a naturalistic worldview?

Naturalism fails to account for this type of beauty through its lack of ability to change lives, to improve people in their character, and to bring peace and reconciliation between people. It is doubtful that we will ever

---

12. Colson and Vaughn, *Being the Body*, 149.

hear someone say, "Atheism helped me kick my drug habit!" or "Evolutionary naturalism saved my marriage!" or "Reading Darwin helped me become a better father." On the contrary, people who read works like those of Richard Dawkins can lean toward self-centered despair, not the beauty of virtue. It has often been pointed out that the most horrific violations of human life in the twentieth century—particularly through fascism or communism—were perpetrated by those who denied Christian truth and espoused a naturalistic or atheistic worldview. Alister McGrath describes this well when he writes, "The twentieth century gave rise to one of the greatest and most distressing paradoxes of human history: that the greatest intolerance and violence of that century were practiced by those who believed that religion caused intolerance and violence."[13]

Naturalism does not properly explain the aesthetic value of reformed *character*. One could refer to this, over against the alleged problem of evil for theism, as part of a problem of *good* for atheism. Naturalism fails to explain our shared experience of the beauty of life change. Naturalism cannot even adequately sustain a positive view of restoration, growth of virtue, and reconciliation in human lives and relationships. Why should stronger nations not overrun and dominate weaker ones? Why should individuals get along and treat others, including the weak and disabled among us, with respect and virtuous actions? Survival of the fittest does not demand this; in fact, it discourages it. Allowing the weaker to live and flourish weakens the genetic pool of the race. Forgiving someone who has wronged you and loving them makes you vulnerable to further harm rather than strengthening your chance of survival and reproduction.

But is this most basic ideal of the continuation of the species even grounded properly under evolutionary naturalism? If life is totally an accident, why is it considered a *good* accident that should be perpetuated? This assumption constitutes borrowed capital from a Christian worldview that espouses the sanctity of human life (with its image of God), and it cannot be allowed to stand without challenge. Further, the idea that *any* species should continue to survive and reproduce again represents capital borrowed from the Christian doctrines of the goodness of God's creation and the stewardship of creation held by mankind. Naturalism inwardly collapses when its assumptions are analyzed, and it catastrophically fails to explain the beauty of reformed human character or even why that is a good thing.

13. McGrath, *Twilight of Atheism*, 230.

Conclusion

There is something transcendent we connect to and feel when we experience beauty. C. S. Lewis spoke compellingly of the influence certain instances of art had on his eventual conversion. In *Surprised by Joy*, Lewis explains three particular childhood experiences—a memory of a toy garden his brother had, his reading of Beatrix Potter's *Squirrel Nutkin*, and his resonance with a portion of Longfellow's *Saga of King Olaf*—which gave him an experience of desire for joy.[14] Lewis describes this joy as something transcending mere happiness or pleasure, and it is clear that these aesthetic experiences were instrumental in Lewis's journey of faith from atheism to his confession of faith as a Christian. Interestingly, he had become an atheist *after* these experiences, but he could not shake their effect from his mind and eventually surrendered to the Beautiful One who was the Source of their beauty.

A naturalistic or atheistic view of the world leaves a vast hole in our experience, unable to explain the unmistakable truth that every human inwardly senses, even if it is suppressed: true beauty *does* exist, and it brings with it truth and goodness and meaning. It can be found in aesthetic experiences mediated by our five senses, but it can also be found in the glory of lives changed through an experience with God. All of this beauty points inevitably to God. Naturalism, however, leaves us grasping desperately for a suitable explanation of these things, as well as for a reason just to get out of bed in the morning. In our apologetic work, we must rigorously explain the propositional truth of the gospel, but we also must not fail to *demonstrate* this truth by pointing to examples of God's gift of beauty. There is too much at stake in the clash between Christianity and other worldviews to ignore the apologetic power of beauty.

Bibliography

Colson, Charles, and Ellen Vaughn. *Being the Body*. Nashville: Thomas Nelson, 2004.

Danaher, William J., Jr. "Beauty, Benevolence, and Virtue in Jonathan Edwards' *The Nature of True Virtue*." *Journal of Religion* 87.3 (July 2007) 386–410.

Dawkins, Richard. *The God Delusion*. New York: Houghton Mifflin, 2006.

Dulles, Avery Robert Cardinal. *A History of Apologetics*. 2nd ed. San Francisco: Ignatius, 2005.

Edgar, William. "Aesthetics: Beauty Avenged, Apologetics Enriched." *Westminster Theological Journal* 63 (2001) 107–22.

14. Lewis, *Surprised by Joy*, 16–18.

Edgar, William, and K. Scott Oliphint. *Christian Apologetics Past and Present: A Primary Source Reader.* Wheaton, IL: Crossway, 2009.

Edwards, Jonathan. *The Nature of True Virtue.* Ann Arbor: University of Michigan Press, 1960.

Lewis, C. S. *Surprised by Joy: The Shape of My Early Life.* Orlando: Harcourt, 1955.

Martyr, Justin. *The First Apology of Justin.* In *Christian Apologetics Past and Present: A Primary Source Reader,* edited by William Edgar and K. Scott Oliphint, 62–63. Wheaton, IL: Crossway, 2009.

McGrath, Alister. *The Twilight of Atheism: The Rise and Fall of Disbelief in the Modern World.* New York: Galilee, 2006.

Von Balthasar, Hans Urs. *Seeing the Form.* Volume 1 of *The Glory of the Lord: A Theological Aesthetics.* 7 vols. Edinbugh: T. & T. Clark, 1991.

Williams, Peter. "Aesthetic Arguments for the Existence of God." *Quodlibet Journal* 3.3 (Summer 2001). https://appearedtoblogly.files.wordpress.com/2011/05/williams-peter-22aesthetic-arguments-for-the-existence-of-god22.pdf.

Wooddell, Joseph D. "Jonathan Edwards, Beauty, and Apologetics." *Criswell Theological Review* 5.1 (Fall 2007) 81–95.

Insight from and for the Arts

The function of dissonance within the structure of classical music can help us understand the role of evil in the unfolding of salvation history. Without dissonance, we miss the joy of resolution; without elements of friction, literary and symphonic stories do not take flight. While the musical paradigm does not decisively answer the problem of evil, it gives lie to the notion that an anodyne world is to be preferred.

The Tension of Evil

A Problem to Be Resolved

BRIAN JAMES WATSON

IF YOUR LIFE IS anything like mine—and I suspect that it is—it is far from perfect. Yet even in our imperfect lives, there are times of relative peace and harmony. There are times when our health is adequate, we have enough money to pay our bills, our relationships are strong, and our life's work is satisfying and meaningful. Yet there are also times when such relative peace is disturbed, when the harmony of our lives becomes discordant, when physical or emotional suffering introduces dissonance. Fortunately, there are also times when such problems are resolved, and we feel a great sense of relief. Strangely, that sense of relief may be enhanced *because* we have first suffered. Pain and suffering, when relieved, can make us appreciate what we so often take for granted.

Of course, many issues of pain and suffering do not resolve within this life. Loved ones die. Relationships are irrevocably broken. Those who commit atrocities are not always brought to justice. The process of aging robs us of much even before we reach the grave. Though we know such things are inevitable, we desire a different outcome. We long for a resolution to suffering that isn't found in this life. We hope for a better world to come, a better ending to our stories, one in which there is peace and harmony.

That pattern of pain and resolution gives us some insight into the problem of evil, the subject of this chapter. Evil might be defined as anything that keeps the world from being what it ought to be, anything that causes pain and suffering, whether physical or psychological. Evil is a

problem for everyone, particularly for those who believe in an all-powerful, all-knowing, benevolent, and loving God who created the universe
and all that is within it. Often that problem is stated in the form of questions like these: If God has the power to do anything logically possible, if
God knows that evil will occur and how to prevent evil before it happens
(or how to stop it quickly after it occurs), and if God is good, why is there
any evil in the world? Why is there so much evil in the world? Why is
there such horrific and seemingly pointless evil in the world? Why did
this evil happen to me?

While it may be impossible for finite human beings to answer those
questions fully, many Christians have tried to explain why God would
permit evil to occur. In the project of faith seeking understanding, Christians want to know why God would allow evil to occur and how they
should respond to evil. Some might even question, given the reality of
evil, if such a good and omnipotent God even exists. In fact, the problem
of evil has been called "the rock of atheism."[1]

Most answers to the problem of evil claim that God has a good reason for allowing evil to occur: to bring about something valuable that
wouldn't otherwise be possible. According to Greg Welty, "[T]he pain and
suffering in God's world play a necessary role in bringing about greater
goods that could not be brought about except for the presence of that
pain and suffering. The world would be worse off without that pain and
suffering, and so God is justified in pursuing the good by these means."[2]
Such an explanation of evil is often called a greater good theodicy.[3]

In this essay, I present a new theodicy. I believe that features of some
of the arts, particularly music, can give us tremendous insights into the
problem of evil. I contend that one of the reasons why God allows evil
to occur is to produce a satisfying resolution at the end of history as we
know it, the end of this age. In great pieces of music, composers introduce tension and dissonance in order to achieve a satisfying resolution.
The denouement is deeply satisfying precisely because it was preceded
by that tension and dissonance. Similarly, God has ordained tension and

---

1. Henri Blocher attributes this phrase to the German playwright Georg Büchner
(1813–37) (Blocher, *Evil and the Cross*, 9).

2. Welty, *Why Is There Evil?*, 14. I highly recommend Welty's book for its philosophical clarity and biblical fidelity.

3. Gottfried Wilhelm Leibniz (1646–1716) coined the word "theodicy" by conjoin-
ing the Greek words for "God" and "justice." A theodicy justifies the ways of God with
respect to evil.

dissonance in the form of evil in order to achieve an eschatological world that is greater than any world that never had evil in it. My proposal is not very different from what the apostle Paul writes in 2 Corinthians 4:17: "For this light momentary affliction is preparing for us an eternal weight of glory beyond all comparison." Or, in the words of Augustine, "In every case, the joy is greater, the worse the pain which has preceded it."[4]

A Word on Music

This chapter will focus primarily on an analogy from music. I realize that not all of us are musically literate, even if we enjoy listening to music. Since not all of us read music or have experience with musical theory, I will start with some basics. I ask the reader to persevere—reading about music theory might produce a light momentary affliction, but this information will prepare us for weightier matters. In this essay, I will introduce and develop various themes before tying them together into what I hope will be a satisfying conclusion.

Music is best thought of as a language. The music that we are most familiar with is tonal music. This is the language of classical music (which I shall call art music), folk music, and pop music.[5] There are several elements of musical language: the melody or tune, harmony (the conjunction of various notes at one given time, as well as how such conjunctions, or chords, relate to each other), rhythm, dynamics (roughly, the volume level), and timbre (often related to which instrument or instruments are playing). We will mostly be concerned with harmony in these pages.

One of the important aspects of the language of music is the concept of a key. In Western music, there are usually two varieties of keys: major and minor. Each contains seven different notes that form a scale. For example, the key of C major contains the following seven notes: C, D, E, F, G, A, and B (the white notes on a piano keyboard). The key of A minor contains those same seven notes, beginning with A and ascending to G.[6]

---

4. Augustine, *Confessions* 8.3, 138.

5. What most people call "classical music" I will call "art music," simply because the Classical period of Western music is rather specific. "Art music" is the music of the concert hall and the academy.

6. To complicate matters, the sixth and seventh degrees of a minor scale (in A, these would be F and G) are often raised, depending on context. So, an A minor scale might have F-sharp and G-sharp instead of F and G.

Just as certain combinations of letters form words, certain combinations of notes make sense, while others do not. Depending on which notes are played together, the result will be either consonance or dissonance. According to a standard music theory textbook, "The terms consonant and dissonant can be defined roughly as meaning pleasing to the ear and not pleasing to the ear, respectively, but these are very dependent on context."[7] It is true that what sounds consonant and dissonant is somewhat context-dependent. The same can be said of letters in language. The combination of letters "strz" makes no sense on its own, at least in English. But in the context of the name Yastrzemski, those letters have meaning, at least for baseball fans. There is also a subjective element to music; some find the more complex chords of jazz to be beautiful, while others may hear those same chords as noise. But consonance is not simply a matter of subjective taste. There is an objective undergirding to consonance and dissonance.

Certain pitches sound good together because there is a simple, mathematical relationship between them. For example, there is a 1:2 relationship between any two notes separated by an octave. There is a 2:3 ratio between the tonic and dominant notes, a fifth apart. A major chord has a 4:5:6 ratio, another simple ratio. By contrast, the frequencies of any two neighboring semitones form a 24:25 ratio. This is hardly a simple relationship. If you were to walk up to a piano keyboard and simultaneously depress a B and C, or an E and F (just to stick to those white keys), you would hear this dissonance. Neighboring pitches separated by semitones generally sound bad to our ears. They recall the music that Bernard Herrmann composed to accompany the famous shower scene in Alfred Hitchcock's *Psycho*. Playing two notes that are separated by a whole tone, such as F and G (think of the beginning of "Chopsticks"), also produces a dissonance of kinds, though one not as jarring. The point is that what we understand to be consonant or dissonant is determined by the relationships between the frequencies we hear.[8]

7. Kostka et al., *Tonal Harmony*, 21.

8. For more information on the mathematics behind music, see Maor, *Music by the Numbers*.

The two most important notes in the scale are the first note, the tonic, and the fifth note, the dominant. A triad, or chord consisting of three notes, is usually built on each of these two notes. A tonic chord consists of the first, third, and fifth notes in the scale. The chord built on the fifth degree is known as the dominant. The harmony in most pieces of Western art music moves from the tonic (the C chord, for example) to other harmonies, and then back to the tonic, often by means of the dominant chord (the G chord). In these pieces, the music leaves its home and goes on a journey, but there is a sense that the music must return home in the end.

Great Works of Art

Let's take a step back from music for a moment. Consider any great work of art. What makes that work of art great? Often, we might say that a work of art is great because it's beautiful, because it's pleasing to the eye or the ear. But what makes that work so pleasing? Often, it's a combination of various factors. The artist has technical skill. The composition (of a painting, a novel, a piece of music) is unified and possesses a structure that is symmetrical or orderly. And the composition is varied. A great novel often features several characters, several settings, several times, and several events. Great paintings often depict many objects, sometimes at varied distances (foreground and background), and in many different colors. Likewise, music has structure and variety.

A piece of music that consists of one note would literally be monotonous. Usually, a piece of music that contains several different notes in the melody and only one chord in the harmony is rather monotonous. Even as simple a hymn as "Amazing Grace" has seven different notes in the melody and four different chords in the harmony. Monotonous songs aren't worth listening to, and simple songs can be become boring rather quickly. (Singing "Amazing Grace" twenty times in a row might feel like singing the full version of "99 Bottles of Beer.")

Great pieces of music have more variety than "Amazing Grace" does. Great pieces of music are like great pieces of literature. If music is a language, a piece of music can be thought of as a narrative. A great piece of music is like an aural journey, one in which there is a beginning, a middle, and an end. It gives you the sense of going somewhere and then coming back home. In short, it tells a story. And any great story features conflict.

In her recent book on reading literature, English professor Karen Swallow Prior claims, "All literature—stories most obviously—centers on some conflict, rupture, or lack. Literature is birthed from our fallenness: without the fall, there would be no story."[9] If a group of people get along peacefully, without any conflict, without any type of evil to defeat, there is no story worth telling. No book worth reading would be written about a set of characters who never disagreed or were never threatened by outside forces, characters who lived in a world without fighting, loss, heartache, or death. Some people prefer to read nonfiction, but very few would want to read nonfriction. Using more technical language, Tzvetan Todorov writes, "An ideal narrative begins with a stable situation that some force will perturb." He explains that the result is "a state of disequilibrium," from which a "second equilibrium," or a resolution, needs to be established.[10]

The same is true of large-scale pieces of music. Great pieces of music feature a similar pattern. The Christian theologian and musician Jeremy Begbie identifies this general structure as "equilibrium-tension-resolution."[11] This pattern provides the large-scale framework for many compositions. Within that larger framework, within the movements of a symphony or sonata, there are also many small-scale instances of that

9. Prior, *On Reading Well*, 26.

10. Todorov, *Introduction to Poetics*, 51.

11. Begbie, *Theology, Music and Time*, 45.

pattern. Tension is "the generation of a sense of incompleteness," which can be produced by dissonance but also by unresolved cadences (a dominant chord that doesn't go back home to the tonic) or modulations to different keys, which create a kind of musical exile, a moving away from something stable, our ear's sense of home.[12]

To produce a satisfying homecoming that gives the listener great relief, we first need tension. Tension may be created by moving away from the home key. Jarring dissonances can create greater levels of tension. Yet a piece of music with only dissonance, or with no sense of a home key, would be one that would grate our ears and leave us without any sense of equilibrium, not to mention resolution. (Imagine listening to an interminable loop of those two dissonant notes in that *Psycho* theme or in "Chopsticks"!) So, though tension or dissonance creates drama, such disequilibrium must be set within the context of equilibrium. We desire equilibrium and resolution, but to have a satisfying resolution, there must first be musical tension.[13]

The Drama of Sonata Form

To get a fuller appreciation for how musical tension can lead to satisfying resolutions—and how that tension, when increased, can lead to even more glorious resolutions—let us consider one prominent type of musical composition.

Sonata form is a musical structure commonly found in art music of the late eighteenth and early nineteenth centuries. The sonata form consists of three main parts: the exposition, the development, and the recapitulation. In his classic work on the sonata form, Charles Rosen describes these parts: "The *exposition* presents the principal thematic material, establishes the tonic key and modulates to the dominant or to some other closely related key." So, the exposition establishes the tonal home

---

12. Begbie, *Theology, Music and Time*, 38.

13. It is true that some pieces of music that we enjoy, such as folk and pop songs, contain only small amounts of tension. These songs contain simple harmonies, and they are almost never dissonant. These songs are arguably not great pieces of art, but they are satisfying. The reason why they are satisfying is because we desire the peace and simplicity of these songs. Our lives are not simple; they are dissonant. Popular songs provide the peace, harmony, and order that are sorely lacking in our lives. In other words, the tension of our lives finds resolution in these songs. Great works of narrative art, including musical compositions, are self-contained stories. They heighten the tension so that the delayed resolution seems sweeter and more gratifying.

of the movement, along with its main themes (melodies). The first theme is presented in the tonic key, and the second theme is usually stated in the dominant key.[14] That movement away from home gives the listener a sense of a journey, and leaving home creates a small amount of tension, perhaps in the form of a question: How will we get back home?

Though tension may be present in the exposition, it increases greatly in the development section. According to Rosen, "It is in this part of sonata form that the most distant and most rapid modulations are to be found, and the technique of development is the fragmentation of the themes of the exposition and the reworking of the fragments into new combinations and sequences."[15] This section of the sonata has greater dissonance. But, as stated above, dissonance is only one variety of tension. Tension is also created by rapid key changes. Not only do we have a sense of being exiled from our tonic home, but the shifting harmonies can introduce a sense of confusion and instability. If there's not literal dissonance, perhaps some cognitive dissonance on the part of the listener has been created. There are times when the key is not clear, and this is often referred to as tonal ambiguity. Tension is also created by the fact that we do not hear the main themes of the exposition in their original form. We want to hear the whole tune, but we only get snippets. Those themes do return in full, in the tonic, during the recapitulation. As Rosen explains, "The *recapitulation* starts with the return of the first theme in the tonic. The rest of this section 'recapitulates' the exposition as it was first played, except that the second group and closing theme appear in the tonic."[16] The recapitulation brings us home, and such homecoming, that resolution, is more satisfying because of the previous journey, with all its tensions and ambiguities.

A work by Franz Schubert (1797–1828) provides an example of how a piece written in sonata form features dissonance that leads to resolution. Schubert's Piano Sonata in B-flat major, D. 960, was composed during the last year of his life.[17] The first movement of the sonata begins with

14. Rosen, *Sonata Forms*, 1–2 (emphasis original).

15. Rosen, *Sonata Forms*, 2.

16. Rosen, *Sonata Forms*, 2.

17. One can hear this piece while reading the sheet music at www.youtube.com/ watch?v=MAZ8PA5_gVA. Though the word of the Lord endures forever, websites and URLs do not. Should that link fail to work, one can search for "Schubert piano sonata 960 score" at www.youtube.com. Several similar videos exist. Similarly, PDF versions of the score can easily be found online, as can audio recordings through various music

the first theme in the tonic, B-flat major. The first theme is pleasing but not out of the ordinary. But something interesting occurs at the end of the first phrase, in measure 8: there is a low, trilled G-flat that resolves to F. Charles Fisk calls this trill "remarkable, even strange."[18] That low G-flat trill is strange because it is foreign to the B-flat major scale. (One would expect to hear a G-natural.) G-flat is indeed part of the parallel minor key, B-flat minor, but nothing in the music thus far suggests a move to the minor key. Fisk believes that this trill foreshadows the modulation to different keys, which will occur shortly in the piece. But when the audience first hears that G-flat, the note sounds ominous and threatening. That is so because the G-flat clashes with the F held in the right hand. (The two notes are a semitone apart; again, think of that *Psycho* theme.) The trill oscillates back and forth between a G-flat and an A-flat, another foreign note that clashes with the A-natural in the right hand, producing another semitone dissonance.

That brief use of dissonance foreshadows exile to foreign harmonic lands. The development section begins in C-sharp minor, shifts to D-flat major (the parallel major of C-sharp minor, enharmonically spelled), and then starts to move quickly through several keys before transitioning back to B-flat for the recapitulation.[19] Interestingly, in his analytical outline of the movement, Fisk labels the beginning of the development section "Memory and reflection and exile." At the beginning of the rapid modulations through various keys, Fisk writes, "WILDERNESS."[20] It is easy to see, as we soon will, how this structure maps on to the narrative presented in the Bible.

At the beginning of that "wilderness" wandering through various keys, which starts at measure 158, semitone dissonances are introduced in succession. These dissonances don't last long, and Schubert uses them to prepare modulations to different keys. Yet those dissonances sound like pain. The wandering through foreign keys is confusing. There is no sense of rest. The listener wants the music to return home, but that homecoming is delayed. Like all movements in sonata form, the resolution comes

---

streaming services.

18. Fisk, "What Schubert's Last Sonata Might Hold," 179.

19. Those keys are E major, C major, A-flat minor, B minor, and D minor.

20. Fisk, "What Schubert's Last Sonata Might Hold," 180. Fisk's essay is not explicitly Christian, which is why his labels are interesting. Fisk's diagram also identifies that G-flat trill as a "protagonist" who seeks to assert his individuality, is then banished, and seeks to be reincluded, only to be exiled before returning home.

in the recapitulation section, which brings us back to the original key, B-flat major, and the main theme. The relevance of this use of dissonance and exile to foreign keys will become clear when we look at the narrative presented in the Bible.

The Biblical Story as Musical Narrative

Let us now turn to the biblical narrative and employ musical metaphors to see how God uses tension to achieve a glorious resolution. The first musical metaphor is God as composer. In eternity past, God has composed all that will occur in human history. Such a view of God assumes a particular view of providence, that God has meticulous control over all events that will ever occur. I believe that God exercises this kind of meticulous providence because of the testimony of Scripture.[21] Though Christians disagree about the extent to which God controls the affairs of creation, all should agree that God knows the end from the beginning due to his omniscience, and that, while knowing everything that will ever occur, he decided to create this world and not another.

In deciding to create a world, God must decide whether the world will possess any evil or not. God has sufficient moral reasons for allowing evil if that evil produces some good that cannot otherwise be obtained. One such good is God's maximal glory: God is more glorified through the incarnation and atonement of Jesus, which would not occur without there first being sin for which to atone. One of the reasons, perhaps among many, why God ordains the occurrence of evil is to create conditions that necessitate the incarnation of the Son of God, his sacrificial death on the cross, and his resurrection. The tension of evil leads to a glorious resolution secured by Christ. This complex of events brings God more glory, reveals more clearly who God is and what he is like, and demonstrates his love for his people.

Just as Schubert had the option of writing a piano sonata without dissonance, God could have chosen to create a world with no sin. However, if Schubert wrote a sonata that consisted of only four chords, all of which are native to the key B-flat, there would be no suspense, no drama, no satisfying resolution. In a word, it would be boring. We wouldn't know

21. For a detailed look at what Scripture says about evil, see Blocher, *Evil and the Cross*, 84–127. For a more accessible and still thorough account of what the Bible says about evil and God's providence, see Welty, *Why Is There Evil?*

Schubert's name if that were all he wrote in his brief life. If God did not allow evil to occur, there would be no need for the incarnation, no need for Jesus' sacrifice on the cross, no triumph over the grave, and no yearning on the part of his people for Jesus' glorious return.

If we accept the idea that God is like a composer, we can see how the story of the Bible resembles sonata form. The opening chapters of Genesis are like the exposition. The unspoiled creation is the home key, and many principal themes are introduced, including the kingdom of God, the glory of God, the image of God, the temple, and the covenant. Soon, an ominous note is introduced: God warns Adam that if he doesn't obey, he will die. Another ominous note, one foreign to the home key, is the voice of the serpent tempting Eve. The harmony of the garden of Eden is shattered by the dissonance of Adam and Eve's sin. This tragic event leads to tonal exile; the development section has begun. The music of Scripture moves to new, strange keys, in which snippets of the exposition's themes, echoes of Eden, resound. There are even times when resolution appears imminent. After the flood, Noah and his family seem to emerge like a new creation from the waters of chaos. Solomon appears to be the promised Son of David. When he inaugurates his glorious temple, we wonder if he will reign forever and bring blessings to the world. But these men and so many others fail. These events lead to frustrated and deceptive cadences. The tension heightens.

Then, in a surprising turn of events, God himself becomes a human being, picks up an instrument, and starts playing. His playing is authoritative; his technique is masterful. He performs all the old themes, reintroducing them in new and beautiful ways. But instead of resolution, the greatest dissonance the world has ever known occurs when the God-man dies. Yet this was no accident, no failure on his part to play the score that was written in eternity past. From one perspective, the sound of Jesus' death is the ugliest event that has ever occurred. From another perspective, that dissonance is beautiful, because it leads to resolution.

With the resurrection, a new key is introduced. Hope for a resolution is restored. Yet we have not reached the recapitulation section. Occasional dissonance occurs, and while the theme of Jesus is played throughout the world, it is accompanied by discordant harmonies.

Our lives do not start in the exposition, but rather in the development section. We enter a world of ambiguous situations and uncertainty about where our lives are headed. When evil occurs, often without warning, the result is cacophony. From our perspective, the dissonance may last a long time. In the case of Schubert's sonata, the dissonance may last a couple of seconds before resolving, at least temporarily. Even Richard Wagner's *Tristan und Isolde*, one of the longest operas and a preeminent example of beautiful resolution after tonal ambiguity and dissonance, resolves after four hours of music. But dissonance in our lives may last days, months, or years. Cancer may slowly consume a spouse. A debilitating disease eats away the body year after year until death. Great evils like murder and even genocide appear to be meaningless noise. But we remember that God's timing is not ours. What appears to be endless dissonance now is almost nothing in the expanse of eternity. We are not able to interpret the dissonance of our lives because we do not understand how it fits into the larger composition God has written.

Yet God has promised us a good ending. So, we wait for the recapitulation. At that time, all the old themes will be played in the original key. However, this time they will be played by an orchestra of innumerable players in the amphitheater of a new garden, a new Jerusalem, and a new cosmos. The music will sound sweeter than anything we have ever heard because of the preceding dissonance, disorienting modulations, tonal ambiguities, and deceptive cadences. We will then realize that each instance of evil, now completely resolved, contributed to the grand symphony God composed. There is no meaningless noise, for every note has a purpose.

Objections

When people consider the evil that is apparent in the world, they may want to have an easy answer as to why, if God exists, there could ever be such evil. However, I don't think there are any easy answers to the problem of evil. One of the reasons why evil is so confounding is that it doesn't make sense. So, this theodicy might not be a quick and easy answer. It might not convince atheists of the reality of God's existence. But it hews closely to the biblical narrative, it presents the gospel clearly, and it shows at least one reason why God would allow evil to occur.

Still, some may object to this theodicy. Limited space permits me to address briefly only two objections. The first possible objection is that if what I argue is true, we should be resigned to our fate and should therefore not attempt to fight against evil. However, that would not be a correct conclusion to make. There is a difference between God's having composed all of history and our knowing what will happen. We can affirm *that* God has composed all that occurs without knowing *what* the various notes of the score are. So, when evil occurs, if we can bring criminals to justice or cure a disease, we should do so. Though finite humans are not able to bring about the ultimate resolution of all evil, we can achieve small-scale resolutions. Large-scale pieces of music have moments of local resolution before achieving global resolution; the same is true in this life.

In fact, knowing that God has composed the whole of reality imbues life with a great sense of meaning and purpose. And when tragedy strikes, though we may not know why evil has occurred, we can trust that God has a purpose for it, and we can trust that he will, in the end, make all things well. Such knowledge gives us hope.

A second objection may be that any kind of aesthetic theodicy is not adequate to explain the horrors that have occurred throughout human history. I do not claim that aesthetic considerations alone can bear the weight of justifying why God permits evil. I agree with Philip Tallon that achieving beauty, in this case a beautiful story, is not enough to justify permitting evil.[22] I believe that my theodicy can and should be combined with various other theodicies and/or defenses. There are in fact many goods that can only be obtained by way of evil. Without evil and its accompanying suffering, there would be no compassion, sacrifice, bravery, victory, and many other desirable outcomes. There may be other reasons why God permits evil to occur, ones that we have yet to imagine or could not conceive given our limitations as finite creatures.

Yet the greatest good that emerges out of evil is the revelation of God in Jesus Christ. Sin necessitates the incarnation of the Son of God, his atoning death, and his triumphant resurrection. In these events, God most clearly reveals himself, God demonstrates his love for his people, and God is most glorified.

Bibliography

Augustine. *Confessions*. Translated by Henry Chadwick. Oxford World's Classics. Oxford: Oxford University Press, 1991.

Begbie, Jeremy. *Theology, Music and Time*. Cambridge: Cambridge University Press, 2000.

Blocher, Henri. *Evil and the Cross*. Translated by David G. Preston. Downers Grove, IL: InterVarsity, 1994.

22. "Theodicists rightly understand that beauty and intensity as values are probably not enough to justify any grave evil, but they wrongly think that this means that theodicy's project has no place for aesthetics" (Tallon, *Poetics of Evil*, 200).

Fisk, Charles. "What Schubert's Last Sonata Might Hold." In *Music and Meaning*, edited by Jenefer Robinson, 179–80. Ithaca, NY: Cornell University Press, 1997.

Kostka, Stefan, et al. *Tonal Harmony: With an Introduction to Post-Tonal Music*. 8th ed. New York: McGraw-Hill Education, 2018.

Maor, Eli. *Music by the Numbers: From Pythagoras to Schoenberg*. Princeton: Princeton University Press, 2018.

Prior, Karen Swallow. *On Reading Well: Finding the Good Life through Great Books*. Grand Rapids: Brazos, 2018.

Rosen, Charles. *Sonata Forms*. Rev. ed. New York: Norton, 1988.

Tallon, Philip. *The Poetics of Evil: Toward an Aesthetic Theodicy*. Oxford: Oxford University Press, 2012.

Todorov, Tzvetan. *Introduction to Poetics*. Translated by Richard Howard. Minneapolis: University of Minnesota Press, 1981.

Welty, Greg. *Why Is There Evil in the World (and So Much of It)?* Fearn, Scotland: Christian Focus, 2018.

Though fantasy literature does not present a literal account of real-ity, it models truths and aspirations and melds apparent conflicts into a plausible template for understanding the workings of the universe under God. We see the interplay of his sovereignty and our creatureli-ness, a map of good and evil, of heroism and villainy. At their best, at the hand of Christian writers, they give us versions of a paradigm far superior to the Darwinian fairy tales trafficked abroad today.

Fantasy, Fairy-Stories, and Understanding Free Will

GEORGE SCONDRAS

PODO HELMER, A REFORMING pirate, had decided to abandon the life of the sea and settle down to a quieter occupation in the Green Hollows, greatly disappointing Zola May, the woman who had envisioned adventure, travel, and excitement by his side. Later recalling his response to her objections, Podo explains that he had simply "wanted to follow the Maker's[1] wind, and it was blowing me straight and true away from the wild of the waters and to solid ground."[2] Unwilling to accept this unromantic domesticity, Zola May had protested, and so Podo had broken off his courtship of her. Transformed by the incident, Podo found his affections being directed toward a servant girl, Wendolyn: "All of the things that were plain about Wendolyn shone like rubies."[3] Eventually, Podo married Wendolyn, and their daughter became the mother of the three Wingfeather children who defeat the nameless evil one's attempt to enslave all of Aerwiar.

---

1. In this story from Andrew Peterson's *The Monster in the Hollows*, "the Maker" is a reference to a personal divinity who created the world ("Aerwiar"). There are many similarities between Peterson's presentation of "the Maker" and the Christian understanding of God.

2. Peterson, *Monster in the Hollows*, 95.

3. Peterson, *Monster in the Hollows*, 96.

This portion of what J. R. R Tolkien would likely categorize as a "fairy story" demonstrates the value that such stories can have for exploring complex themes, including the relationship between sovereignty and freedom. The choices and actions of the characters in this story are presented as free actions, and yet there is a sense of direction within the story, that what exists is not simply "what is" but "what must be." In this essay, I will explore the relationship between divine sovereignty and human free will as expressed within the framework of fairy stories. I will first lay out some thoughts on the ways that fairy stories can provide insight for these questions. Second, I will consider several aspects of both sovereignty and then free will as presented in stories. Finally, I will conclude with some thoughts about a synthesis between the two motifs.

Learning from Fairy-Stories

In his seminal essay entitled, "On Fairy-Stories,"[4] Tolkien described a category of fiction that he termed "fairy-stories," similar but not identical to the stories widely known as "fairy-tales." For Tolkien, a fairy story provides a means for a reader to understand aspects of truth through a "piercing glimpse of joy"[5] that "has the very taste of primary truth."[6]

---

4. Tolkien, "On Fairy-Stories," 38. This essay is also more widely available in an updated form in Tolkien, *Tree and Leaf.*

5. Tolkien, "On Fairy-Stories," 82.

6. Tolkien, "On Fairy-Stories," 84.

Commenting on what Tolkien has identified, Clyde Kilby notes that, "Unreality becomes the best road to realism"[7] through "disarming the reader of his normal inattention and disbelief";[8] the fairy story is able to communicate a message where propositional statements may find difficulty. Mary Shideler similarly notes, "Myths and fairy-tales may not be true, but they reveal truths. They give us not philosophies, but visions."[9] In fact, C. S. Lewis, himself a well-known author of such stories, credits fairy stories with being instrumental in awakening his heart to the joys of Christian faith.[10]

Fairy stories create a world that is recognizable[11] so that a reader, by relating to the story, may perceive truths about reality. These stories are "not primarily concerned with possibility, but with desirability."[12] Shideler notes that entering "imaginary worlds, we return with gifts of refreshment and wisdom that are hard to come by in any other way."[13] Though there is no specific theology of fairy land,[14] the stories, as creations of an author, are in many ways expressions of the author's conception of reality. Indeed, a Christian theistic worldview is evident in the fairy works of Christian authors such as Tolkien,[15] Lewis, George MacDonald, and Andrew Peterson, and through these works the Christian reader is led to understand the world Christianly. The fairy story isn't a proof for the Christian worldview or even for specific Christian truths, but it guides the Christian to understand, interpret, and apply what he believes.[16] Just

7. Kilby, "Meaning in *The Lord of the Rings*," 76.

8. Kilby, "Meaning in *The Lord of the Rings*," 76.

9. Shideler, "Philosophies and Fairy-Tales," 24.

10. Lewis writes of first reading MacDonald's *Phantastes*: "That night, my imagination was, in a sense, baptised" (Lewis, *Surprised by Joy*, 222). Kreglinger describes this event as setting Lewis on a "journey of transformation" (Kreglinger, "Storied Revelations," 307).

11. Mary Shideler describes the function of this recognizability and internal coherence as a means to allow the reader to have the experience desired by the author (Shideler, "Philosophies and Fairy-Tales," 20).

12. Tolkien, "On Fairy-Stories," 62.

13. Shideler, "Philosophies and Fairy-Tales," 21.

14. Williams, *Mere Humanity*, 61.

15. Williams identifies the impact of Tolkien's worldview on his stories as well as demonstrates that the deficient (nontheistic) worldview of Peter Jackson results in a deficient retelling of the story through his movies (Williams, *Encouraging Thought*, 17–54, 70–89).

16. Williams, *Mere Humanity*, 61.

as joy is experienced by children long before linguistic and reasoning skills are available to analyze the concept, stories bring the reader to an imaginative grasp[17] of weighty or complex subjects.[18]

Sovereignty in Fairy-Stories

Sovereignty, even in theological contexts, is a broad topic. A simple theological definition might be that it is God's "absolute right to do all things according to his own good pleasure,"[19] but for evaluative purposes, more clarification is likely needed, specifically with regard to what extent the sovereign right is actually exercised. For present use, the understanding of sovereignty largely melds with "providence,"[20] which is "generally used to denote God's preserving and governing all things by means of second causes."[21] John Calvin dedicates a section in the first book of his *Institutes of the Christian Religion* to the subject of providence, describing it specifically as action rather than merely knowledge of a conclusion beforehand.[22] It includes the actions and thoughts of humans,[23] as well as the occurrence of natural events.[24] Calvin explicitly precludes the category of "coincidence," noting that, although events may seem fortuitous, God should be perceived as the providential actor behind the occurrence.[25] In a similar vein, though following Aquinas rather than Calvin, Tolkien understands a world where "all events are always the effect of God's will."[26]

17. Williams, *Mere Humanity*, 67. Williams demonstrates the epistemological value in Lewis's presentation of nonhuman moral beings without asserting that beings such as hrossa and seroni actually exist.

18. This imaginative grasp has some advantages, even, over rational consideration. "We intellectualize in order to know, but, paradoxically, intellectualization destroys its object" (Kilby, "Mythic and Christian Elements in Tolkien," 120).

19. Easton, "Sovereignty," in *Illustrated Bible Dictionary*, 641.

20. John Piper's recently published volume, *Providence*, similarly treats "providence" specifically as purposefully active sovereignty (Piper, *Providence*, 29).

21. Easton, "Providence," in *Illustrated Bible Dictionary*, 564.

22. Calvin, *Institutes*, 1.16.4.

23. Calvin, *Institutes*, 1.16.6.

24. Calvin, *Institutes*, 1.16.7.

25. Calvin, *Institutes*, 1.16.9. Similarly, Peter Kreeft notes that sovereignty (providence) is not something that can be strictly proven but must rather be perceived (or not perceived) (Kreeft, *Philosophy of Tolkien*, 58).

26. Wood, "Conflict and Convergence," 325.

Sovereignty: Prophecy

Sovereignty is evident in fairy stories in the expectation that prophecies will come true despite contrary efforts of characters in the story. If
a prophecy can be made and intentionally fulfilled, some level of sovereignty must exist within the world. In the first book of C. S. Lewis's
Chronicles of Narnia, the malevolent White Witch, who has enslaved
Narnia for years under an unending winter,[27] is on the lookout for "sons
of Adam" and "daughters of Eve," hoping that by finding them she might
thwart the fulfillment of a prophecy that the winter, her reign, and even
her life would end when two sons of Adam and two daughters of Eve sit
on the four thrones of Cair Paravel.[28] Victory seems near when Edmund
is lured into betrayal by false sweetness, but the witch's winter suddenly
begins to falter, and spring appears when Aslan, an expression of the
divine,[29] approaches. Through the sovereign working of Aslan, subtle
and mysterious, the witch is defeated, the four children are enthroned at
Cair Paravel, and the prophecy is fulfilled.

Lewis's Narnia also demonstrates sovereignty through the speaking of prophetic words that are eventually accomplished, not through
direct divine actions but through the innumerable contingent actions of
creatures. Early in *The Silver Chair*, Aslan gives Jill four signs to guide
the rescue of the missing Prince Rilian.[30] Jill is often forgetful, arrogant,
ignorant, and inobservant, but despite the missteps that she and Eustace
take, the signs continue to appear in succession. As the children repeatedly blunder, the signs end up functioning more as indicators that they
are still participating in the quest than as instructions for action. Finally
when the fourth sign appears, the children are hesitant to act, but trusting

27. Lewis, *Lion, the Witch, and the Wardrobe*, 82. By referring to this as "the first
book" in the series, I am using Lewis' publication order rather than the chronological
order in which the books are commonly presented now.

28. Lewis, *Lion, the Witch, and the Wardrobe*, 79–82. "When Adam's flesh and
Adam's bone/Sits at Cair Paravel in throne,/The evil time will be over and done." There
is also a second prophecy concerning the end of the winter that deals with the advent
of Aslan: "Wrong will be right, when Aslan comes in sight,/At the sound of his roar,
sorrows will be no more,/When he bares his teeth, winter meets it death,/And when
he shakes his mane, we shall have spring again."

29. A later book in the series, *The Magician's Nephew*, reveals that Aslan is, in fact,
the creator of Narnia.

30. Lewis, *Silver Chair*, 25–26.

Aslan, they do.[31] Their trust is justified, and the quest is completed. Aslan's providence is evident in the three fulfilled signs, even when the children fail to live up to the ideals of the quest, as well as in the fourth sign, whereby the children finally accomplish the task for which they were sent.

Sovereignty: Providence in Action

Tolkien's stories of Middle Earth demonstrate a pattern of providence through the history of the one ring, particularly in that it comes to be possessed by a hobbit named Bilbo and passes on to his nephew Frodo. The ring is discovered blindly[32] and remains unappreciated for many years. When momentous events begin to occur, the wizard Gandalf discovers the true nature of the ring, and, revealing the terrifying reality to Frodo, he looks for hope in a curious direction. Though the servants of the Dark Lord are inexorably approaching, Gandalf tells Frodo, "Behind that [Bilbo's discovery of the Ring] there was something else at work, beyond any design of the Ring-maker. I can put it no plainer than by saying that Bilbo was *meant* to find the Ring, and *not* by its maker. In which case you also were *meant* to have it. And that may be an encouraging thought."[33] Rather than finding hope in anonymity, stealth, or strength, Gandalf expresses an understanding of the world that recognizes an active providence that is greater than the Dark Lord. Indeed, the prospects for a Ring-bearing hobbit seem bleak, but the quest is not a fool's errand if Gandalf's perception is correct. Based on this hope, Frodo sets off into a world that is bigger and more perilous than he ever could have imagined. His smallness in a big world mirrors that of his uncle Bilbo when, years earlier, he had recognized the purposeful orchestration of the world.[34] Though hardships abound, the good end is certainly coming.[35]

31. Lewis, *Silver Chair*, 166–68.

32. Tolkien, *Hobbit*, 79.

33. Tolkien, *Fellowship of the Ring*, 65 (emphasis original). I am indebted to Williams, *Encouraging Thought* for pointing out the significance of this passage.

34. Tolkien, *Hobbit*, 317. Gandalf remonstrates with Bilbo after the latter's return following his completed quest: "Surely you don't disbelieve the prophecies, because you had a hand in bringing them about yourself? You don't really suppose, do you, that all your adventures and escapes were managed by mere luck, just for your sole benefit?"

35. All creation works toward its purposed end (Urang, "Tolkien's Fantasy," 103).

The winter is whispering, "green and gold,"
And the heart is whispering, too—
It's a story the Maker has always told
And the story, my child, is true.[36]

Sovereignty: Eucatastrophe

One of the most important aspects of Tolkien's presentation of fairy stories is what he famously terms the *eucatastrophe*, or the "Consolation of the Happy Ending."[37] He asserts that, with this turn-of-events leading to the final victory of good, the "*eucatastrophic* tale is the true form of fairytale, and its highest function,"[38] that is, to bring a joy and longing in the reader.[39] At this point, the fairy story resembles the *evangelium* that is the Christian story.[40] Against all odds, the triumph of good is finally secured.

One of the most remarkable examples of this *eucatastrophe* in fairy stories is the story of Gollum in Tolkien's *The Lord of the Rings*. Through long years of slavery to a soul-gnawing greed,[41] this once-pleasant creature has been reduced to a wretch, slinking and stalking in the shadows, desiring to possess the precious ring. When Frodo expresses a desire to be rid of the treacherous creature, the wizard Gandalf presciently notes that, though he is guilty, Gollum may yet play some important role in the story of the ring.[42] As the tale proceeds, Gollum, having sworn fealty by the ring, is bound to guide Frodo and Sam to the entrance to Mordor,[43] where Frodo aims to destroy the ring in the fires of Orodruin. Gollum, however, breaks his troth and betrays Frodo and Sam. Despite this, and beyond expectation, Frodo and Sam reach the fires, but Frodo is overcome by the power of the ring. He puts it on and claims it for his own, dooming not only the quest but also all that is good in Middle Earth. At the moment of despair, the lurking Gollum leaps upon Frodo, bites off his finger, claims the ring for himself, and, in ecstasies over regaining

36. Peterson, *Warden and the Wolf King*, 517.

37. Tolkien, "On Fairy-Stories," 81.

38. Tolkien, "On Fairy-Stories," 81 (emphasis original).

39. Duriez, "Theology of Fantasy," 42.

40. Tolkien, "On Fairy-Stories," 83.

41. Tolkien, *Fellowship of the Ring*, 62.

42. Tolkien, *Fellowship of the Ring*, 69. Echoes occur throughout the narrative.

43. Tolkien, *Two Towers*, 224.

his treasure, falls bodily into the fires, destroying himself and the ring.[44] Gandalf's words come true; salvation comes, neither by might nor by wisdom, but, when least expected, by the providential greed of a creature. *Eucatastrophe* indeed.

Free Will in Fairy-Stories

Like sovereignty, creaturely freedom is hardly ever explicitly discussed in stories, and yet it is often presented through the thoughts, words, and actions of characters in those stories. While acknowledging the lack of scholarly consensus on the entailments of such a term, the operative understanding of free will in this essay will be an ability to act in accordance with desire in a noncoerced manner, bounded by conditions appropriate to a creature.[45] This is an experience-oriented concept of freedom rather than a strictly philosophical freedom. In what follows, the focus will be on three modes of exercised will in fairy stories: participation in the quest, the moment of crisis, and the freedom to choose good or evil.

Free Will: Heroes, Quests, and Companions

Almost universally, fairy stories include some form of quest,[46] and though the quest is often thrust upon a hero[47] there is also a struggle as to whether or not to accept the responsibility offered. Bilbo's memorable objection illustrates this point: "We don't want any adventures here, thank you!"[48] Additionally, the hero of the quest is accompanied at various times by companions who likewise give their willing assent: Sam, Merry, and Pippin join Frodo,[49] Mr. and Mrs. Beaver join the Pevensie children,[50] and Puddleglum joins Jill and Eustace.[51] Once on the quest, companions

---

44. Tolkien, *Return of the King*, 223–25.

45. Limitations considered here would include things like physical laws, natural capacities, aptitudes, etc. This is, in many ways, an Augustinian view of freedom.

46. The theme of quest can be distinguished in three parts: the perilous journey, the crucial struggle, and the exaltation of the hero (Urang, "Tolkien's Fantasy," 100).

47. Heroes don't purpose to be heroes on their own.

48. Tolkien, *Hobbit*, 13.

49. Tolkien, *Fellowship of the Ring*.

50. Lewis, *Lion, the Witch, and the Wardrobe*.

51. Lewis, *Silver Chair*.

often face moments of decision, whether to remain, possibly to leave, or even to attempt to co-opt it for their own purposes, sometimes tragically.[52] In the end, none are compelled; each must choose whether or not to remain faithful.

> The landscape's always changing. There is no
> Map that can be trusted once you swerve
> Aside; your only compass is your quest.
> If, true to friend, implacable to foe,
> You're faithful to the vision that you serve,
> You'll find the country which the muse has blessed.[53]

Free Will: Crises

In addition to participation in the quest, fairy stories often involve crises of will with regard to ultimate allegiance. Some of these take the form of desires for power where a once-good character is tempted to assert himself beyond his rightful place, falling into evil. Others are crises of endurance: Why not give up if the cause is hopeless?

Tolkien's *The Lord of the Rings* contains several examples of such crises. Saruman, the erstwhile arch-wizard of the Council of the Wise, abandons his given white robe to reach for even greater power, becoming Saruman of Many Colours.[54] He abandons wisdom and puts his faith in power and in the machinery and engines of war.[55] Rather than resisting evil through virtue, Saruman relishes dominion. This moral failure leads to his humiliation[56] and an ignoble death.[57] In contrast, Galadriel, an ancient elf-lady, is presented with an opportunity, even an offer,[58] to possess the great Ring of Power. Of all of the creatures in Middle Earth, she is among the most worthy to claim the power that the ring possesses,

52. The story of Boromir in Tolkien's *The Lord of the Rings* is an example of a will that refused to conform to the task of the quest. His choice is contrasted with that of his brother, Faramir, who, though only tangentially connected with the quest, still submitted to it (see Tolkien, *Fellowship of the Ring*, 413; also Tolkien, *Two Towers*, 280).

53. Williams, *Mere Humanity*, 165. Only the last lines of Williams's sonnet are represented here.

54. Tolkien, *Fellowship of the Ring*, 272.

55. Tolkien, *Two Towers*, 159.

56. Tolkien, *Two Towers*, 189.

57. Tolkien, *Return of the King*, 300.

58. Tolkien, *Fellowship of the Ring*, 381.

and yet, at the moment of doubt, in humility she overcomes her own desires and rejects the offer, choosing to lose what she had made for the freedom of others.[59] Galadriel's virtue empowers her will to choose what is best. These two prominent characters portray the freedom of creatures to follow the path they most desire, for good or for ill.

Free Will: Who Does Evil

One of the things that is easy to identify in fairy stories but often difficult to discern in ordinary existence is a truly evil character. Middle Earth has its Melkor and its Sauron, Narnia has its White Witch, its Calormenes, and its Tash, and Aerwiar has Gnag the Nameless and Ouster Will. In addition, arch-villains have evil servants: orcs, balrogs, hags, minotaurs, and fangs.[60] These creatures, masters and slaves alike, are all presented as acting in accord with desire.[61] Evil characters consistently choose evil, and often the choice is for more evil rather than less.[62] Their wills, at least in some measure, are free, but not free enough to choose good. In Christian terms, this might be expressed as a depravity present in some creatures that, short of a transformation, renders them incapable of doing good.[63] On the other hand, other characters are portrayed as having the

59. Tolkien, *Fellowship of the Ring*, 381.

60. "Fangs" are man-beast meldlings in Andrew Peterson's *Wingfeather Saga*. Of all the evil characters listed here, they most poignantly portray the impact of personal desire on actions and outcomes. Peterson's work, however, is relatively obscure in comparison with Tolkien and Lewis, and so the "fangs" will not be discussed at length in this essay.

61. The will of the master is often portrayed as being the primary motivator for the servants, particularly as seen in the disarray and bewilderment that occurs among the servants when the masters are defeated. However, subjection to the will of the master is always seen as contingent; servants retain some measure of autonomy. As a result, frequent conflicts erupt between rivals. See Tolkien's orcs of Cirith Ungol, who end up destroying each other in their greed to possess Frodo's mithril coat.

62. The orcs of the previous footnote portray this. They could choose to hand Frodo and his valuable possessions over to Sauron, or they could choose to take some of the treasures for themselves and turn over Frodo and the remaining possessions. The second choice is more evil in that it consists of the first evil with the addition of treachery, theft, etc. Given their commitment to evil, what isn't a possible option for the orcs is to turn Frodo loose (or any other such act of goodness).

63. This transformation is beautifully portrayed at the end of Peterson's *The Warden and the Wolf King* when, after Gnag's death, some "fangs" are restored and given new names.

potential for choosing good, whether or not they in fact do. One of the most noted examples of this is Tolkien's character of Gollum. While he is wretched and duplicitous, until the last he is presented as having the potential for choosing good. The total picture, then, is that the ability to choose good is not a universal condition, even among free creatures. Choices are constrained by the nature of the creature.

Synthesis of Sovereignty and Free Will

Fairy stories have been presented here as a way of perceiving and understanding Christian truths about the real world through imagination. In this concluding section, the themes of divine sovereignty and creaturely freedom, previously addressed separately, will be looked at in concert under three headings intended to demonstrate some ways in which the two seemingly divergent themes can be understood coherently through the vehicle of story.[64]

Synthesis: God as Creator and Determiner

In Tolkien's discussion of what a fairy-story is, he emphasizes the role of the author as subcreator.[65] An author defines the world in which the story takes place as well as the characters and their actions. The author is god to the story analogous to God, who created the world.[66] Likewise Lewis, working from the *imago Dei* nature of mankind, posits an analogous relationship between the control that an author exerts over his work and the providential work of God in creation.[67] As creator, God must necessarily

---

64. Peter Kreeft suggests that the artifact of a story is itself a model for providence and free will. A story is under the providence of an author while the characters portray free actions (or else the story would be simply the description of a machine) (see Kreeft, *Philosophy of Tolkien*, 63). While Kreeft's argument may be worthy of discussion, this essay treats elements within stories. The role of an author is not a part of the present argument.

65. Tolkien, "On Fairy-Stories," 51.

66. Williams, *Mere Humanity*, 44.

67. Williams, *Mere Humanity*, 50. Here Williams argues based on Lewis's *Miracles: A Preliminary Study*. Jesus is "like the corn-king [a reference to the Roman deity Ceres] because the corn-king is a portrait of Him." We can understand some of God's creative role through understanding the way that subcreators operate in his image.

exercise some level of control over his creation,[68] and the freedom of his creatures' wills must at least be limited to the created paradigm.

In his *The Silmarillion*, Tolkien presents a story of creation that provides some insight into the interaction of the will of the creator and the wills of creatures.[69] Illuvatar's music of creation is interrupted by the discordant music of Melkor, who desires to fill "the void" with his own imaginations, and, as a result, introduces evil to Illuvatar's creation. As the struggle between the musics progresses, Melkor's "loud, and vain, and endlessly repeated" music, "a clamorous unison as of many trumpets braying upon a few notes,"[70] is contrasted with Illuvatar's theme: "wide and beautiful, but slow and blended with an immeasurable sorrow."[71] The sovereignty of Illuvatar is apparent: "[Melkor's song] essayed to drown the other music by the violence of its voice, but it seemed that its most triumphant notes were taken by the other and woven into its own solemn pattern."[72] At its most self-assertive, the music of the rebellious creature appears paradoxically to be a harmonious part of the great creator's work. Melkor's boasting is actually an affirmation of Illuvatar's sovereignty; the creature's will is always according to the will of the creator.

Synthesis: The Heart as the Center of Activity

Near the end of the last book of the *Wingfeather Saga*, after Gnag the Nameless has been defeated and only the devastating effects of his regime remain, Kalmar Wingfeather, the High King of Anniera, enters the Fane of Fire to meet face to face with the Maker. His older brother, Janner, is left outside, struggling with resentment, jealousy and unanswered questions. Sitting there, in the glow of light from the Fane, Janner senses a change, an illumination and identification of the dark secrets in his own heart. He realizes, "What was happening inside of him was the Maker's doing."[73] His will is deficient and in need of reformation, or in the apostle

---

68. This can't be limited to merely establishing initial conditions as in a deistic framework.

69. Williams, *Encouraging Thought*, 41–42. His treatment focuses on the demonstration of a theistic worldview for Tolkien's works, connecting this creation narrative with subjects throughout Tolkien's works concerning Middle Earth.

70. Tolkien, *Silmarillion*, 17.

71. Tolkien, *Silmarillion*, 16.

72. Tolkien, *Silmarillion*, 17.

73. Peterson, *Warden and the Wolf King*, 477.

Paul's language, he must "be conformed."[74] The Maker is reshaping Janner's will so that he would desire better things. As Janner sits by the Fane
of Fire, aware of the deficiencies of his heart, he hears the voice of the
Maker repeat: "Be still."[75] Janner's transformation will not be accomplished by his own efforts and determination but by the Maker. Indeed,
as the story continues to unfold, Janner embraces the role for which he
had been born; he is the Throne Warden, purposed to protect his brother
the High King. Soon after his transformation beside the Fane of Fire, the
Throne Warden heroically gives his life for his brother.[76] Janner's self-
sacrifice portrays a free will that is, at the moment of decision, neither
governed by circumstances nor externally coerced, but one that chooses
in accordance with the desires of the heart. By conforming the heart, the
Maker draws the will to his purposes.

Synthesis: Submission and Freedom

Finally, a Christian context for understanding the relationship between
a human free will and a sovereign divine will is this: a good God and a
fallen humanity. In a fallen state, the will of man is, to use Lewis's term,
"bent,"[77] and the bent will does not prefer the good.[78] In such a case, a
good God might sovereignly restrain the desires of a bent person so that
a particular evil is freely chosen without God's incurring guilt for that
evil.[79] Lewis portrays this necessary creaturely submission to the good
will of God in *Perelandra* through the image of floating islands, moved

74. Rom 8:29. The passive voice of the verb is significant both for the present argument and for Paul's.

75. Peterson, *Warden and the Wolf King*, 477.

76. Peterson, *Warden and the Wolf King*, 510.

77. Lewis, *Space Trilogy*, 62. In the first of his trilogy, *Out of the Silent Planet*, Lewis
describes this term as the nearest English equivalent to an alien language expression.
In reality, the use of "bent" serves to make an ordinary concept foreign to readers so
that, as the fairy story itself is doing, the concept can be more deeply considered.

78. Though Plato's discussion in *Republic* concerning virtue-formation is relevant,
the Pauline discussion of the fallenness of the will in Romans 7–8 is particularly in
mind here. While the details of interpreting Romans 7 are debated, it seems clear that
apart from the work of the Spirit of God, the will is unable to effect a choice that
pleases God.

79. The problem of evil is not the focus of this essay and is addressed here only
incidentally.

about by currents of the sea and wind.[80] In God's world, if freedom is limited, it is for the best, and that is an encouraging thought.

Conclusion

When Podo Helmer spoke of following the Maker's wind, he was expressing a common theme in fairy stories. The fairy world we have examined is created and ordered by a personal deity; it is neither atheistic nor deistic. Instead, the one who made the world is the one who is also acting providentially within the world in order to effect ultimate victory over evil. He directs the actions of his creatures and his creation, he makes prophecies and fulfills them, even when his creatures oppose his plans, and at the very point where evil seems triumphant, he works his greatest victory. Yet in all of this, the experience of the creatures is that they are free. Evil creatures continue to work the evil that they desire, and good creatures must decide where their allegiances lie. Will they join the quest? Or will they leave it? Will they seek their own good or that of others? Creatures are not coerced against their desires, but the creator of the world cannot be discomfited by their choices either. He conforms their desires so that his will is done, and the result is good. The Maker's wind blew Podo precisely where he needed to be.

Bibliography

Calvin, John. *The Institutes of the Christian Religion*, edited by John T. McNeill. Translated by Ford Lewis Battles. Philadelphia: Westminster, 1960.

Duriez, Colin. "The Theology of Fantasy in Lewis and Tolkien." *Themelios* 23.2 (1998) 35–51.

Easton, M. G. *Illustrated Bible Dictionary*. New York: Thomas Nelson, 1894.

Kilby, Clyde S. "Meaning in *The Lord of the Rings*." In *Shadows of Imagination: The Fantasies of C. S. Lewis, J. R. R. Tolkien, and Charles Williams*, edited by Mark R. Hillegas, 70–80. Carbondale, IL: Southern Illinois University Press, 1969.

———. "Mythic and Christian Elements in Tolkien." In *Myth, Allegory, and Gospel: An Interpretation of J. R. R. Tolkien/C. S. Lewis/G. K. Chesterton/Charles Williams*, edited by John Warwick Montgomery, 119–43. Corona, CA: New Reformation, 2015.

Kreeft, Peter. *The Philosophy of Tolkien: The Worldview Behind The Lord of the Rings*. San Francisco: Ignatius, 2005.

Kreglinger, Gisela H. "Storied Revelations: The Influence of George MacDonald upon J. R. R. Tolkien and C. S. Lewis." *Sewanee Theological Review* 57.3 (2014) 301–20.

80. Williams, *Mere Humanity*, 70.

Lewis, C. S. *The Lion, The Witch, and the Wardrobe*. New York: Harper Trophy, 2000.

———. *The Silver Chair*. New York: Harper Trophy, 2000.

———. *The Space Trilogy, 75th Anniversary Collector's Edition*. London: Harper Collins, 2013.

———. *Surprised by Joy*. New York: HarperOne, 2017.

Peterson, Andrew. *The Monster in the Hollows*. Nashville: Rabbit Room, 2011.

———. *The Warden and the Wolf King*. Nashville: Rabbit Room, 2014.

Piper, John. *Providence*. Wheaton, IL: Crossway, 2020.

Shideler, Mary McDermott. "Philosophies and Fairy-Tales." *Theology Today* 30.1 (1973) 14–24.

Tolkien, J. R. R. *The Fellowship of the Ring*. Second Edition. New York: Houghton Mifflin, 1965.

———. *The Hobbit*. Collectors Edition. New York: Houghton Mifflin, 1997.

———. "On Fairy-Stories." In *Essays Presented to Charles Williams*, edited by C. S. Lewis, 38–89. Grand Rapids: Eerdmans, 1966.

———. *The Return of the King*. Second Edition. New York: Houghton Mifflin, 1965.

———. *The Silmarillion*. Edited by Christopher Tolkien. Boston: Houghton Mifflin, 1977.

———. *Tree and Leaf*. London: Harper Collins, 2001.

———. *The Two Towers*. Second Edition. New York: Houghton Mifflin, 1965.

Urang, Gunnar. "Tolkien's Fantasy: The Phenomenology of Hope." In *Shadows of Imagination: The Fantasies of C. S. Lewis, J. R. R. Tolkien, and Charles Williams*, edited by Mark R. Hillegas, 97–110. Carbondale, IL: Southern Illinois University Press, 1969.

Williams, Donald T. *An Encouraging Thought: The Christian Worldview in the Writings of J. R. R. Tolkien*. Cambridge, OH: Christian, 2018.

———. *Mere Humanity: G. K. Chesterton, C. S. Lewis, and J. R. R. Tolkien on the Human Condition*. Nashville: B&H, 2006.

Wood, Ralph C. "Conflict and Convergence on Fundamental Matters in C. S. Lewis and J. R. R. Tolkien." *Renascence* 55.4 (2003) 315–38.

Other major world religions—Islam, Hinduism, Buddhism—don't countenance complaints to God for one's circumstances. The Bible not only permits them, but gives us the very words to express dismay and despair—the literature of lament. Not only that, but God in Christ shared in our suffering and used the Psalms himself to cry out to the Father.

A Savior Set Apart

*How Christ's Use of the Biblical Laments Calls
Believers into Empathetic Fellowship*

Ann Ahrens

If we have never sought, we seek Thee now;
Thine eyes burn through the dark, our only stars;
We must have sight of thorn pricks on Thy brow;
     We must have Thee, O Jesus of the Scars.

The heavens frighten us; they are too calm;
     In all the universe we have no place.
Our wounds are hurting us; where is the balm?
Lord Jesus, by Thy Scars, we claim Thy grace.

If, when the doors are shut, Thou drawest near,
     Only reveal those hands, that side of Thine;
We know to-day what wounds are, have no fear,
Show us Thy Scars, we know the countersign.

The other gods were strong; but Thou wast weak;
     They rode, but Thou didst stumble to a throne;
But to our wounds only God's wounds speak;
     And not a god has wounds, but Thou alone.

—EDWARD SHILLITO, "JESUS OF THE SCARS"[1]

1. Shillito, "Jesus of the Scars," 191.

OF THE MANY EXPERIENCES common to all humankind, suffering is the most universal, and even perhaps the most unifying. Not one of us can escape the experience of suffering, and few of us will bear no scars having experienced it. For some, suffering will come in brief waves which will eventually dissipate into periods of calm, while for others it will last a lifetime. Either way, it is the signature shared theme of all humanity.

Within the body of Christ, the experience of suffering remains universal, as becoming a believer in Christ brings no guarantee that sorrow will no longer be a part of life. One could even argue, as does author and preacher Tim Keller, that for Christians the experience of suffering is often amplified and should even be *expected* as one grows in grace.[2] Drawing from Ezekiel 11:19, in which the prophet declares that God would give the people a "new heart of flesh," Keller reminds believers that a supernaturally changed heart is a heart which becomes *more* touchable, vulnerable, and moved by suffering.[3] In growing to become more like Christ, Christians must *accept*, and therefore *expect,* that they will weep. Indeed, one could go so far as to say Christians should *welcome* expressions of suffering, for without them there is no growth in grace, no true fellowship with Christ.

Why does becoming more like Christ produce tears? In his poem "Jesus of the Scars," Edward Shillito (1872–1948) recognizes that the "balm" for our wounds is only to be found in a wounded Savior, in one who has experienced human suffering:

> We know to-day what wounds are, have no fear,
> Show us Thy Scars, we know the countersign.

The "countersign" or signal by which we indicate that we know the scars of Christ, is our own scars, our own wounds, our own weeping. Only in our wounds can we recognize the wounds of Christ and, in turn, those of the world. More importantly, we can know and embrace our own wounds *because* of the wounds of Christ. Remarkably, Shillito concludes,

> The other gods were strong; but Thou wast weak;
> They rode, but Thou didst stumble to a throne;
> But to our wounds only God's wounds speak;
> And not a god has wounds, but Thou alone.

---

2. Keller, "Praying Your Tears," sermon series.

3. Keller, "Praying Your Tears."

In this final verse, Shillito proclaims the truth that sets Christianity apart from all other religious belief systems: "Not a god has wounds, but Thou alone." The idea and reality of a suffering Savior is unique to Christianity. While other religions have developed processes for dealing with suffering, or philosophies to explain suffering, Christianity alone reserves worship for a God who carries wounds and who invites followers to bring their own wounds to him as an act of worship and means of fellowship.

Scope of This Brief Study

A brief comparative study of the religions of Buddhism, Hinduism, Islam, and Christianity reveals that Christianity's God, Jesus Christ, is the only one who empathetically suffered substitutionally for and with his followers. Importantly, of these religions, Christianity's Holy Scripture, the Bible, is the only book which dedicates major portions towards the subject of suffering, giving its followers actual words of protest, complaint, and lament to pray during times of suffering.

Considering the presence of such a substantial number of prayers of protest, complaint, and lament in Scripture, the case can be made that God accepts and even encourages this type of dialogue between himself and believers. In his suffering, Jesus modeled for us "a vocabulary of need and a rhetoric of affliction."[4] Jesus' use of Old Testament prayers from the Psalms of Lament gives permission to his followers to bring raw, unfiltered expressions of emotion to him in prayer. As such, these prayers of protest, lament, anger, and complaint become the very dialogue through which believers come into fellowship with Christ, as Paul explained in Philippians 3:10: "That I may know him and the power of his resurrection, and may share his sufferings, becoming like him in his death."

Finally, when one explores the scriptural foundations for lament as dialogue, and thus worship, the *absence* of such expressions in corporate musical worship becomes a glaring omission, and one which should raise serious concern. That such expressions have been almost completely replaced by exclusively triumphalist declarations should give believers pause in considering the state of corporate worship and its effectiveness in forming believers to hold in tension the reality of lived experience with eschatological hope.

Buddhism

There are many Buddhist traditions, and suffering is not viewed universally amongst them all. Consistent among traditions, however, is the belief that all of life, from birth to death, is infused with suffering.[5] Given that suffering is a part of human existence and cannot be eliminated, the goal is to carefully observe its causes and sources in order to effectively eliminate them from the individual life, and ultimately the world.[6]

In transcending suffering, according to the Buddha, one must avoid the "extremes" of self-indulgence and self-mortification and instead forge a "middle path" called "The Noble Eightfold Path": right view, right thought, right speech, right action, right livelihood, right effort, right mindfulness, right concentration.[7] This path leads one to detach oneself from anything or anyone tending to produce cravings or selfish desires. Ultimately, as believers pursue The Noble Eightfold Path, the transformation from ordinary to holy person occurs, resulting in *Arahat*, or a perfect human freed from all suffering.[8]

---

4. Mays, *Psalms*, 22.

5. Shim, "Evil and the Overcoming," 14.

6. Shim, "Evil and the Overcoming," 11.

7. Bowker, *Problems of Suffering*, 238.

8. Shim, "Evil and the Overcoming," 16–17.

Hinduism

In Hinduism, the origin of suffering is rooted in *karma* or "the cause and effect in the moral sphere."[9] *Karma* is similar to a "bank deposit," the balance of which is predicated on one's actions, and from which one can withdraw.[10] Like Buddhism, how much one feels or experiences suffering is, therefore, dependent upon the work of the individual.

Since Hinduism teaches that God is infinite, and therefore, the ways in which one might approach him are equally varied, there is no seminal approach to dealing with suffering.[11] Instead, individuals must work to accept suffering as a part of life, using it as a means to attain *moshka*, or the release from the cycles of *samsara*, or rebirth, ultimately reaching a state of transcendence.[12]

As for the cause of suffering in Hindu religion, there is a variety of thought. Most believe that it is a direct result of human choice and not connected to any action on the part of a particular god. This idea is directly connected to karma and the need for samsara in order to purify the mind and body, eventually "becoming fully pure and spotlessly clean."[13] Karma dictates that the actions humans beings take to fulfill various desires, good or bad, produce fruit, which result in either pleasure or pain. Release from suffering is, therefore, the work of the individual person and is refined throughout the many rebirths which must inevitably take place.

Islam

Suffering in Islam is not viewed as a problem as much as an opportunity. While in Christianity, suffering is problematic due to its alleged conflict with the love of God, in Islam it becomes troublesome when it challenges the belief that God is all-powerful.[14] To prevent this conflict, Islam concludes that all suffering is the result of human disobedience, which is permitted by an omnipotent God. As John Bowker explains,

9. Anantharaman, "Hindu View," 106.

10. Anantharaman, "Hindu View," 107.

11. Anantharaman, "Hindu View," 104.

12. Bowker, *Problems of Suffering*, 197.

13. Anantharaman, "Hindu View," 106.

14. Bowker, *Problems of Suffering*, 102–3.

It is this sense that the "problem of suffering" is, in the Quran, almost dissolved. In effect, the Quran says, "Take the concept of omnipotence seriously: if your imagination of God is not too small, then suffering cannot be a problem, because the fact of suffering must necessarily be contained within the omnipotence of God." Suffering occurs only within creation, which is *God's* creation—and assuming that the universe has not got out of his control, then suffering is not out of his control either.[15]

Because of God's undeniable omnipotence, suffering is therefore purposeful as it is part of God's plan. All followers who endure suffering are promised paradise as a reward for their faithfulness. Such a standard leaves no room for fear or questions around the reasons for suffering and results in blasphemy if feelings of despair arise.[16] Thus, there is no place for lament and no space given to "bear one another's burdens," as Paul admonished in Galatians 6:2.

Since suffering is expected and viewed as a means to approval, and ultimately paradise, followers must suffer alone and seek individual rewards for endurance; suffering in community is not an option. This, coupled with Islam's rejection of the fall, original sin, and the resulting need for atonement, is perhaps the greatest contrast between Islam and Christianity, which teaches that its leader, Jesus Christ, suffered and died to atone for and bear the burden of the sins of his followers.[17]

The Place and Role of Suffering in Christianity

While there are multiple ways in which these religions differ from Christianity, five common threads highlight the major differences: First, unlike Christianity, these major world religions possess no historic canon of lament prayers offered by sufferers which can serve as a model for future believers. This absence of a canon of historic prayers of suffering is likely due to the fact that prayers or cries of lament to a deity are prohibited. Second, suffering serves to refine the believer, and therefore must be endured until the end goal of release from all suffering is achieved in this life. Third, believers are not invited to dialogue with the deity regarding their suffering. Fourth, the fact of a suffering savior or leader

15. Bowker, *Problems of Suffering,* 103 (emphasis original).

16. Bowker, *Problems of Suffering,* 112.

17. Aslan, "Fall and the Overcoming of Evil," 35.

who empathetically and substitutionally suffers and dies for his followers is absent. Finally, the act of shared suffering amongst believers is completely absent.

An Historic Canon of Lament

Following the creation story in the opening chapters of Genesis, one of God's first actions is in response to the voice of the sufferer, Abel, whose spilled blood cries out from the ground. Patrick D. Miller notes that "the sounds of these human cries run through Scripture from beginning to the end."[18] Indeed, lament is the persistent theme that pervades Scripture, from the cries of Abel in Genesis to the final verses of The Revelation in which John records, "Amen. Come Lord Jesus!"

Central to the Scriptures around suffering is the book of Psalms, in which a dominant theme is that of lament, with fully one-third of its 150 psalms centering around it.[19] This largest book in Scripture, Israel's official songbook, is filled with expressions of pain, suffering, loss, protest, anger, complaint, darkness, depression, guilt, anxiety, and fear. The large number of laments found in the psalter is no coincidence, but they aren't the product of a group of writers who somehow lacked faith or trust in the faithfulness, steadfast love, goodness, mercy, and longsuffering nature of Yahweh. Indeed, these expressions point to the very *opposite*, and serve as signs of unwavering faith and trust in God, a trust that reaches back to the history of God's faithfulness to his people, a faithfulness which the psalmist looks to in his time of trouble. Glenn Pemberton comments,

> Israel did not think about lament as we do. The overwhelming presence of the language of complaint, questioning, and protest in the Psalms suggests that Israel had a different view of the nexus among lament, faith, and praise. The headings of the book of Psalms place lament on the lips of God's most faithful followers—Moses (once in Ps. 90), David (thirty-eight times, e.g. 22, 38), and various temple leaders (Ethan [89], Korah [42–43], Heman [88], Asaph [77, 79])—and assigns lament for occasions ordained by God (e.g., the memorial offering [38, 79]). In the Psalms it is not those who lack faith who lament but those

---

18. Miller, "Heaven's Prisoners," 16.
19. Nowell, *Pleading, Cursing, Praising*, 21, 87.

recognized for strong faith who bring their most honest and passionate feelings to God.[20]

Indeed, it seems that God in his providence has invited us to engage him in and with our sorrows, giving us the very words to pray, thus validating their use.

The End of Suffering

The predominant belief in Buddhism, Hinduism, and Islam is that the work of overcoming suffering must be done by the individual and that it can be accomplished in one's lifetime, whether through cycles of reincarnation or through denial of self and the exercise of human perseverance. Christian Scripture, however, teaches that hope and suffering are bound up together in the tension of human experience and that only in the new heaven and new earth will this tension be released, as stated in Revelation 21:3–4:

> And I heard a loud voice from the throne saying, "Behold, the dwelling place of God is with man. He will dwell with them, and they will be his people, and God himself will be with them as their God. He will wipe away every tear from their eyes, and death shall be no more, neither shall there be mourning, nor crying, nor pain anymore, for the former things have passed away.

Until this time, Christians rejoice and lament within what Pemberton calls "liminal space," or "two states of being"—when we are no longer this, but not yet that. "In a liminal state, we are caught by circumstances in an in-between time or space of ambiguity, and as result we feel displaced, confused, frustrated, or even angry."[21] Indeed, this liminal space is a main theme in 1 Peter 1:3–9, in which the apostle writes to suffering believers about this very tension of suffering and hope. Reminding believers of the "living hope" which is bound up in their "inheritance" in heaven, which is "imperishable" and "undefiled," Peter acknowledges that they have been "grieved by various trials," but that these trials would ultimately reveal "the tested genuineness of your faith" at the "revelation of Jesus Christ." Though believers have no guarantee that suffering will end in this life, they hold in tension their suffering with the "living hope" noted in 1 Peter.

20. Pemberton, *Hurting with God*, 33.
21. Pemberton, *Hurting with God*, 63.

A Dialogical Relationship

The undeniable message of the Psalms of Lament is this: Worship is not pain denial.[22] This is supported, as stated above, by the very presence of the Psalms of Lament in Scripture. Old Testament scholar Walter Brueggemann consistently argues,

> All such experiences of disorder are a proper subject for discourse with God. There is nothing out of bounds, nothing precluded or inappropriate. Everything properly belongs in this conversation of the heart. To withhold parts of life from that conversation is in fact to withhold part of life from the sovereignty of God. Thus these psalms make the important connection: everything must be *brought to speech*, and everything brought to speech must be *addressed to God, who is the final reference for all of life*.[23]

Simply stated, God wants to speak with his people, a fact that is present throughout Scripture. Unlike the deities in other religions, Christianity's God is one who invites dialogue, who longs to hear the joys, sorrows, cries of suffering, and complaints of his people. Indeed, this human cry is, according to Patrick Miller, the "primary mode of conversation between God and humans."[24]

In the same sense that human relationships cannot exist and flourish without the type of dialogue that allows the participants to be deeply known, the relationship between God and believers will wither and fade apart from these authentic conversations. This desire on the part of God was evidenced throughout the Old Testament as God continued to call the people back into relationship even as he meted out judgment (e.g. Jer 32:36–44). The result was the restoration of covenantal discourse between God and believers. These conversations serve as examples of the rich dialogical relationship God has always desired between himself and believers. These texts remind us that we do not have to bear our suffering alone, but that God himself has provided words of lament that serve as expressions of grief—"the voice of the Gospel," God's "good word addressed to God's faithful people"[25]—opening the dialogue so necessary for comfort.

---

22. Runck, conversation with author, April 12, 2014.

23. Brueggemann, *Message of the Psalms*, 52 (emphasis original).

24. Miller, "Heaven's Prisoners," 16.

25. Brueggemann, *Spirituality of the Psalms*, 1–2.

A Suffering Savior: "He Knows Our Frame"

The most profound difference which sets Christianity apart from all religions of the world is the fact of a Suffering Savior or leader who empathetically and substitutionally suffered and died for his followers. The writer of Hebrews captures the weight of it in 4:14–16, reminding Christian believers of just how near Christ came:

> Since then we have a great high priest who has passed through the heavens, Jesus, the Son of God, let us hold fast our confession. For we do not have a high priest who is unable to sympathize with our weaknesses, but one who in every respect has been tempted as we are, yet without sin. Let us then with confidence draw near to the throne of grace, that we may receive mercy and find grace to help in time of need.

Indeed, Christ *is able* to sympathize, even *empathize*, with our suffering because he too suffered. Patrick Miller cites Christ's lament on the cross as "one of the primary *incarnational* clues in all of Scripture," for it signals that all cries before and after Christ's "are taken up in the laments of Christ."[26]

Christ's use of the lament Psalms in processing his own emotions, as found in the Gospels, serves as an example for believers, e.g., Jesus' lament over the sin of Jerusalem (Matt 23:1–37), which echoes the city lament in Psalms 46 and 48; his tears at the death of Lazarus (John 11) modeled after Psalm 6:3 and 77:4b; his prayer of agony in the garden of Gethsemane (Matt 26:36–46), which borrowed the "cup" metaphor found throughout the Psalms (e.g., 11:6; 16:5; 75:8); his cry of dereliction from the cross (Matt 27:46), a direct quote of Psalm 22:1; and his final words on the cross (Luke 23:46) which directly quote Psalm 31:5.[27] In these examples, believers not only are invited to share in Christ's suffering (Phil 3:10), but are assured that Christ also shared in their sufferings.

While Christ's sacrificial death on the cross signaled once-for-all atonement for sin that was unachievable by humankind on their own, his death also atoned for our suffering. Miller comments,

> The lament opens to us not only the meaning of the *person* of Christ. The lament is also critical for understanding *the work of God* in Jesus Christ, for it is our chief clue that Christ died not simply as one *of* us but also as one *for* us, both *with* us and *in*

---

26. Miller, "Heaven's Prisoners," 20 (emphasis original).

27. Ahrens, "Suffering, Soul Care, and Community," 59–67.

our behalf. As we hear our human voice of lament on the lips of the dying Jesus, it now becomes crystal clear: Jesus died for our *suffering* as much as for our *sins.*[28]

Thus, Christ died not only for sin, but for our suffering: abuse, neglect, abandonment, loss, sickness, pain, grief, fear. Indeed, within his death is bound up the entirety of the broken human condition.

Implications for Corporate Worship

The suffering of Christ for his followers is unique among all world religions. While Christ's suffering atoned for the sins of humankind, within it was bound up the *suffering* of all who follow. Even as he suffered, Christ modeled for all believers how to approach God with and in their pain. His prolific use of the Psalms of Lament proved that the great songbook of Israel can continue to serve as both template and teacher for all believers. These cries of protest, complaint, anger, and suffering prove that God not only tolerates but *invites* us into intimate dialogue with him as we "pre-reflectively" process our pain, praying the very emotion in his presence.[29] Unlike other religions, Christian believers must never suffer alone, for he hears when we cry.

Despite the multitude of lament Psalms and Christ's regular use of them, Christian believers today often prefer to sing songs of triumph, avoiding the breadth of expressions in the Psalms. While life may have seasons of balance and stability, it is also often "savagely marked by disequilibrium, incoherence, and unrelieved asymmetry."[30] Perhaps the insistence on a triumphalist tone is an act of bold faith in the face of suffering, a "great evangelical 'nevertheless,'" according to Brueggemann.[31] Given the aversion of society to weakness, and the seemingly relentless quest for power, it would appear that avoidance of lament in musical worship is more likely a "numb denial" and refusal or inability to sit with sorrow, to hold it in tension with hope—a difficult process, without doubt.[32] Brueggemann concludes, "a church that goes on singing 'happy songs' in

28. Miller, "Heaven's Prisoners," 21 (emphasis original).

29. Keller, "Praying Your Tears," sermon series.

30. Brueggemann, *Message of the Psalms*, 51.

31. Brueggemann, *Message of the Psalms*, 51.

32. Brueggemann, *Message of the Psalms*, 51.

the face of raw reality is doing something very different from what the Bible itself does."[33]

The turn from the strictly triumphalist tone in worship music can only begin when believers balance confidence in God with expressions of need.[34] As believers join their voices in expressions of sorrow, loss, and lament, they will then more easily turn their focus outward, joining the voices of the marginalized within the congregation as well as those across the world. As lament is practiced, hearts become sensitized anew to suffering and violence within and without the congregation. By avoiding the rush to rejoicing and choosing to sit with the pain, believers learn to hold in tension suffering and hope.

Throughout the history of humankind, one thing is undeniably true: "somber doesn't sell. We prefer to sing and repent, lament and die in silent privacy."[35] Jesus Christ, the "man of sorrows," as he was described in Isaiah 53:3, reversed this, giving to his followers what no other prophet or leader of any world religion gave: wounds. Within his wounds is an invitation to lament in his presence and in community with other believers.

> The other gods were strong; but Thou wast weak;
> They rode, but Thou didst stumble to a throne;
> But to our wounds only God's wounds can speak,
> And not a god has wounds, but Thou alone.[36]

Bibliography

Ahrens, Ann. "Suffering, Soul Care, and Community: The Place of Corporate Lament in Evangelical Worship." PhD diss., The Southern Baptist Theological Seminary, 2017.

Anantharaman, Tanore Ramachandra. "The Hindu View of Suffering, Rebirth, and the Overcoming of Evil." In *The Origin and the Overcoming of Evil and Suffering in the World Religions,* edited by Peter Koslowski, 100–112. New York: Cambridge University Press, 1970.

Aslan, Adnan. "The Fall and the Overcoming of Evil and Suffering in Islam." In *The Origin and the Overcoming of Evil and Suffering in the World Religions,* edited by Peter Koslowski, 24–47. New York: Cambridge University Press, 1970.

Bowker, John. *Problems of Suffering in Religions of the World.* New York: Cambridge University Press, 1970.

33. Brueggemann, *Message of the Psalms,* 52.

34. Pemberton, *Hurting with God,* 40.

35. Towner, "'Without Our Aid,'" 18.

36. Edward Shillito, "Jesus of the Scars," quoted in Carson, *How Long, O Lord?,* 191.

Brueggemann, Walter. *The Message of the Psalms: A Theological Commentary.* Minneapolis: Augsburg, 1984.

———. *The Spirituality of the Psalms.* Minneapolis: Fortress, 2002.

Carson, D. A. *How Long, O Lord?: Reflections on Suffering and Evil.* Grand Rapids: Baker, 1990.

Keller, Tim. "Psalms—The Songs of Jesus." Sermon series, recorded February 20, 2000—March 19, 2000. Redeemer Presbyterian Church, New York. http://www.gospelinlife.com/psalms-the-songs-of-jesus.

Mays, James. *Psalms.* Interpretation. Louisville: John Knox, 1994.

Miller, Patrick D. "Heaven's Prisoners: The Lament as Christian Prayer." In *Lament: Reclaiming Practices in Pulpit, Pew, and Public Square,* edited by Sally A. Brown and Patrick D. Miller, 15–26. Louisville: Westminster John Knox, 2005.

Nowell, Irene. *Pleading, Cursing, Praising: Conversing with God through the Psalms.* Collegeville, MN: Liturgical, 2013.

Pemberton, Glenn. *Hurting with God: Learning to Lament with the Psalms.* Abilene, TX: Abilene Christian University Press, 2012.

Shim, Jae-Ryong. "Evil and the Overcoming of Suffering in Buddhism." In *The Origin and the Overcoming of Evil and Suffering in the World Religions,* edited by Peter Koslowski, 8–23. London: Kluwer, 2001.

Towner, Sibley. "'Without Our Aid He Did Us Make': Singing the Meaning of the Psalms." In *A God So Near: Essays on Old Testament Theology in Honor of Patrick D. Miller,* edited by Brent A. Strawn and Nancy R. Bowen, 17–34. Winona Lake, IN: Eisenbrauns, 2003.

Burial sites present a clash of metaphysical paradigms. The Egyptian and Sudanese pyramids held mummified remains surrounded by provisions for the afterlife; Hindu ashes are poured out into the Ganges; typical Muslim cemeteries feature monochrome chess pieces, free of ornamentation. In contrast, the Christian cemetery, particularly of the rural variety, is spiritually freighted and artistically alive, arguing that the understandings of both the deceased and the mourners are life-giving.

In the Company of the Dead

Reflections on Art, Faith, and the Rural Cemetery

STEVE HALLA

SOMETIMES, A QUIET WALK through an old rural cemetery can breathe new life into a weary soul. This is especially true if the cemetery contains a few good examples of figurative memorial sculpture. Or at least this has been true in my own life. During the nineteenth century, the rise and popularity of rural, or garden, cemeteries provided Americans with a brand-new way of memorializing the dead and encouraging the living. At a time when public parks were a rarity, rural cemeteries offered lush garden settings in which people of all ages could gather and enjoy the beauty of nature and art while mourning lost loved ones and reflecting on the human condition. Today, as rural cemetery directors continue to experiment with new ways of engaging local communities, some urban centers, such as Memphis, Tennessee, are experiencing small-scale rural cemetery revivals. Along with history buffs, bird watchers, curiosity seekers, gardening enthusiasts, service volunteers, and countless others, many rural cemeteries nationwide are now home to movie nights, discussion groups, lecture series, weddings, yoga classes, concert series, recreational biking, and a whole host of other creative activities and events. For me, rural cemeteries provide an aesthetically rich environment where I can reconnect with the past, reflect on the present, and look to the future with hope. In the company of the dead, life abounds.

In this essay, my goal is to share a few thoughts and reflections on three topics: first, the historical relationship between Western Christianity and the dead; second, the rise of the rural cemetery and the role of the imagination; and third, the contemplative richness of Elmwood Cemetery in Memphis, Tennessee. I will then conclude with a few summary remarks concerning Riverside Cemetery, in Jackson, Tennessee, and the role of the rural cemetery in contemporary society. Let us begin.

Western Christianity and the Dead

Prior to the eighteenth century, in the Christian West, the dead were often buried either near, around, or in churches. In 752, Cuthbert, the Archbishop of Canterbury, obtained permission from the Pope and announced that bodies could and should be buried in churchyards, i.e., the area of land surrounding a church building.[1] Although Christian burial customs have varied from age to age and from one ecclesiastical tradition to another, a few of the most frequently cited theological reasons for church-oriented burials include the salvific protection of saints and their relics, the assurance of the future resurrection of one's entire being, and a continual reminder to the living to pray for the souls of the deceased.[2] In nineteenth-century America, as churchgoers commonly passed by graveyards just prior to entering church buildings, they were consistently reminded of the mortality of the flesh, the immortality of the soul, and the brevity of life. A popular graveyard epitaph, of which there were many variations, read:

> Where you are now,
> so once was I.
> Where I am now,
> so you will be.[3]

Nowadays, church property that just a few centuries ago would have most likely been used for graveyards now plays host to other, more pressing needs such as paved parking lots, children's playgrounds, and manicured lawns. Our casual journeys to and from church have become remarkably sterilized and cleansed from the presence of death. Historically speaking, however, this has not been the Christian norm. Whether or not our contemporary practices are a good thing is still open for debate.

1. Sanders, *History and Antiquities*, 27.
2. For these and other reasons see Ariès, *Hour of Our Death*, 29–51.
3. Jackson and Vergara, *Silent Cities*, 10.

An interesting example of the once-intimate relationship between churchgoers and the dead can still be seen in the reformed church known as the Great Church located in the central market of the Dutch city of Haarlem. Consecrated in 1559, the then Catholic Gothic cathedral was soon after confiscated as part of the Protestant Reformation and converted to a Protestant church in 1578. Although much of the church's art and collection of artifacts was either sold or destroyed, one of its most unique features survived, that is, its floor, which consists entirely of gravestones. "The whole floor space of the church is a compartmentalized cemetery," writes Philippe Ariès in his monumental book *The Hour of Our Death*, "and no matter where the faithful turn, they walk on graves."[4] The church's last interior burial took place on June 27, 1829. During the 1980s, a major restoration project helped ensure that congregants will still be able to worship atop the graves of Christians from centuries past for centuries yet to come. In the presence of the dead, life joyously abounds. But then, during the early nineteenth century, the intimate relationship between the church and the dead took a dramatic turn for the worse.

A cringeworthy example of this is London's Enon Chapel and its Baptist minister Mr. W. Howse. Opened in 1822, the chapel consisted of a top floor, which was used for worship and teaching, and a basement, which contained a small space for burials measuring roughly 708 square feet.[5] At the time, graveyard reformers argued that graveyards should contain no more than 136 bodies per 43,560 square feet.[6] The problem, however, was that most urban churches simply did not have the space to accommodate such ideal demands. By the late 1830s, Enon Chapel was home to over 500 annual burials. To make room for new arrivals, Mr. Howse began paying workers to secretly dump bodies into the nearby Thames River.[7] At the same time, back in the chapel's basement, some of the stacked bodies occasionally tumbled down into an open sewer.[8] Although churchgoers frequently complained about the putrid stench rising through the wooden floorboards, there was little anyone could do. Miraculously, the chapel never ran out of burial space. After all, desperate times call for desperate measures, and, besides, by charging less money

---

4. Ariès, *Hour of Our Death*, 48.

5. Arnold, *Necropolis*, 105.

6. Cock-Starkey, "Disgusting Victorian Cemetery," para. 3.

7. Cock-Starkey, "Disgusting Victorian Cemetery," para. 8.

8. Cock-Starkey, "Disgusting Victorian Cemetery," para. 6.

per burial than his neighboring parish competitors, which Mr. Howse did, there was a small fortune to be made.

Thankfully, the ill-gotten charade ended abruptly immediately following Mr. Howse's death in 1842. A few years later, in 1844, the chapel was converted to a dance hall where participants were invited to join in and dance on the dead.[9] But the damage had already been done. By the mid-nineteenth century, urban church graveyards were roundly criticized as unsightly, overcrowded, grossly unsanitary, and, in a word, shameful. Something drastic needed to change. A leading source of inspiration for that change came in the form of a novel new cemetery in Paris, France, called Pére-Lachaise.

Founded by Napoléon Bonaparte and opened in 1804, Pére-Lachaise was situated on forty-eight acres of a former Jesuit retreat complete with winding paths, dense woods, rose gardens, large rocks, grassy knolls, and bountiful fruit groves. Modeled after traditional English garden designs, the cemetery combined the natural beauty of the landscape with a wide assortment of funerary monuments, architecture, and art made by some of Paris's leading architects and artists. In sharp contrast to Paris's overcrowded catacombs and congested church graveyards, Pére-Lachaise offered a spacious environment wherein Parisians could pay their respects to the dead while also being reminded of important theological virtues and philosophical ideas such as love, faithfulness, courage, compassion, and justice, just to name a few. Today, Pére-Lachaise remains one of the most-visited cemeteries in the world and a place where people can still gather and contemplate the big questions of life aided by hundreds of elegantly carved memorial sculptures and thousands upon thousands of impressive monuments, all of which represents "the grand sweep of the human experience."[10] In the company of over a million corpses, visitors can still experience afresh what the celebrated French novelist and playwright Honoré de Balzac (1799–1850) experienced over 150 years ago, that is, bustling crowds, curious onlookers, lively conversations, and melancholic mourners, i.e., "nothing but the living."[11]

9. Arnold, *Necropolis*, 106.

10. Campbell, *City of Immortals*, 32.

11. Quoted in Campbell, *City of Immortals*, 19.

The Rural Cemetery

Inspired, in part, by Pére-Lachaise's revolutionary design and commercial success, European and American architects, landscape designers, visionary leaders, and generous patrons crafted a new kind of public burial space: the rural cemetery. In most cases, rural cemeteries were located in picturesque landscapes on the outskirts of towns and cities. They were exquisitely maintained by professional caretakers; open to all social classes and religious affiliations; decorated with beautiful works of art and architecture; and graced with at least one or two chapels in which services and other important activities could be held. Although a leading function of the rural cemetery was to provide a sanitary and dignified final resting place for the dead, it was equally designed to serve as an open-air museum where people could receive free and informal instruction in matters of theology, philosophy, morality, history, art, architecture, landscaping, and gardening, while at the same time reaping the benefits of physical exercise, social interaction, communal mourning, and, especially in America, a renewed sense of patriotism, unity, and shared cultural values.[12] Little wonder, rural cemeteries quickly became some of the leading civic and cultural institutions of their day.

In America, the first great rural cemetery was Mount Auburn, located in Cambridge, Massachusetts, opened in 1831. In 1861, the then well-known author and naturalist Wilson Flagg (1805–84) edited and contributed to a book titled *Mount Auburn: Its Scenes, Its Beauties, and Its Lessons*. In his essay titled "Rural Burial," Flagg reflected on how the active use of the imagination can help transform the rural cemetery's natural environment into a rich source of spiritual and philosophical reflection:

> As we stroll through the grounds, we read lessons which heaven, through nature, conveys to us in many a pleasing emblem of light and beauty. The winds represent the vicissitudes of life: but they inculcate the lesson that there is no adversity that is not followed by the tranquility of a better day. The flowers bud and bloom, and, in their vernal loveliness, represent the morning of our days and the spring-time of our life; but they perish, like our own corporeal frames, to indicate by their revival that new life, of which death is but the celestial dawning. The trees that shade over the graves of our friends, as a manifestation of that

12. See Brown, *Soul in the Stone*, 2–6; French, "Cemetery as Cultural Institution," 67–91; Gillon Jr., *Victorian Cemetery*, v–xiii; Rutherford, *Victorian Cemetery*, 13–23; Sloane, *Is the Cemetery Dead?*, 32–34.

unseen power that has assembled the departed spirits under his providential care.[13]

In contrast to reason alone, which often casts doubts on things unknown, Flagg argued that the imagination, when enlivened by memory, nature, art, and either the religious faith of believers or the "poetic" faith of nonbelievers, enables the mind to catch glimpses of higher truths that can help soften grief, calm anxieties, and tranquilize sorrows.[14] Working in harmony with humanity's innate aesthetic and sacred sensibilities, the designers of Mount Auburn crafted a serene garden of consolation, offering reassurance of things not fully known until "mortals have become immortals."[15]

A few years after the opening of Mount Auburn, a rural cemetery movement swept across the country, resulting in the creation of over 100 new ones, including Mount Hope in Bangor, Maine, opened in 1834; Laurel Hill in Philadelphia, Pennsylvania, opened in 1836; Mount Hope in Rochester, New York, opened in 1838; Green Mount in Baltimore, Maryland, opened in 1839; Cave Hill in Louisville, Kentucky, opened in 1848; and one of my personal favorites, Elmwood in Memphis, Tennessee. Opened in 1852 and spread out across eighty gently rolling acres, Elmwood is an historic Tennessee state treasure. On the glamorous side of things, Elmwood played host to a funeral scene in the 1993 cinematic legal thriller *The Firm,* starring Tom Cruise. On the practical side of things, Elmwood remains an active burial site and contains a rich collection of both cemetery art and stories from the past that are still worth reflecting upon, especially when considered in the larger context of art and theology and enlivened by the imagination. Here are three examples.

Etta Grigsby Partee

One of Elmwood's most beautiful monuments commemorates the life of Etta Grigsby Partee, who was born in 1884 and died in 1911 at the age of twenty-six.

---

13. Flagg, "Rural Burial," 9.
14. Flagg, "Rural Burial," 11.
15. Flagg, "Rural Burial," 11.

Carved from white Italian Carrara marble and mounted on a granite base, the monument depicts a seated young woman dressed in a long, flowing, Classically inspired garment, and with Easter lilies lain across her lap. The Easter lilies serve as a symbol of innocence, purity, and the resurrection of Christ. Although her youthful appearance suggests a sense of vitality, and even a hint of sensuality, her overall melancholic demeanor suggests something more sorrowful. A poetic inscription carved on the east side of the monument reads:

> Warm summer sun shine brightly here
> Warm southern wind blow gently here
> Green sod above lie light, lie light
> Good night dear heart, good night, good night.

Tragically, Etta died of Bright's disease, a kidney disorder, on the day of her wedding.[16] Of all days, on her wedding day.

When I first learned about Etta's story, I was immediately reminded of a sixteenth-century woodcut print titled *New-Married Lady* by the German artist Hans Holbein the Younger.[17] In the print, a recently married husband and wife delight in each other's company while a skeletal figure, representing death, beats a drum in front of them. In the lower right-hand corner, a small hourglass, along with the print's title, lets us know that death has come for the young lady. At a moment when she least expects it, death is waiting for her. Originally published in 1538 as

16. McCollum and Bearden, *Images of America*, 25.
17. Holbein, *Holbein's Dance of Death and Bible Woodcuts*, 35.

part of a series of prints commonly known today as the *Dance of Death,* the image was designed, in part, as a reminder that death is the final destiny of us all and can occur at any moment.[18] Expect the unexpected. If something can happen, then it can (generally speaking) happen to you.

Etta's monument and Holbein's print are stark reminders that life is a precious gift from God that we should never take for granted. No one is guaranteed tomorrow. As such, never put off anything for tomorrow that you know you could and should do today. Tell the people you love that you love them. Do not wait. A quick text will take you no more than five seconds: I ♥ U. SEND. Make the absolute most of the life God has graciously given to you and live each day for his glory and the betterment of those around you. Always be ready to give an account for your life, especially when you least expect it.

Kate Simpson McCormick

In contrast to the size, beauty, and elegance of Etta's monument, Kate Simpson McCormick's memorial is barely even noticeable. In fact, if you blink, you are likely to miss it. In 1875, Kate found herself in a terrible situation. After being seduced by one of her father's friends, she became pregnant. Not knowing quite what to do, the unwed twenty-one-year-old traveled to Memphis seeking an illegal abortion. Sadly, Kate died as a result of the abortion procedures. When Kate's mother was called

18. Holbein, *Holbein's Dance of Death*, 150.

in to claim her daughter's body, she left behind a single white rose, and then, essentially, disowned her. A county undertaker had Kate buried at Elmwood. One hundred and twenty-one years later, in 1997, a pair of benefactors paid for a small gravestone to commemorate Kate's life and prick the conscience of visitors.[19] The inscription carved on the gravestone reads:

> Kate McCormick
> Seduced and pregnant by her father's friend,
> Unwed, she died from abortion, her only choice.
> Abandoned in life and death by family.
> With but a single rose from her mother.
> Buried only through the kindness of unknown benefactors.
> Died February, 1875, age 21
> Victim of an unforgiving society
> Have mercy on us.

Every human being is made in the image of God and worthy of dignity and respect. If no human being is ever outside of the reach of God's love, then no human being should ever be outside of the reach of our willingness to love and care for them. You do not have to personally like everyone. In fact, there are probably some people in your life right now that you simply cannot stand, and maybe for good reason. And it's fair to argue that abortion was not Kate's "only choice." But we are called, regardless, to faithfully extend God's love and kindness to them, even if we might personally feel that they do not deserve it. Genuine love requires real actions. Do the people in your circle of influence, from your closest friends to the cashier at the local grocery store, see the love of God flowing in and through everything you do? Today, Kate's monument rests peacefully beneath the outstretched arms of a large oak tree, finding in death what she could not find in life, a place of safety and shelter from the storms.

Statues of Hope

Scattered throughout the landscape in which both Etta and Kate are buried, are numerous examples of a popular nineteenth-century funerary monument known as the statue of Hope. It is one of seven uniquely designed figurative statues representing the seven Christian virtues:

19. McCollum and Bearden, *Images of America*, 25.

prudence, justice, temperance, courage (the cardinal virtues), and faith, hope, and love (the theological virtues). Often displayed atop towering monoliths, the statue of Hope depicts a standing female figure dressed in ancient Roman clothing and calmly gazing upward while supporting a large maritime anchor. In some instances, she is shown with either one or both of her hands on her heart, a symbol of faithfulness and devotion. In other instances, she simply raises one of her hands high into the air and symbolically points towards heaven. A five-pointed star can sometimes be seen on the top of her forehead, a symbol of the immortality of the soul. Creative variations abound.

The symbolic use of the anchor, the statue's main feature, has been historically associated with Hebrews 6:19–20, which reads, "This hope we have as an anchor of the soul, a hope both sure and steadfast and one which enters within the veil, where Jesus has entered as a forerunner for us, having become a high priest forever according to the order of Melchizedek." At the time of their construction, statues of Hope were designed to encourage family and friends of the deceased that, one day, they would be reunited with their lost loved one(s) in heaven. As time passed, however, those same family and friends grew old themselves and, like their lost loved one(s), passed away. In turn, their family and friends then received the same encouragement from the same statues, thus establishing a living legacy of hope passed down from one generation to the next. People change. Circumstances change. Hope remains.

The Christian hope that statues of Hope represents is a steadfast confidence anchored in the death and resurrection of the Lord Jesus Christ and the faithfulness of God. It rests secure in the belief that because God will do all he says he will do, we can confidently step out in faith, reach out in love, and be who God created us to be, come what may. It is a hope that can stand in the presence of death and still have reason to rejoice. Elmwood is a place firmly rooted in the past. But its vast assortment of statues of Hope compels us, the living, to keep striving forward with our heart's gaze fixed on the one who knows us better than we will ever know ourselves. With God, all things are possible. Whom or what shall we fear?

The nineteenth-century rural cemetery movement provided several generations of Americans with picturesque settings in which people could mourn the dead, reflect on life, and even enjoy an afternoon stroll or picnic. But things change, and so too did the rural cemetery. During the mid- to late nineteenth century, as American values, beliefs, and tastes gave way to more modern sensibilities, a new kind of burial space emerged known as the lawn-park cemetery, which then gave way to the memorial park cemetery. In sharp contrast to rural cemeteries, lawn-park cemeteries were characterized by relatively flat landscapes, less vegetation, fewer works of art, and smaller grave markers.[20] Rural cemeteries were designed to tell stories and instruct the masses. Lawn-park cemeteries were designed to kindle private memories in the hearts and minds of close family and friends. And so, just like that, the rural cemetery movement lost its momentum and quietly slipped into the pages of history and the backdrop of everyday life. But they have not been entirely forgotten.

Riverside Cemetery

In Jackson, Tennessee, the city I now call home, is historic Riverside Cemetery, a small, ten-and-a-half-acre urban cemetery established in 1824. Although Riverside is not a rural cemetery, it does contain several examples of popular rural cemetery memorial sculpture, including a statue of Hope.

---

20. Sloane, *Is the Cemetery Dead?*, 39–44.

Unfortunately, the statue is barely recognizable except for a small part of the anchor that rests at the base of the woman's left foot. Time and the elements have dramatically taken their toll. Even still, she tirelessly raises her right arm towards the heavens and quietly proclaims her message of hope to all those who have the eyes to see and the ears to hear. But what about those who have neither the eyes to see nor the ears to hear? In an age that no longer readily speaks the symbolic language of cemetery art or encourages the active use of the religious imagination, can rural cemeteries still play a meaningful role in contemporary society apart from being merely culturally rebranded, repurposed, or reimagined? I believe they can.

The rural cemetery is a place of death, plain and simple. "Even the gravestones that we raise," laments the poet Shloyme Ettinger (1803–56), "Soon reach the end of their days."[21] Death is humanity's greatest enemy and the source of its deepest sorrows. In his essay "Sorrow and Its Recompense," Wilson Flagg noted that death's sorrows are so deep, in fact, that any consolation derived amid them typically results in near rapturous joy and happiness.[22] A leading source of such consolation was the statue of Hope:

> One of the most delightful of our sacred emblems is that which represents Hope as the image of a female leaning upon an anchor, the symbolic representation of steadfastness and

21. Ettinger, "On the Occasion of the New Year," 19.
22. Flagg, "Sorrow and Its Recompense," 371.

confidence, without which hope cannot exist. This is a very appropriate emblem for a cemetery, where our only consolations
are derived from our confidence in a future life, and our faith in
the assurances of religious hope.[23]

By employing the use of universally recognized human gestures, e.g.,
a slight upward glance, a hand resting gently on the heart, etc., statues
of Hope were designed to communicate their basic message of hopeful
longing to both learned and unlearned audiences alike. Along with a wide
variety of other Christian-themed memorial artworks, rural cemeteries
enabled visitors to mourn lost loved ones and reflect on the mysteries of
life from a uniquely Christian perspective.

Today, rural cemeteries remain among the most Christian-faith-af-
firming public spaces in all Western society. In lieu of secularism's current
ideological rise and dominance in the West, rural cemeteries continue to
serve as palpable expressions of what it means to think Christianly about
life, death, the nature of humanity, and the world in which we live. At a time
when Christian apologetic discourse is often either culturally ignored or
brazenly dismissed as racist, sexist, homophobic, xenophobic, etc., rather
than honestly and vigorously debated, the Christian testimony of rural
cemeteries might just be one of their greatest contemporary strengths and
lasting legacies. In the company of the dead, the hope-filled tradition of
Christian worldview thinking lives on. As Wilson Flagg once wrote:

> Let us go to the resting place of the dead, where the turfs lie in
> verduous heaps, and the flowers of the field scatter their incense
> over them and consecrate their repose. Here will the gentle
> mother receive us, and when we can no longer be comforted by
> reason and philosophy, she lulls us to rest by the assurances of
> religion . . . [24]

Sometimes, a quiet walk through an old rural cemetery can breathe new
life into a weary soul. Or at least this has been true in my own life.

Bibliography

Ariès, Philippe. *The Hour of Our Death.* New York: Knopf, 1981.
Arnold, Catherine. *Necropolis: London and Its Dead.* New York: Pocket, 2006.

23. Flagg, "Funeral Emblems and Devices," 188–89.
24. Flagg, "Sorrow and Its Recompense," 371.

Brown, John Gary. *Soul in the Stone: Cemetery Art from America's Heartland.* Lawrence: University Press of Kansas, 1994.

Campbell, Carolyn. *City of Immortals: Père-Lachaise Cemetery, Paris.* New York: Goff, 2019.

Cock-Starkey, Claire. "The Disgusting Victorian Cemetery That Helped Change Burials in London Forever." *Mental Floss*, October 3, 2018. https://www.mentalfloss.com/article/559169/disgusting-victorian-cemetery-helped-change-burials-london-forever.

Ettinger, Shloyme. "On the Occasion of the New Year—To My Friends." Translated by Jessica Kirzane. In *Poems About Death*, edited by Eric Luft, 19–20. North Syracuse, New York: Gegensatz, 2018.

Flagg, Wilson. "Funeral Emblems and Devices." In *Mount Auburn: Its Scenes, Its Beauties, and Its Lessons*, edited by Wilson Flagg, 187–91. Boston: James Munroe, 1861.

———."Rural Burial." In *Mount Auburn: Its Scenes, Its Beauties, and Its Lessons*, edited by Wilson Flagg, 8–13. Boston: James Munroe, 1861.

———."Sorrow and Its Recompense." In *Mount Auburn: Its Scenes, Its Beauties, and Its Lessons*, edited by Wilson Flagg, 367–71. Boston: James Munroe, 1861.

French, Stanley. "The Cemetery as Cultural Institution: The Establishment of Mount Auburn and the 'Rural Cemetery Movement.'" In *Death in America*, edited by David E. Stannard, 67–91. Philadelphia: University of Pennsylvania Press, 1975.

Gillon, Edmond V., Jr. *The Victorian Cemetery.* New York: Dover, 1972.

Holbein, Hans. *Holbein's Dance of Death.* New York: Penguin, 2016.

———.*Holbein's Dance of Death and Bible Woodcuts.* New York: Sylvan, 1947.

Jackson, Kenneth T., and Camilo José Vergara. *Silent Cities: The Evolution of the American Cemetery.* New York: Princeton, 1989.

McCollum, Kimberly, and Willy Bearden, eds. *Images of America: Elmwood Cemetery.* Charleston, SC: Arcadia, 2016.

Rutherford, Sarah. *The Victorian Cemetery.* New York: Shire, 2008.

Sanders, Harry. *The History and Antiquities of Shenstone, in the County of Stafford, Illustrated.* London: J. Nichols, 1794.

Sloane, David Charles. *Is the Cemetery Dead?* Chicago: The University of Chicago Press, 2018.

Generations of aestheticians have sought to harness the arts to secular causes, whether economic, hedonistic, political, or cultural. In one way or another, they presume to liberate the artist, his calling, and his audience from the shackles of biblical sanctification, but this liberation has proven to be a cruel taskmaster. In contrast, artists can find a gracious master in the living God, who infuses their work with his grace and power.

The Pretense of Artistic Autonomy

Matthew Raley

MRS. GERETH WAS A woman so aesthetically sensitive that, having to sleep in an ugly mansion, she was "kept awake for hours by the wallpaper in her room."[1] Yet Mrs. Gereth found a soulmate there, Fleda Vetch, a young woman who saw the difference between true art and commercialized imitations. Henry James's novel, *The Spoils of Poynton*, tells how Mrs. Gereth tried to rescue her vast art collection from her son's grubby fiancée, maneuvering him to fall in love with Fleda instead. The art must not be defiled.

Like Mrs. Gereth, art theorists guard the holy precincts around aesthetic pursuits. Human creativity is so pure that no other endeavor should violate the temple. The unclean ethics of commerce, religion, bourgeois sentimentality, and political propaganda must never constrain or pervert human expression. The temple, furthermore, shelters the works themselves, just as Mrs. Gereth's house Poynton both displayed and protected her collection. The concert hall sequesters the performance of pure music away from common sounds. The museum frames visual art and paces its reception, quarantining it from the values outside. The temple of purity seems to have an axiom carved high on its edifice: "Art for art's sake." Fine art is separate, autonomous, serving only itself.

Among theorists, however, this axiom is more problematic than might appear. For example, art has been independent of religion for a

1. James, *Spoils of Poynton*, 5.

long time. Yet freeing art from religious constraints, according to James Elkins, has effectively banned religious conviction from artistic expression unless it conforms to a broad gnostic spirituality—replacing one constraint with another.[2] Other theorists note the folk origins of many artworks. Nicholas Wolterstorff (citing André Malraux) has argued that many of the objects in museums have been housed there on false pretenses. An African mask was not conceived on the same theory of art as an Expressionist painting. Such objects are venerated together as art in museums though they were designed and made for other purposes.[3]

More fundamentally, many theorists argue for art's purity but cannot actually separate art from the grubby world. They promise to take initiates to the pinnacle of the holy precincts, the autonomy of art. Once there, however, art merely serves some larger design—just as it would when harnessed to religion, commerce, or ideology. Friedrich Schiller (1759–1805) said that man needed a pure spring of free virtue—an "aesthetic education" from fine art. His approach was affirmed by G. W. F. Hegel (1770–1831). Painters such as Piet Mondrian (1872–1944) and Wassily Kandinsky (1866–1944) saw themselves as the prophetic avantgarde of human evolution. Modernists like Theodor Adorno (1903–1969) and Walter Benjamin (1892–1940) derived a concept of artistic purity from Hegelian philosophy, showing how the arts might awaken human consciousness. The aesthete Walter Pater (1839–1894) was the most notorious for making artistic purity an explicit axiom of wisdom. "Of this wisdom," he famously wrote, "the poetic passion, the desire of beauty, the love of art for art's sake has most."[4] But each of these theorists left the arts in the same servitude they claimed to reject.

There are other ways to understand art's importance. Many twentieth-century theorists, such as Wolterstorff and Susanne Langer (1895–1985), sought to integrate art into life. In particular, contemporary painter Makoto Fujimura argues that the act of making must be understood as a participation in God's activity in the world. His argument, examined below, establishes the holiness of artistic expression without claiming a specious autonomy. In fact, it embraces art's mission to serve something larger than itself.

2. Elkins, *On the Strange Place.*

3. Wolterstorff, *Art in Action,* 204.

4. Pater, *Studies in the History,* 121.

Schiller's Impulses

Schiller's influential work, *On the Aesthetic Education of Man,* asserted that the fine arts were the means for achieving human freedom, both individually and culturally. Published in 1794, this series of letters reflected Schiller's disillusionment with the French Revolution and the failure of successive governments to achieve its ideals. How could the character of a people be ennobled? "We should need, for this end, to seek out some instrument which the State does not afford us, and with it open up well-springs which will keep pure and clear throughout every political corruption." Schiller proposed that external duties could be reconciled with internal feelings when an awareness of beauty raised a person's consciousness. The fine arts educated human beings by liberating them from slavery to sense impressions with a reflective appreciation of beauty.[5]

On his account, there were three impulses. Human beings were slaves to the sense impulse, the power of the physical world, and the form impulse, the power of intellect. Our senses are stimulated by a block of marble. Our intellect is stimulated when the marble is sculpted into a statue of David. But there is a third impulse. "The aesthetic creative impulse is building unawares a third joyous realm of play and of appearance, in which it releases mankind from all the shackles of circumstance and frees him from everything that may be called constraint, whether physical or moral."[6] The play impulse is stimulated by the David statue's beauty. Art provides the freedom human beings need.

Schiller had an answer for his disillusionment with the French Revolution, which had the right goals, but inadequate means. The path to the fulfillment of human potential ran through the aesthetic. His account created a holy mission for the arts, one that seemed to place the arts in a commanding position in human life. Yet Schiller was arguing that the arts serve human freedom, advancing the larger goals of creating a virtuous society—however that was defined. Holy and separate as the artistic temple appears, Schiller tethered the artist to a social agenda—and the consequences of his idea would be unrecognizable to him.

5. Schiller, *On the Aesthetic Education of Man,* 50–51.
6. Schiller, *On the Aesthetic Education of Man,* 137.

Hegel's Dialectic

Hegel saw where Schiller was headed, and he approved. Adopting the idea of aesthetic education, Hegel thought it might give form to sensuality and passion to make them "rational in themselves, and by the same process reason, freedom, and spirituality may . . . be invested with flesh and blood."[7] Specifically, Hegel adopted Schiller's account of freedom and reason: fine art brings the subjective world of experience into voluntary agreement with the objective world of duty. Hegel also continued Schiller's optimism about aesthetics. Freedom could live on through the fine arts—the holy mission of creativity.

Freedom could live on, that is, if artists recognized their duties to culture. Hegel said that Christian European culture was "beyond the stage at which art is the highest mode" of human consciousness. "We are above the [ancient classical] level at which works of art can be venerated as divine, and actually worshipped; the impression which they make is of a more considerate kind, and the feelings which they stir within us require a higher test and a further confirmation. Thought and reflection have taken their flight above fine art."[8] Statues of David were not adequate for this stage. An opera about David would stimulate greater freedom— an immersive spectacle with music. Artists must participate in Hegel's dialectic, the process by which history realizes its own spirit.

Painters' Theories

For Piet Mondrian (1872–1944) and Wassily Kandinsky (1866–1944), painting both revealed and spoke to the deeper order of the universe—an order humanity badly needed to experience. Mondrian grew up in Dutch Calvinism and learned to draw as he made devotional illustrations with his father. Even as he moved further toward abstraction (and after leaving Calvinism for theosophy), he retained a fascination with such forms as found in church facades.[9] Mondrian's religious heritage lived on in his fervor for the relationships between forms and the order those relationships expressed. Kandinsky derived his sense of mission in painting from

7. Hegel, *Introductory Lectures,* 68.
8. Hegel, *Introductory Lectures,* 12.
9. Anderson and Dyrness, *Modern Art,* 175–79.

his early experiences of Russian orthodoxy, in particular his love of the "beautiful corner" in Orthodox homes where icons were displayed.[10]

Kandinsky famously describes the arts in spiritual terms and the holy mission of the artist as heroic and prophetic. A craven arts community is dominated by museum-goers who consume paintings like pastries and by artists who strive to turn their "aimless, materialistic art" into wealth.[11] Artists have forsaken their duty to educate the senses aesthetically. Humanity is not reaching its potential.

> It is then that there unfailingly arises some human being, no different from the rest of humanity but for a secret power of "Vision" within him. He sees and points the way. Sometimes he would prefer to lay aside his power, as it is a heavy cross to bear; but he cannot do so. Though scorned and hated, he never lets go but drags the cartload of protesting humanity after him, ever forcing it forward and upward, over all obstacles in his way.[12]

This artist is at the apex of a triangle, where in his solitude he is considered a fool. Since the masses of humanity below him in the triangle "have never solved any problem independently, but have always been dragged in the cart of humanity by self-sacrificing fellowmen, who stand high above them, they know nought of this progress which they always have observed from afar."[13] This is Kandinsky's account of the avant-garde, which leads the revival of aesthetic education for the masses. As with Schiller, the fine arts change the character of the populace. But these masses of individuals are not quite the free agents Schiller envisioned. They're dragged in a cart by a holy prophet.

Mondrian also saw his move to abstraction as part of a historical process, "a turning point of culture" toward goals that were spiritual. He saw the process as dictated by logic, which demands that art must "be the direct expression of the universal in us which is the exact appearance of the universal outside us." Where Schiller saw art as reconciling the subjective and the rational, Mondrian saw logic in art actually abolishing the subjective. He described subjectivity in terms of tragic suffering. "The tragic in life leads to artistic creation: art, because it is abstract and in opposition to the natural concrete, can anticipate the gradual

10. Anderson and Dyrness, *Modern Art*, 197–98.

11. Kandinsky, *On the Spiritual in Art*, 12–13.

12. Kandinsky, *On the Spiritual in Art*, 15–16.

13. Kandinsky, *On the Spiritual in Art*, 21.

disappearance of the tragic. The more the tragic diminishes, the more art gains in purity."[14] Mondrian assumed that the dialectical evolution of humanity was driving these changes. But, again, there was not much room for freedom. Mondrian was a missionary for a new kind of subjective life, one that history demands.

In the view of these two preeminent modernist painters, art is supposed to have a sacred presence. But the purity of art is in harness to a severe mission on behalf of human progress. In their vision, the power and suffering of David as a human being needs to be driven out of painting entirely, replaced with an abstract, universal logic, like the squares and rectangles Mondrian is famous for. Again, art does not exist for itself, but for history.

Modernists' Marxism

Adorno wrote *Dialectic of Enlightenment* with Max Horkheimer (1895–1973) in exile from Germany, when the outcome of World War II was still in doubt. They believed that individual freedom had been destroyed by capitalism—the modern expression of rationality. Those who are employed in the system are slaves to their standard of living. The unemployed are "mere objects of the administered life . . . Each individual is unable to penetrate the forest of cliques and institutions which, from the highest levels of command to the last professional rackets, ensure the boundless persistence of status."[15] Schiller's hope for human freedom was dead. But Hegel's grind of history went on.

What had art become in modern society? For Adorno and Horkheimer, the "culture industry" of capitalism had violated the temple of the fine arts, leaving artists to produce corrupted works for "mass deception." Their writing seethes with fury at this violation: "Films, radio and magazines make up a system which is uniform as a whole and in every part. Even the aesthetic activities of political opposites are one in their enthusiastic obedience to the rhythm of the iron system."[16] The industry has a "technical and personnel apparatus which, down to its last cog, itself forms part of the economic mechanism of selection."[17] The

---

14. Mondrian, "Neo-Plasticism," 289.

15. Horkheimer and Adorno, *Dialectic of Enlightenment*, 38.

16. Horkheimer and Adorno, *Dialectic of Enlightenment*, 120.

17. Horkheimer and Adorno, *Dialectic of Enlightenment*, 122.

very technological perfection of film, for instance, dominates viewers' imaginations and allows them no response.[18] In all these ways, Adorno and Horkheimer charged, the culture industry had destroyed the ability of the intellect to affect culture.

> By subordinating in the same way and to the same end all areas of intellectual creation, by occupying men's senses from the time they leave the factory in the evening to the time they clock in again the next morning with matter that bears the impress of the labor process they themselves have to sustain throughout the day, this subsumption [of culture by industry] mockingly satisfies the concept of a unified culture which the philosophers of personality contrasted with mass culture.[19]

Adorno and Horkheimer were not attacking artistic output that they found banal. They were attacking capitalism as the historical rationality that had enslaved the individual. With the bourgeois dream of human freedom dead, the only role for pure art was to reveal the truth without pity. Art needed to be the antithesis of poisonous capitalism. Instead, it had become the vehicle for capitalist ideology dominating the human imagination. This fraudulent art abandoned the David of statues, painting, or operas. Instead, it made *David: The Movie*, "occupying men's senses" with gripping violence and hot sex scenes, lulling them into a satisfied stupor before their next day of slavery in the factory.

Benjamin was a less formal Marxist than his friend Adorno. Still, Benjamin argued for the same pure mission of art—to the degree that not only capitalism but even art's audience must be cast out of the temple: "In the appreciation of a work of art or an art form, consideration of the receiver never proves fruitful ... [Art] posits man's physical and spiritual existence, but in none of its works is it concerned with his response. No poem is intended for the reader, no picture for the beholder, no symphony for the listener."[20]

For Benjamin, the mass audience's very existence proved that a writer who portrayed the lives of ordinary people was merely pleasing his customers. Furthermore, he argued that when artworks are designed for reproducibility, "the total function of art is reversed. Instead of being

18. Horkheimer and Adorno, *Dialectic of Enlightenment*, 126.
19. Horkheimer and Adorno, *Dialectic of Enlightenment*, 131.
20. Benjamin, "Introduction," 69.

based on ritual, it begins to be based on another practice—politics."[21] Ritual kept artworks for the few, while reproducibility made propaganda for the masses—like films. "The cult of the movie star, fostered by the money of the film industry, preserves not the unique aura of the person but the 'spell of the personality,' the phony spell of a commodity."[22]

How could such a sophisticated observer make so many judgments about mass audiences without evidence, without analysis of actual artworks, and without anything even resembling an attempt to argue the case? Benjamin could do it—and apparently get away with it—because he wrote from so far within a dialectical narrative that the intellectual system, powered by his considerable rhetorical fluency, seemed to justify itself. Is there a mass audience or not? Is art being reproduced for the masses or not? Is history moving or not? Well, there you are. The film actor in *David: The Movie* is nothing more than a commodity. Benjamin knew a thing or two about spells.

Marxists like Adorno and Benjamin claimed to uphold a holy mission for art, kept pure from capitalism. But this claim masked a reality that would ultimately prove to overthrow the modernist art movement itself. Artists either served history or were exposed as phonies, and mass audiences were contemptible. Audiences saw that reality and left the temple.

Pater's Moments

Of all the claims that the fine arts have an autonomous, holy mission in human life, Walter Pater's is regarded as the most sweeping.

Pater depicted physical life as a "perpetual motion" of sense impressions, "the concurrence, renewed from moment to moment, of forces parting sooner or later on their ways." The human body continually receives intricate combinations of physical energies. In our inward experience, "the whirlpool is still more rapid," seeming to drown us in experiences. Human reflection "begins to act upon these objects," creating groups of impressions. "Every one of these impressions is the impression of the individual in his isolation, each mind keeping as a solitary prisoner its own dream of a world."[23] Pater's "moments" are the relentless, unre-

---

21. Benjamin, "Work of Art," 224.
22. Benjamin, "Work of Art," 231.
23. Benjamin, "Work of Art," 118–19.

peatable experiences that human beings have physically and inwardly, a cascade of impressions that individuals receive in absolute solitude.

Unlike Schiller, Pater has no place for duties of reason and no role for a "play impulse" to mediate between the senses and rationality. There is no human consciousness participating in history, as in Hegel's dialectic. The goal of life is the individual's "experience itself," a goal that philosophy, religion, and culture all serve. These fields of inquiry all "startle [the human spirit] into a sharp and eager observation." Pater said, "To burn always with this hard gem-like flame, to maintain this ecstasy, is success in life." No precept, habit, or abstract idea should sacrifice anything of this passionate experience. The moments are of the essence to success: "We have an interval, and then our place knows us no more." The wisest people spend their moments in art and song. "For our one chance is in expanding that interval, in getting as many pulsations as possible into the given time."[24]

Thus Pater's love of art for art's sake is not at all a devotion to art as an autonomous pursuit with no purpose beyond itself. Art has a deeply practical purpose. It serves individual success in life, helping each one "burn always with this hard gem-like flame," and thereby expand the passion of their moments. A beautiful David, no matter what artistic form he takes, exists to make a moment's ecstasy feel greater, deeper, and longer. Individuals imprisoned in their dreams seize upon this David, not for art's own sake, but for "those moments' sake." Pater is no different from the other thinkers surveyed above. He claims that art is holy. But it remains a tool. In Pater's case, the artist is in harness to the voracious hunger of human subjectivity for passion. Only the specific servitude of the fine arts is different.

Fujimura's Theology

Why is art important to human life? There is something holy about artistic expression, something ineffably powerful. Yet in each account of this distinct role surveyed above, art is in service to some ideology, vision for society, or personal need. How can we say that art is holy, deserving of reverence, if it ends up harnessed to an earthly agenda? None of the accounts in the foregoing discussion solves the problem. Each one of them

---

24. Pater, *Studies in the History*, 119–20.

would have artists push away corrupting programs, only to impose yet another human program on them.

Makoto Fujimura, in *Art and Faith: A Theology of Making*, shows why art is important to human life by explaining both the holiness and the service of artistry. The act of making art is holy because it participates in God's life. "I now consider what I do in the studio to be theological work as much as aesthetic work," he writes. "I experience God, my Maker, in the studio. I am immersed in the art of creating, and I have come to understand this dimension of life as the most profound way of grasping human experience and the nature of our existence in the world."[25] Genesis is "not just about the idea of Creation, but about the actual process of the Incarnation, of God's love to create the universe."[26] God also redeems and restores what is broken in human life, much as *kintsugi* artists make new bowls or vases by repairing broken ones with gold.[27] Human artists are bringing God's abundance to the poverty of the world in the same way God does—through making.

25. Fujimura, *Art and Faith*, 3.

26. Fujimura, *Art and Faith*, 7.

27. Fujimura, *Art and Faith*, 52–53.

Through the holy work of participating in God's life, art serves God's redemptive purposes. "The true and lasting understanding of the gospel is not whether we can recite our creeds, or even are able to convey the information of the gospel to others; the ultimate understanding of the gospel is what we make, and what we love, with what we know, or that deepest realm of knowledge that is garnered through our making."[28] Deeper still, the artist renders the most profound service through grief, making lament, expressing trauma, giving comfort.[29] In this account of art, service comes from the whole being of the artist in response to God's redeeming love.

For these reasons, Fujimura argues that the act of making is a form of knowledge. If the artist participates in God's life and serves his love, then the artist's making becomes an experiential intimacy with God's heart. This idea could be mistaken for a generalized spirituality in Christian language. But Fujimura is precise in linking our redemptive service to the substitutionary atonement of Christ for human sin, his resurrection, and the new creation.[30] He is also precise in grounding our knowledge of God in the Bible. But in that historic Christian context, our experiential knowledge of God comes from all kinds of making: "I have come to believe that unless we are making something, we cannot know the depth of God's being and God's grace permeating our lives and God's Creation."[31]

In Fujimura's account, any number of artistic expressions might capture something of David—a marble statue, an oil painting, an opera, a film, a piece of music, or an abstract image. Any number of people might be edified by that expression—a few people in a gallery or unseen masses. There are no specious criteria for authenticity imposed on artists, nor are there presumptuous duties demanded of them by ideology. The criteria for evaluating the expressions flow from the giving and redemptive nature of God, reaching into the artist's own aspiration to be like David himself: "Bless the Lord, O my soul, and all that is within me, bless his holy name" (Ps 103:1).

---

28. Fujimura, *Art and Faith*, 72.

29. Fujimura, *Art and Faith*, 119–31.

30. Fujimura, *Art and Faith*, 45.

31. Fujimura, *Art and Faith*, 7.

Poynton's Spoils

Mrs. Gereth's Poynton was a temple for her art collection. Her energy was spent guarding it against the philistine values of her son's fiancée, straining to keep her from taking possession of the holy things. Mrs. Gereth was willing to use Fleda Vetch to lure her son out of his engagement. Henry James ends his parable about aestheticism in a way that seems fitting for modernist art theorists, who were determined to guard the fine arts against the corrupting masses. Arriving at the train station near Poynton, Fleda is enveloped by the odor and sting of smoke. She learns that the house has burned to the ground with all its contents. She boards the next train home.[32]

The art world has struggled to reconnect with audiences after the long contempt they endured from modernism. What had been a flourishing culture of interaction with the arts among the middle class was left a smoldering ruin. The arts may refuse to serve anything but themselves in theory. But in practice, human creativity must serve something. Though powerful, the fine arts are not autonomous. Though holy, they cannot be sequestered. If the fine arts embrace their service to the Creator, they may become humane.

Bibliography

Anderson, Jonathan A., and William A. Dyrness. *Modern Art and the Life of a Culture: The Religious Impulses of Modernism*. Downers Grove, IL: IVP Academic, 2016.

Benjamin, Walter. "An Introduction to the Translation of Baudelaire's Tableaux Parisiens." In *Illuminations*, translated by Harry Zohn, 69–82. New York: Schocken, 2007.

———. "The Work of Art in the Age of Mechanical Reproduction." In *Illuminations*, translated by Harry Zohn, 217–51. New York: Schocken, 2007.

Elkins, James. *On the Strange Place of Religion in Contemporary Art*. New York: Routledge, 2004.

Fujimura, Makoto. *Art and Faith: A Theology of Making*. New Haven: Yale University Press, 2020.

Hegel, G. W. F. *Introductory Lectures on Aesthetics*. Edited by Michael Inwood. Translated by Bernard Bosanquet. New York: Penguin, 1993.

Horkheimer, Max, and Theodor W. Adorno. *Dialectic of Enlightenment*. Translated by John Cumming. New York: Continuum, 1999.

James, Henry. *The Spoils of Poynton*. New York: Penguin Classics, 1983.

Kandinsky, Wassily. *On the Spiritual in Art*. Edited by Hilla Rebay. New York: Solomon R. Guggenheim Foundation, 1946.

32. James, *Spoils of Poynton*, 190–92.

Mondrian, Piet. "Neo-Plasticism: The General Principle of Plastic Equivalence." In *Art in Theory, 1900—2000: An Anthology of Changing Ideas*, edited by Charles Harrison and Paul Wood, 289–92. 2nd ed. Malden, MA: Blackwell, 2002.

Pater, Walter. *Studies in the History of the Renaissance*. New York: Oxford University Press, 2010.

Schiller, Friedrich. *On the Aesthetic Education of Man*. Translated by Reginald Snell. Mineola, NY: Dover, 2004.

Wolterstorff, Nicholas. *Art in Action: Toward a Christian Aesthetic*. Grand Rapids: Eerdmans, 1980.

Unless we anchor Beauty in the transcendent realm, along with Truth and Goodness, we find ourselves adrift on a sea of feelings and superficial preferences. Losing our grasp on the objective, we are carried away by the subjective, and so into all sorts of vanity, shabbiness, and madness. The Greeks and Medievalists had it right: denizens of the Enlightenment and Romanticism got it wrong, and we are the victims of their muddled zeal.

Beauty and Its Malcontents[1]

Rod Miller

In Fellini's 1953 film, *La Dolce Vita*, the vapid American actress, Sylvia, when asked by reporters her three favorite things in life, answers: "I like lots of things, but there are three things I like most: love, love . . . and love."[2] Within the context of the movie, the superficial Sylvia means something like: "The things I love most are pleasure, emotion and passion." Have we not heard Sylvia's response before? Is not her response that which is typically offered to the question of beauty? And is there not a sad irony? Sylvia, the bombshell beauty, is shown to be a superficial dud. In spite of appearances, she is revealed by her shallowness to be devoid of love—and beauty. This sort of discourse has dominated Western thought for at least the past 200 years, and pursued a reductionism of beauty to the aesthetic, to sensation and emotional responses. This tiresome reduction necessitates a denial of transcendence and meaning. Without the transcendent, beauty and love have no object, and our pleasures, emotions, and passions, indeed our lives, are rendered meaningless.

About the same time the word *aesthetics* was coined by Alexander Gottlieb Baumgarten in the mid-eighteenth century, Kant was developing aesthetic beauty as a theory. Kant's main contribution may be, as one philosopher suggests: "The idea that it [the beautiful] is the formal features of a thing or artwork, considered independently of any 'content' it may have,

---

1. A version of this essay was published in *American Art Quarterly*, Spring 2006.
2. Fellini, *La Dolce Vita*, 28:07–28:11.

which are the proper objects of aesthetic appraisal . . ."[3] In brief, beauty is revised to be thought of as our response to a thing, an aesthetic event, one of rationalized sensation and emotional response. This modern answer to beauty is one of eliciting a personal response.[4] However, this concept is rather thin, to say the least, and stands in conflict with common sense and many other traditions. How did we descend from the ancient, lofty, and more widely embraced idea of beauty as the manifestation of what is known to be true and good in reality to that of pleasure, emotion, and passion? Why did we embrace the notion that there is no such thing as objective, intelligible, universal beauty? Without knowing that Beauty is an alternative to beauty, meaning superficial aesthetics, we can never succeed in reclaiming our ability to love what is good and, therefore, truly beautiful.

Roots of the modern transformation of beauty into aesthetics (and thinking into feeling) can be found in the Renaissance, with its alleged separation of faith and science. Dante was in conflict with Galileo and Raphael was in conflict with Leonardo. Areas of contention revolved around the changing understanding of reason and the new assumption that science focuses on empirical fact whereas faith focuses on subjective feeling. It is not just a distinction between fact and feeling, but one of fact and feelings versus the pursuit of truth, of an aesthetic and quantifiable universe versus a beautiful and qualitative universe. The aesthetic approach is rooted in the Aristotelian tradition returned recently to Europe via Averroes.[5] Even this early on, the West had a choice to make and did so, tragically. Rather than reconciling faith and reason as had Augustine (i.e., *credo ut intelligam*, "I believe in order that I may understand"), there were statements that sound more familiar to contemporary ears: *credo quia absurdum*, "I believe because it is unreasonable."[6] This alleged separation of faith and reason had a profound affect upon much thought in the West, including the concept of beauty. If human reason could stand alone, without being grounded in a purposeful reality, then what need

---

3. Cooper, *Aesthetics*, 95.

4. Of course, Kant had more to say in this regard, particularly about the Genius, the one who imaginatively recognizes beauty [sic] in the object under consideration.

5. The Paduan School became a hotbed of heresy, as scholars attempted to dilute Christianity of its metaphysical elements by claiming a different sort of theological knowledge, based only on rationalism, for the intellectual class (see Molnar, *Pagan Temptation*).

6. Molnar, *Pagan Temptation*, 60.

was there for faith in the existence of truth? Similarly, if an object could have an intrinsic coherent perfection, or a perfection of a kind apart from any considerations of objective and meaningful content, then how important was any content?

By the seventeenth century, during what is commonly called the Enlightenment, the shift from beauty to aesthetics, from quality to quantity, continued to widen and play out in the West. Thinkers like Descartes, for example, intending to support faith, deny it via rationalism, a rationalism which contributed to the destruction of traditions (and their wisdom) which were not rationalistic. Debates ranged from two extremes: a traditionalist notion that knowledge other than that given by revelation is false, and a progressive notion that knowledge not based on verifiable empirical method is false. To be traditional meant to embrace the former; to be progressive, the latter. The reduction of meaning to subjective feeling proved vulnerable to the assault of empirical fact and the power it promises:

> To be no longer at the mercy of nature, no longer to be encompassed by arbitrary mystery—these benefits were to be accompanied by the great new gift of power, power to control natural forces and to turn them, in Bacon's phrases, to the "occasions and uses of life," and "the relief of man's estate." All this the new thought promised and indeed performed; no wonder, then, that the types of explanation which it offered seemed the only "true" ones.[7]

Reason and purpose were thereby enervated. Now the Aristotelian final and formal causes would belong to a suspect metaphysics, efficient causes and matter to a power-based physics. Effectively, this meant that an Averroist separation of science and faith was established. There was a shift towards the how, that is, the means of causation, as opposed to the why, or ultimate explanations of that causation, a shift from objective purpose and hope to subjective purpose and power. What began with Galileo was now carried to its logical conclusion.

But as these things will, this would have other effects. "The mechanical explanation was *the* 'philosophical' explanation; all others were . . . vulgar, superstitious, and superficial."[8] Thus was the realm of metaphysics rendered seemingly impotent. With this way of considering beauty, what is there to which human creative endeavor might aim? Indeed, the entire

7. Willey, *Seventeenth-Century Background*, 15.
8. Willey, *Seventeenth-Century Background*, 16 (emphasis mine).

question of whether there can be a distinct category of objects imbued with notable value was raised by Wilhelm Worringer in his book *Abstraction and Empathy*:

> Modern aesthetics, which has taken the decisive step from aesthetic objectivism to aesthetic subjectivism, i.e., which no longer takes the aesthetic as the starting point of its investigations, but proceeds from the behavior of the contemplating subject, culminates in a doctrine that may be characterized by the broad general name of the theory of empathy.[9]

What might all of this advancement in thinking have provided for, say, beauty in architecture? In 1892, architecture professor A. D. F. Hamlin hit upon what would become the lingering problem of modernity, claiming that the myriad styles seemed "to have been determined by no more serious consideration than the architect's personal predilection."[10] One can find versions of this thinking at least as early as English architect Christopher Wren (1632–1723). He distinguishes between what he names "natural" beauty and "customary" beauty; the former followed nature, and the later followed individual sense perception.[11] Similarly, Jean-Nicolas-Louis Durand's (1760–1834) architectural theory was "replete with the Modern architect's obsessions, thoroughly specialized, and composed of laws of an exclusively prescriptive character that purposefully avoid all reference to philosophy or cosmology. Theory thus reduced to a self-referential system . . . must pretend that its values, therefore its meaning, are derived from the system itself."[12]

Eighteenth-century architectural theory had almost nothing to do with the ontological significance of classical design or the analogical significance of the Gothic. It was no longer about reality, but rather about design—or rationality—itself. Neither design alone, nor rationality

9. Worringer, "Abstraction and Empathy," 79.

10. I am indebted to Professor Keith Morgan for this quote and for his fine book, *Charles A. Platt* (see also Hamlin, "Battle of Styles").

11. Kruft, *History of Architectural Theory*, 234. But Wren was not so "liberating" as that: "He permits the architect a certain latitude in his measurements, but then immediately restricts this by maintaining that 'the true Test is natural or Geometric Beauty'" (234).

12. Pérez-Gómez, *Architecture and the Crisis*, 4. In Durand's major work, *Précis et leçons d'architecture* (1802), he posits an ideal of pure functionalism. It is clear that Durand's design criteria, as well as that of all architects whether they are conscious of it or not, are simply based on a philosophical choice. In Durand's case the choice is a kind of utilitarianism.

alone, can direct how or why one should design. There was, and remains, a metaphysical void, one noted by historian John Mordaunt Crook. He notes the "abandonment of the idea of objective standards of beauty—absolute values—and in particular the rejection of Classical harmonies as the eternal verities of architectural taste. What occurred was a kind of aesthetic Reformation, in which private judgment—in this case stylistic multiplicity—triumphed over prescriptive authority."[13] And yet a dilemma immediately rises: architecture, indeed all the arts, cannot avoid values, for decisions are made. There is always some grounding for how to build, how to design, and for what good art and architecture might be. The effects of this dilemma, or confusion, or duplicity, or stupidity, can be quite astonishing. See, for example, the tsunami of Modern architecture that rolled over western and eastern Europe and America starting in the early twentieth century.

Architectural writer Deyan Sudjic notes that architecture had been a "visible expression of cultural and civic values. It has a history of being at the very heart of statecraft. And yet for most of the second half of the last century its discussion has been marginalized . . . not least because the architectural elite withdrew into an ever-smaller ghetto, erecting barriers of incomprehensibility against the world."[14] Examples of that incomprehensibility include much: the razing of entire old neighborhoods in favor of new buildings, or the trendiness and faddish nature of Modern architectural styles. The latter was particularly an issue in architectural education. Modernism ridiculed the past and posited a deceptive (and weird) claim to functionalism. What was produced, and endured, were often simply hideous structures: raw concrete, stripped ornament, and disregard of local setting and tradition. Most emblematic of the problem, those god forsaken and utterly daft flat roofs: they are not in the least functional, are more expensive to build and maintain, and were embraced for decades as the right way to build hospitals, schools, and myriad commercial endeavors.

Examples of why this way of thinking developed so quickly can be found in many places. Consider the following statement by architectural historian Walter Creese: "[A] truly democratic architecture may benefit by accepting new impulses from whatever origin. A free building tradition must rely upon its power of intelligent inclusion rather than blind

13. Crook, *Dilemma of Style*, 19.
14. Sudjic, *Edifice Complex*, 370.

exclusion. Selective judgment and creative synthesis are the means to this end."[15] "Yes," one wishes to reply, "but inclusion of *what*, and judgment and synthesis to *what end*?" For his part, the ridiculously influential French architect Le Corbusier (1887–1965) was enamored with fascism, ingratiated himself with Vichy France, and was "autocratic himself, contemptuous of democracy and elections, and lov[ed] power."[16] One need not imagine his effects upon buildings and city planning in France, and elsewhere, as one can see them and their damage firsthand. In an extraordinarily meticulous dissecting of the Modern movement, architectural historian James Curl points to the failed utopias and the "annihilation of historic cities and whole districts" and suggests these were "a crime against civilization, a policy of wanton destruction swallowed whole by adolescents of all ages."[17] Significantly, Curl notes that tossed aside in the moment were "any transcendental spiritual aspirations."[18]

Thus, no longer would beauty pursue or attempt to manifest eternal verities, for it was thought by some there was little certainty as to what those might be, if they existed at all. Did this represent an advance in human thinking or was it a step towards tragedy and folly? How can a category of objects known as beautiful ever exist?[19] The subject of beauty was largely avoided in the twentieth century. Beauty was rejected, yet for what? A rather duplicitous way to dodge qualitative considerations of beauty and value is to merely play the art card. Labeling something as art removes it from mere mundane objects; a work of art contains some particular characteristic that allows it to rise above, to be more than mere material, more than what is now referred to by the oxymoronic term, material-culture. But how can the material ever be anything more than mere material to a materialist? Is St. Peter's merely an amalgam of gathered materials (like marble and gold) and prepared minerals (bricks and mortar)?

15. Creese, "Architecture and Learning," 138.

16. Curl, *Making Dystopia*, 201–5. Curl's book is an astonishingly complete history of the destructive story of Modern architecture. Curl shines light upon why so many traditional buildings or town squares were razed in favor of an abstract, and often authoritarian, stripped-and-bare Modern aesthetic. He also provides the much-needed documentation and evidence for the bizarre, but perhaps not unexpected, connections many of the most famous architects of the period had to the National Socialist movement in Germany.

17. Curl, *Making Dystopia*, 347.

18. Curl, *Making Dystopia*, 347.

19. August Zamoyski suggested: "Art is all that which has arisen out of a need for shape" (quoted by Tatarkiewicz, *History of Six Ideas*, 29).

For a materialist, one who denies the transcendent but who embraces the chilly peaks of purposeless or atheistic materialism, the world is a vast, level playing field, where nothing is, or can be, more than anything else. And yet, some things are called art and valued to extraordinary levels. The experts decide what is art, focusing on tradition or progressivism, and in today's academy the latter have the power.[20] Neither position, however, is particularly reasonable or beautiful.

For beauty to exist, there must also be a state of existence that is higher. Since, it is thought, there is no God, transcendence is an illusion or a lie. Therefore, beauty is also an illusion or a lie. Claims to beauty *can only be* a claim for preference. When we say something is beautiful, if we want that statement to mean anything more than "I like it," we must assume that in some measure that object contains something special. Plato might say that object is beautiful because it participates in, contains a pale reflection of, the form of beauty. A Jew, a Buddhist, or a Christian would suggest that an object is beautiful when it conforms to that which is true of the divine. A work of art may be called beautiful when it corresponds to something transcendent. Beauty (again, meaning more than mere aesthetic preference) presumes ontological purpose, or the divine, a higher realm, a transcendent realm to which the notion of higher can appeal. Ironically, artists who deny the transcendent, who reject beauty, must still embrace a position, for who can act and not think? Philosopher Michael Potts writes, "If the self is the highest reality, the church, the family, the country, the individual state, and all values associated with the 'establishment' must be rejected. 'I,' says the narcissist . . .'will believe as I want and do as I want, and no one has the right to question me—or else.'"[21] Potts points out that this creates an inherent contradiction as these persons are, in fact, following a set of beliefs they think better. Tragically, this position thus suggests a purpose that is purposeless: a theology of existentialism. That theology of existentialism ultimately does not deny the divine but subjectifies it.

---

20. Mostly the battles between the Moderns and the Postmoderns are done, the latter winning. This has led to the situation in the arts wherein rather than coming up with some Modern, dull-witted material qualifications for why something is art, or better art (i.e., form, color, texture, act-of-making), we all now enjoy the increasingly frightening expressions of Postmodern power (i.e., all work is suspect as it benefits some group; only work from oppressed groups attempting to fight oppression is thought good, or just art anyway).

21. Potts, "Narcissistic Subjectivism," 47.

> The essence of modernity is to deny that there are any transcendent stories, structures, habits, or beliefs to which individuals must submit and that should bind our conduct. To be modern is to be free to choose. *What* is chosen does not matter; the meaning is in the choice itself. There is no sacred order, no other world, no fixed virtues and permanent truths. There is only here and now and the eternal flame of human desire. *Volo ergo sum—* I want, therefore I am.[22]

This transcendence problem was noticed by some who recognized that not only beauty, but also ethics, required grounding if they were to have any meaning. They attempted to repair the modernist rift by connecting beauty to something else. Rousseau thought nature to be a suitable replacement for religion after its decline in the face of the skepticism of the Enlightenment. Barzun writes: "Its beauty and harmony gave warrant for the feeling of awe which he [Rousseau] said that men experienced natively."[23] Kant, influenced by Rousseau in many ways, supported this concept of beauty; among other things, it should have the appearance of nature.[24] He wished to make something more substantial of beauty, as he attempted with ethics. Kant focused on the sublime, the feelings of awe that are not, he suggested, the same as beauty, but exist in a "realm of being beyond the grasp of our understanding."[25] The Romantics would latch onto this concept to suggest a similar sort of function for the arts, a subjectively spiritual function: "Two persons—and more than two—can then commune through art alone in a spiritual event divorced from creeds. This power of art to evoke the transcendent and bring about this unity is what has led artists and thinkers in the last two centuries to equate art and religion, and finally to substitute art for religion."[26] The modernist mysticism finds popular expression in new age theology (embraced as well by Kandinsky), advocating a self-deification as an

---

22. Dreher, *Live Not by Lies*, 115 (emphasis original).

23. Barzun, *The Use and Abuse of Art*, 26.

24. I would suggest this was at the basis for the revival of classical architectural styles during an historical moment that does not seem especially classical. Proponents argued that classicism was the most appropriate style as the proportions appeared in nature, only not everyone agreed. Of course, the whole edifice came crashing down when thinkers such as doctor and architect Claude Perrault (1613–1688) asked where those proportions were in nature. He went on to suggest a theory of architecture that was culturally based upon mere preference.

25. Cooper, *Aesthetics*, 95.

26. Barzun, *Use and Abuse of Art*, 26.

alternative to transcendence. Certainly, two of the most prolific propo-nents of modernism, critics Roger Fry and Clive Bell, were on the same page: "Art is a religion. It is an expression of and a means to states of mind as holy as any that men are capable of experiencing," and historian Gertrude Himmelfarb noted: "It is towards art that modern minds turn, not only for the most perfect expression of transcendent emotion, but for an inspiration by which to live."[27]

But what could faith mean anymore after the empirical questioning of the seventeenth and eighteenth centuries? The linkage of materialism and mysticism is historically consistent around the world. So, too, are the consequences of rejecting reason as a means of pursuing the true, good, and beautiful. Barzun notes: "But when the artist's religious impulse is individual only, no longer linked with doctrine or ritual, then, while faith may strengthen his hand, it leaves him to invent his own symbols with no guarantee that they will be intelligible or moving."[28] A clear example of this is found in Kant's thinking. Unlike the traditional understanding of beauty in the West, and in many other cultures and periods, wherein beauty had a cognitive role in discovering meaning, Kant's view of beauty is noncognitive: it cannot reveal transcendent knowledge about reality, for there is none. He based both his ethics and his notions of beauty in the subjective realm, rather like a subjective objectivity, a reality but only in our minds. Writes art historian Arthur Pontynen, "Within this subjective-objectivity there is no knowledge beyond meaningless fact, chance, or mechanical or biological necessity. This constitutes a shift from beauty to aesthetics, but it is important to recognize that this is also a significant step on the path towards folly—and tragedy."[29] Kant stated that objects judged to be beautiful are those with a particular ordering form which causes "a more lively play of both mental powers [imagina-tion and understanding]."[30]

27. Johnstone, *Bloomsbury Group*, 36.

28. Barzun, *Use and Abuse of Art*, 25.

29. Pontynen continues warning, "By reducing the pursuit of knowledge to the pursuit of individual facts and subjective experience, all attempts to comprehend the meaning of reality and life are condemned to be a matter of meaningless fact and meaningless subjective experience. And when knowledge is reduced to meaningless experience, or to a subjective-objectivity, then reality, life, and art are reduced to ex-pressions of power and violence" (Pontynen, *For the Love of Beauty*, 13).

30. Beardsley, *Aesthetics*, 215.

It ought to come as no surprise then that by 1948, artist Barnett Newman could state,

> I believe that here in America, some of us, free from the weight of European culture, are finding the answer, by completely denying that art has any concern with the problem of beauty and where to find it. The question that now arises is how, if we are living in a time without a legend or mythos that can be called sublime . . . if we refuse to live in the abstract, how can we be creating a sublime art?[31]

In the same article he put it more succinctly: "The impulse of modern art was this desire to destroy beauty."[32]

And now, is it possible to reclaim beauty? The choices have been seemingly limited to the leveling limitations of modern empiricism, where transcendence was allegedly rejected, yet replaced with a self-deification. All concepts of beauty were relegated to the self, or to some nebulous concept of the beautiful as it related to the undefined, which, in practice, turned one back on the self. Beauty must be grounded in the transcendent, the transcendent understood as theology or ontology. When the transcendent is denied, all that remains is the mundane. How then might Beauty be reclaimed?

The classical understanding of beauty finds the profound link between beauty and goodness to be compelling and meaningful. Indeed, it is only by avoiding the emptiness, or silliness, of mere aesthetics that beauty or art can make anything like a substantial contribution to our lives. The classical understanding seeks this contribution, above aesthetic, technical, or nostalgic convention. It pursues an understanding of meaningful reality rather than the trivial or superficially pleasurable. Plato recognized this and suggested that beauty must be connected to the universal, the absolute, to Being itself. If we can see objects that participate in mundane physical beauty, we must be able to conceive of a higher and even higher beauty, and so on, until we can conceive of Ideal Beauty or a Supra-Being, the ground of all.[33] And this is what we ought to do, suggests Plato: "Now if a man believes in the existence of beautiful things, but not of beauty itself, and cannot follow a guide who would lead him

---

31. Newman, "The Sublime Is Now," 574.

32. Newman, "The Sublime Is Now," 573.

33. It ought to be noted here that this argument is also one of the classical, so to speak, demonstrations for the existence of God.

to a knowledge of it, is he not living in a dream?"[34] But why ought it to be followed? Plato has an answer for that, too. Imitation leads to virtue. To quote one scholar on this topic: "The musician imitates divine harmony, the good man imitates the virtues, the wise legislator imitates the Form of the Good in constructing his state."[35] Greek architecture was based on mathematical proportion and harmony drawn from the human body; an understanding of the divinely proportioned body and the workings of the divinely ordered universe would make one wise. Furthermore, these clearly delineated values all contributed to a particular ontological view, one that considers the universe as orderly, sensible, and knowable. As the harmony and mathematical proportions of the architecture are clear and intelligible, so is the universe. It is a cosmos rather than a chaos.

34. Hamilton and Cairns, *Collected Dialogues of Plato,* 715.
35. Beardsley, *Aesthetics,* 34.

The Greeks, of course, were not the only ones to make the connection, to understand the significance of the relationship of beauty to the Ideal. Christians learn in Genesis the proper relationship to creation: We are to care for the creation without worshipping creation, but with thankfulness. Similarly, the Christian artist is to avoid worshipping creative art but is rather to extol works that lead to worship, works of art that lead to the Transcendent. Christian artists in the past often (but not always) understood this. The cathedrals of Europe attempted to emulate a mathematical precision that echoed the perfection of God. Wrote Abbot Suger (1081–1151): "The dull mind rises to truth through that which is material and, in seeing this light, is resurrected from its former submersion."[36] St. John of Damascus (c. 675–c. 749), a Byzantine scholar and defender of visual art works at a critical moment, wrote: "I do not worship matter, I worship the God of matter, who became matter for my sake, and deigned to inhabit matter, who worked out my salvation through matter. I will not cease from honoring that matter which works my salvation. I venerate it, though not as God."[37] And continuing, "Gregory, who is so eloquent about God, says that the mind, which is set upon getting beyond corporeal things, is incapable of doing it. For the invisible things of God since the creation of the world are made visible through images.[38]

Augustine, a primary intellectual influence upon Western culture in general, including beauty, believed, "Physical beauty is not without its value, since it is the work of God; but it is only a reflection of the highest beauty; it is a transitory and relative beauty, whereas the highest beauty is eternal and absolute."[39] Early-twentieth-century American architect Ralph Adams Cram wrote,

> [W]hen we build here in America, we are building for now ... It is art, not archaeology, that drives us. From the past, not in the past. We must return for the fire of life to other centuries, since a night intervened between our fathers' time and ours wherein the light was not. We must return, but we may not remain. It is the present that demands us—the immutable Church existing in times of the utmost mutability. We must express the Church that is one through all ages; but also we must express the endless

---

36. Suger, *De Administratione*, sect. XXVII.

37. St. John Damascene, *St. John Damascene on Holy Images,* 10–17.

38. St. John Damascene, *St. John Damascene on Holy Images,* 10–17.

39. Tatarkiewicz, *History of Aesthetics,* 54. The quote is from Tatarkiewicz in regards to Augustine's concepts of Beauty.

changes of human life, the variation of environment. This is church architecture; the manifestation through new modes of the ecclesiastical past; unchangeableness through variety; the eternal through the never-fixed.[40]

All of these considered beauty not as mere aesthetics, nor as ill-defined spirituality, but as a substantial manifestation of the true and the good. As such, beauty is not guided by our preferences, our random aesthetic responses; it is real, it is objective, it is true. Beauty is to be carefully sought, thoughtfully manifested, always treasured.

This, then, leaves us with a choice. One may choose, with Sylvia, to embrace the empiricism of modernity, where beauty is reduced to aesthetics, art is trivialized, and purposiveness in living is generated by a narcissistic desire for meaningless power. Or one may choose the path where beauty is anchored to an optimistic vision where there is an Ideal realm in both art and life. We can then love the good, as we are reminded by Plato that such love is the desire to possess beauty.

Bibliography

Barzun, Jacques. *The Use and Abuse of Art*. Princeton: Princeton University Press, 1973.

Beardsley, Monroe, ed. *Aesthetics: From Classical Greece to the Present*. Tuscaloosa: University of Alabama Press, 1975.

Cooper, David E., ed. *Aesthetics: The Classic Readings*. Oxford: Blackwell, 1997.

Cram, Ralph Adams. *Church Building*. 3rd ed. Boston: Marshall Jones, 1924.

Creese, Walter. "Architecture and Learning: A Collegiate Quandary." *Magazine of Art* 43.4 (1950) 133–39.

Crook, John Mordaunt. *The Dilemma of Style: Architectural Ideas from the Picturesque to the Post-Modern*. Chicago: University of Chicago Press, 1987.

Curl, James Stevens. *Making Dystopia: The Strange Rise and Survival of Architectural Barbarism*. Oxford: Oxford University Press, 2019.

Dreher, Rod. *Live Not by Lies*. New York: Sentinel, 2020.

Fellini, Federico, dir. *La Dolce Vita*. New York: Astor Pictures Corporation, 1960.

Hamilton, Edith, and Huntington Cairns. *The Collected Dialogues of Plato, Including the Letters*. Bollingen Series LXXI. Princeton: Princeton University Press, 1961.

Hamlin, A. D. F. "The Battle of Styles." *Architectural Record* 1 (March 31, 1892) 265–75 and (June 30, 1892) 405–13.

Himmelfarb, Gertrude. *Marriage and Morals among the Victorians*. New York: Knopf, 1986.

Johnstone, J. K. *The Bloomsbury Group*. London: Secker and Warburg, 1954.

Kruft, Hanno-Walter. *A History of Architectural Theory from Vitruvius to the Present*. New York: Princeton Architectural, 1994.

40. Cram, *Church Building*, 13.

Molnar, Thomas. *The Pagan Temptation*. Grand Rapids: Eerdmans, 1987.

Morgan, Keith. *Charles A. Platt: The Artist as Architect*. Cambridge: MIT Press, 1985.

Muccigrosso, Robert. *American Gothic: The Mind and Art of Ralph Adams Cram*. Washington, DC: University Press of America, 1979.

Newman, Barnett. "The Sublime Is Now." In *Art in Theory: 1900–1990*, edited by Harrison and Wood, 571–74. Oxford: Blackwell, 1998.

Pérez-Gómez, Alberto. *Architecture and the Crisis of Modern Science*. Cambridge: MIT Press, 1983.

Pontynen, Arthur. *For the Love of Beauty: Art, History, and the Moral Foundations of Aesthetic Judgement*. London: Routledge, 2017.

Potts, Michael. "Narcissistic Subjectivism, the Transcendence of Truth, and Academic Freedom." *Journal of Faith and the Academy* 12.1 (Spring 2020) 40–56.

St. John Damascene. *St. John Damascene on Holy Images*. Translated by Mary H. Allies. London: Thomas Baker, 1898.

Sudjic, Deyan. *The Edifice Complex: The Architecture of Power*. London: Penguin, 2011.

Suger, Abbot. *De Administratione*. http://employees.oneonta.edu/farberas/arth/arth212/liturgical_objects/suger_excerpts.html.

Tatarkiewicz, Wladyslaw. *History of Aesthetics: Medieval Aesthetics*. New York: Thoemmes, 1999.

———. *A History of Six Ideas: An Essay in Aesthetics*. Warsaw: Polish Scientific, 1975.

Willey, Basil. *The Seventeenth-Century Background*. New York: Doubleday, 1953 ed.

Worringer, Wilhelm. *Abstraction and Empathy: A Contribution to the Psychology of Style*. Eastford, CT: Martino Fine Books edition, 2014.

Hollywood is notoriously unfriendly toward, or uncomprehending of, a Christian perspective on life, culture, and history, so believers have been wary or largely dismissive of the blandishments of the silver screen. But technology has changed the game, with excellent, affordable equipment available to the small film producer, so it's time for us to show what we can do. And we need to up our game if we hope to strengthen the faithful and impact the culture.

Cut the Kitsch

Unleashing the Potential of Christian
Film as Apologetics

Daniel Cabal

CERTAIN INDICATIONS SIGNAL THAT Christian cinema may soon enter a golden age. Christian filmmakers are beginning to intuit what their brothers and sisters in other art forms discovered long ago: movies of the highest quality serve both artistic *and apologetic* purposes. (Certainly, those with sub-Christian and anti-Christian agendas have known this, and acted upon it, right along.) The sad truth is that Christian movies have largely failed, first as art and then as apologetics. This chapter explains why Christian movies have been, frankly, disappointing, even kitschy, and then it draws both from filmmaking experience and apologetics approaches to suggest steps towards the improvement of Christian film.

While many people have a vague notion of what constitutes kitsch,[1] deciding precisely what it means can be a challenge, sparking disagreement and confusion among scholars.[2] Laymen who have heard the word

---

1. In German, from which the term derives, nouns are capitalized. When the word appears in English texts, it often begins with a lower case k. That will be the practice here, except in quotes, where the writer stayed with the German approach.

2. Yale philosopher Karsten Harries elaborates, "The term Kitsch seems to have originated in the second half of the nineteenth century, perhaps in Munich art circles. There are two theories concerning its derivation. The first relates it to the English word 'sketch.' When English visitors to the Bavarian capital wanted to take some cheap artistic mementos home with them, they demanded sketches, quickly done pictures, depicting perhaps some icy peak; or a lovely Alpine valley complete with morning

often associate it with trinkets and figurines, and this connects with the term's common usage. But in this chapter we'll look below the typical embodiments to the underlying idea.

Older Understandings of Kitsch

The common element in older definitions of kitsch is oversweetness, going beyond that which is native to the subject. William-Adolphe Bouguereau, Norman Rockwell, and Thomas Kinkade have been disparaged as producers of kitsch for their tendency to portray their subjects as more pleasant, innocent, or kind than they are. By this standard, Christian movies might fit the bill when they portray conversion as the instant solution to life's problems.

Yale philosopher Karsten Harries understands this view's claim that sweetness destroys a level of separation from reality. Yet Harries stumbles when he says that "the sugary stickiness of Kitsch is opposed to the sense of distance which is said to be characteristic of art."[3] The opposite of sweetness is not contemplative, aesthetic distance. Rather, bitterness is the opposite of sweetness.

Continuing with gustatory metaphors, Harries references Hermann Broch's idea that "there is sweet Kitsch and there is sour Kitsch,"[4] concluding, "The nineteenth century preferred the sweet [Kitsch], the twentieth prefers the sour. If we think that in changing sweet into sour we have escaped from Kitsch, we are ourselves victims of an illusion."[5] So which is it? If saccharine art objects separate themselves from reality, do overly sour ones do so too? Or does the overly sweet definition still rule the day?

One may recall the movie *Pollyanna*, with its reputation for looking at life with a sense of irrepressible (kitschy?) optimism. But the story

---

sun, milkmaid, and handsome young forester; or some jolly monks, brandishing beer steins and huge white radishes. A second, more plausible theory, relates Kitsch to the obscure German verb *kitschen* which suggests playing with mud, smoothing it out. Anybody familiar with nineteenth-century painting can appreciate how well this verb suggests both the color and the texture of much that was produced at that time. Regardless of which version we adopt, it seems likely that the term Kitsch was first applied to certain genre paintings, such as the innumerable works celebrating the life of the mountaineer" (Harries, *Meaning of Modern Art*, 75).

3. Giesz, *Phenomenologie des Kitsches*, 50.

4. Broch, *Dichten und Erkennen*, 295–350.

5. Harries, *Meaning of Modern Art*, 82.

is also about an orphan who ends up paralyzed from the waist down. Perhaps one could count the portrayal of her plight as melodramatically kitschy in itself. Surely, one does not wish to argue that sweetness, kindness, and gentleness in and of themselves make an artwork kitsch, especially when they are tempered with the harsh realities of life. After all, to find some hope in such an awful situation would not seem to be objectionable. In real life, for instance, Betsie Ten Boom, while living in the concentration camp where she died, told her sister Corrie that she was grateful for the fleas since they kept the prison guards from entering their living area.[6] Her statement here was not cheap positive thinking; it was the outflow of her faith in a caring and compassionate God.

Of course, art that shuns the portrayal of evil, wickedness, or grime is not very real to life, but art that looks down on the kindness, tenderness, and joy of life is equally problematic.[7]

Twentieth-Century Kitsch Theory

In the twentieth century, kitsch garnered a fair amount of academic interest. For instance, Professor of Russian literature Phillip Bullock wrote, "To see kitsch merely as bad art is to miss the point."[8] He explained that "a more cogent argument can be made against kitsch on ethical rather than aesthetic grounds, since kitsch offers an account of the world that is not so much artistically deficient as willfully mendacious,"[9] an observation with application to apologetics.

The most popular definition of kitsch in literature—ascending so quickly it became the definition referenced by many scholars—belongs to Milan Kundera in his novel *The Unbearable Lightness of Being*:

> Kitsch causes two tears to flow in quick succession. The first tear says: how nice to see children running on the grass! The second tear says: How nice to be moved, together with all mankind, by

6. Ten Boom, *Hiding Place*, 198, 209–11.

7. Kitsch should not be conflated with camp. The critical difference between kitsch and camp lies in the way the aficionado of camp knowingly appreciates crudeness, vulgarity, or over-the-top tendencies in taste. Camp constitutes an attitude toward kitsch, namely, taking kitsch ironically but in a celebratory way, while the intended response to kitsch takes its sentiments sincerely. The difference either in the creation or enjoyment of kitsch versus camp is therefore rooted in ironic awareness.

8. Bullock, "Andrei Platonov's *Happy Moscow*," 204.

9. Bullock, "Andrei Platonov's *Happy Moscow*," 205.

children running on the grass! It is the second tear that makes
kitsch kitsch.[10]

The core of Kundera's definition initially seems to be that kitsch is rooted
in self-satisfaction. One is not only pleased with the artwork; one is
pleased with one's pleasure at the artwork, pleased that one gets it.

However, self-satisfaction is likely not what Kundera meant. It is
more likely that Kundera intended the recognition of shared feeling to
be the primary attribute of kitsch. Kundera certainly places this communion in a universal scope, applicable when one shares (or thinks one
shares) the appreciation of the artwork with all humanity. Philosopher
Denis Dutton echoes Kundera by saying kitsch entails "an enjoyment of
the fact of universality. So, when Bambi appears on screen, and everyone
sighs, 'Awaaah,' part of the appeal of the event is the recognition that everybody's awaahing at the same time."[11]

Clement Greenberg's Conception of Kitsch

Greenberg shot to fame from his article "Avant-Garde and Kitsch,"
wherein he thundered that any art which affects users too emotionally or
too easily is kitsch. His essay deals at length with the painter Ilya Repin,
whom Greenberg treats as a surrogate for kitsch. Greenberg describes
Repin, and by extension kitsch, as any work that "predigests art for the
spectator and spares him effort, provides him with a short cut to the pleasure of art that detours what is necessarily difficult in genuine art. Repin,
or kitsch, is synthetic art."[12] So he derides an artwork as kitsch when it
grants an emotion to the audience without requiring them to work hard
for it; it affects them too emotionally, quickly, or easily.[13]

In all Western literature, the most famous example of purportedly
engaging an audience's emotions too much is Charles Dickens's depiction
of Little Nell's death in his novel *The Old Curiosity Shop*. Although the
word "kitsch" had not been invented yet, Oscar Wilde perhaps prefigured

10. Kundera, *Unbearable Lightness of Being*, 252.
11. Dutton, "Tomas Kulka on Kitsch," 208–11.
12. Greenberg, *Art and Culture*, 15.
13. Greenberg, "Avant-Garde and Kitsch," 34–49. Greenberg offers additional nu-
ance, which is helpful for identifying kitsch (including its mass production, its relationship to capitalism, and its potential status as a side effect of peasant migration to
cities), but these nuances are not part of the core identity of kitsch.

its meaning when he quipped, "One must have a heart of stone to read the death of Little Nell without dissolving into tears . . . of laughter."[14] When used in that sense, kitsch judges a work of art as being too heavy-handed or too manipulative in its attempts to get the audience to feel.

Greenberg ranged well beyond such easy examples, lashing out, for instance, at *New Yorker* magazine as "high-class kitsch"[15] and calling John Steinbeck a "puzzling borderline" author.[16] He contrasts the work of Maxfield Parrish to the output of Michelangelo and compares the illustrations of Norman Rockwell to the disjointed paintings of Georges Braque. Greenberg laments: "It is lucky . . . that the peasant is protected from the products of American capitalism, for he would not stand a chance next to a *Saturday Evening Post* cover."[17]

Certainly, there is truth to kitsch's being easily grasped. As with many television shows, most kitsch requires little mental effort. People fall asleep in front of their TVs and kitsch trinkets all the time, but it is difficult to imagine falling asleep from boredom in Michelangelo's Sistine Chapel. (Writing of the cinema, Mark Coppenger explicates Greenberg's objection in the context of films which "demand too little of the viewer. Their accessibility, their willingness to do the work, surely marks them as second rate. How can anything of value come forth without willful and studied attention?"[18])

Yet Greenberg's definition of kitsch has been powerfully challenged. Notre Dame Professor Erika Doss cautions against allowing the nakedly ambitious manipulation of emotion to cause one to dismiss emotions altogether because "capitalizing on popular and public response suggests the significance, rather than the triviality, of emotions and prompts questions about what, in fact, generates such response."[19] Doss's cautioning re-

14. Eaton, "Laughing at the Death," 269. This supposed quote may be a gloss on an earlier phrase that ended by saying "without laughing." Regardless of who first said it or how they said it, Marcia Eaton recognizes that the phrase simultaneously shows that "it is appropriate even for people without hearts of stone to laugh at the death of an impossibly good child [while at] the same time we still find something odd about such laughter" (269).

15. Greenberg, *Art and Culture*, 11.

16. Greenberg, *Art and Culture*, 12. One wonders, in passing, if budding authors may feel their enthusiasm dampened when Nobel prize-winners like Steinbeck are labeled possible writers of kitsch.

17. Greenberg, *Art and Culture*, 14.

18. Coppenger, "Christian Perspective on Film," 291.

19. Doss, "Makes Me Laugh," 3–4. Along these lines, Sidney questions, "But what,

veals that Greenberg believes certain emotions to be immoral. However, the root problem with Greenberg's definition does not lie in determining which emotions are immoral, but in Greenberg's assertion that kitsch stirs emotions either too quickly or too easily.

Coppenger addresses head-on the concern that some art may be too easy to understand or too straightforward with its emotion. In regard to critics condemning certain movies for being too easy to digest, Coppenger observes that their condemnation

> reflects a curious value structure. They seem to elevate the obscure, the difficult, the esoteric. Of course, experience teaches us that some of the finest things are available to only the diligent. And so we might insist that the viewer encounter a range of difficulties, for his own good. But surely this misses the point of the filmmaker's art. It is his task to appropriate the inaccessible, the obscure, and render it accessible and clear. He should eliminate obscurity, not transmit it.[20]

Coppenger is not simply dismissing critics' concerns about artworks which affect audiences immediately. He is rather suggesting that the audience should contemplate a range of artworks. His practical solution strikes one as sensible for most laypeople,[21] but Greenberg's followers would likely suggest that it does not address their actual theories. In other words, advising someone to engage with artworks of various degrees of difficulty constitutes prudent advice, but it does not adjudicate between the qualities of kitsch versus good art. Yet because Greenberg claims kitsch engages the audience's emotions too much but never mentions how much emotion is too much, critics have been able to lob the accusation of "kitsch" upon any artwork that affects them uncomfortably. Greenberg never offers an explanation for how kitsch engages the audience's feelings so easily, and, in fact, one wonders how supposedly bad art could manipulate emotion so easily. In most fields, having more power is considered a good trait, after all.

---

shall the abuse of a thing make the right use odious?" (Sidney, *Selected Prose*, 138).

20. Coppenger, "Christian Perspective on Film," 291.

21. Coppenger's solution, to be fair, is not at all an attempt at addressing the Greenberg theory of kitsch. Rather, he is writing in the specific context of "invisible films," his term for movies that hide their very createdness and thus engulf viewers in such a way that the viewers temporarily forget they are at the cinema. The quote above is Coppenger's response to an attack on invisible films, but its appropriateness as a response to Greenberg's definition of kitsch validates its inclusion here.

The most helpful challenge to Greenberg's view of kitsch arises through acknowledging its scope. Simply put, Greenberg's definition casts too widely; it is too easily applicable to objects with nothing in common. When a definition of kitsch captures Repin's *Ivan the Terrible and His Son Ivan on November 16, 1581* (1885: Tretyakov Gallery) and Precious Moments figurines in the same net, the definition is too broad. The upcoming appraisal of kitsch situates it in the realm of art (unlike scholars who view it as nonart) while simultaneously articulating why it is bad art.

Situating Kitsch in a Theory of Art

Kitsch evokes an emotionally freighted referent while taking credit for the emotional power of its referent. It is, in a sense, parasitic. The philosopher Robert Solomon picks up on this referential aspect:

> It is the critic of kitsch, not the kitsch lover, who assumes that the saccharine velvet painting of Jesus is the object of devotion or the Bouguereau children are themselves the object of tender affection. Quite the contrary, the objects of such emotions— what they are really "about"—are God and children (perhaps one's own children) respectively, and the artistic quality of the cause has little to do with the appropriateness of the actual object or the genuineness of the emotion.[22]

A card saying "Happy Anniversary" in understated font is not kitsch. It simply intends to share an emotion toward an event, and thus it is very simple art. A card with "Happy Anniversary" printed in pseudo-handwritten font on top of a picture of diamonds and roses is kitsch, because it pretends that its emotions are important and self-generated, although no diamonds, roses, or handwritten letters are present. Kitsch is holographic, visually recalling people, places, or things which are not actually present. And this makes it susceptible to shortcuts, whereby they can make their references without good craftsmanship. This is probably why scholars have thought of kitsch as synonymous with bad taste.

Denis Dutton observes that "the perfect example of kitsch is the religious souvenir: ugly taken by itself, it begs for acceptance by reason of its associations, the meanings it derives from spirituality. In this sense,

22. Solomon, "On Kitsch," 11.

kitsch objects are parasitic."[23] Unfortunately, he is right: a substantial sub-set of kitsch is religious.

In sum, kitsch's worth lies in its reference to an object or idea not actually present, while masquerading as if it were; anything which refer-ences something else but claims credit for its emotional impact consti-tutes kitsch.

Practical Guidance on Improving Christian Film

Believers will benefit not just from avoiding kitsch but from unleashing the power of Christian film as it transcends kitsch and enters into the realm of apologetics. Let's look at three groups who have a role in this strategic enterprise:

Christian Filmmakers

Film production immensely complicates the process of artistic creation due to the many people involved. The first step for Christian filmmakers is to identify their target audience. An apologist considers beforehand what he knows about the age, education level, and culture of the people he will engage. Then, he customizes his presentation to fit them, intro-ducing one kind of humor instead of another and increasing or decreas-ing the amount of academic reference and terminology. (Of course, the discursive apologist has an advantage Christian filmmakers lack, and that is the ability to gauge his viewers in real time, tailoring his responses to the nuances of their questions.) The filmmakers will therefore need to speak the same language of the target audience and even move that audi-ence's subculture forward, which requires exceptional knowledge of it.[24]

23. Dutton, "Literary Theory," 23–34, 36.

24. Expanding this point about culture a bit, good art fits into its culture, but great art enriches its culture. The linguistic examples from great American film art simultaneously broadened and deepened the public parlance through shared conno-tations; American adults hear someone say "We're not in Kansas anymore" or "You can't handle the truth!" and immediately understand far more about a situation than the words themselves denote. Perhaps even more compelling—because it remains un-noticed—is the impact of film on seeing. Insofar as it was the cinema which provided people with their initial visuals of how things they had never seen appeared, a society's perception even of sight is likely influenced by movies. Thus, it is not inconceivable that if Christian movies were of high enough quality, they could not only be received by their target audience, but go on to benefit the entire culture.

Secondly, Christian filmmakers can learn from the way a traditional apologist prepares for a talk, identifying one or two attacks against Christianity to neutralize while also presenting a couple of strong reasons in support of the faith. The apologist does not throw the book at the audience, attempting to skim over dozens of reasons to accept the veracity of the Bible and counterattacking the accusations proffered against it. Likewise, when deciding whether to handle an apologetics-related subject, filmmakers should significantly narrow their scope.

Furthermore, books and conversations can go on for many hours, but movies last conventionally less than two hours. Non-Christian directors long ago realized they have enough time to tell one tight story, hammering home just a couple themes. By 1928, legendary film director and theorist Sergei Eisenstein was proclaiming that a film should have a "monism of ensemble," by which he meant that everything present should be working for the same effect.[25] Heeding Eisenstein's words in preproduction will yield Christian films feeling substantially less disjointed to their target audiences.

Christian films are almost always aimed at Christians.[26] One might reasonably think that since apologetics is defined as the defense of the faith, Christian filmmakers should consider expanding their range to unbelievers.[27] However, apologetics is not simply the defense of the faith; it also strengthens believers' faith as they learn they have powerful reasons to believe. So, it is perfectly legitimate for Christian movies to have an emphasis in apologetics, even when Christians are the target audience.

Thirdly, Christian film does well, paradoxically, to focus away from their messages. Christian movies do themselves a grave disservice when they present themselves as if their value lies primarily in their message. The problem arises when, in making their message paramount, they undercut everything else which makes cinema unique, powerful, and enjoyable. A movie is primarily not a message-delivery vehicle. Before film is a vehicle for the gospel, it is an art. A Christian bakery would fail in its primary purpose if it had horrible food but wrote John 3:16 on top of every muffin. So, Christian films need to become better art first.

To substitute the value of the gospel as an excuse for a bad-quality film is lazy, and it may repulse the very non-Christian audience who needs to accept the gospel. For that matter, a film which presents a biblical message in a ham-handed way is actually worse than a public speaker who mumbles a poorly developed sermon, because people do not pay to hear sermons but they do to watch a film. And since the competition for

25. Eisenstein, *Film Form*, 20, 22–27.

26. What makes an artwork "Christian" (or whether Christian art even exists) has been virulently argued. However, these steps bypass that discussion entirely to focus instead on the quality and effects of the artwork, regardless of one's belief about what constitutes Christian art.

27. Despite being targeted at Christians, far more Christian films are evangelistic than apologetic. Almost inevitably, their plots feature a main character needing to have faith, with the faith resulting in a victory. While the filmmakers might eschew a health-and-wealth philosophy in real life, their films' happy-ever-after endings present a different picture of the purpose of evangelism. Despite their evangelistic purpose, a significant number of Christian movies have historically offered three reasons to become a believer: 1) having one's personal problems solved, 2) getting to be raptured, or 3) at least escaping the horror of the final judgment (because the rapture already happened in the movie). When laid out like this, it should be obvious that these reasons match neither those of most people who become Christians nor the reasons listed in the Bible.

Christian movies is other Christian movies, the entire field suffers from
low expectations.

Pastors

In a stern warning for pastors, preaching professor Johan Cilliers shows
Christians that God embraces the totality of life and not just the beautiful.

> The cross of Christ was "ugly," and yet it embodies the strange
> "aesthetics" of God. It has its own scandalous "beauty." It under-
> lines the fact that that which we deem "ugly" could in fact be
> "beautiful." This means that the Gospel of the (ugly) cross does
> not shrink away from the ugliness of life, does not gloss over it
> and does not try to dish up a sanitized version of it. Kitsch does
> exactly that. But the cross is not kitsch. Unfortunately, however,
> the cross can be kitschified, can be swept along in theological
> and liturgical strands that sentimentalize and sugarcoat it.[28]

While most pastors would be horrified to make light of the cross, one
hopes pastors will also avoid showing movies which treat the cross as
little more than a self-help tool.

Christian Audiences

Of course, the vast majority of Christians are neither filmmakers nor
pastors, but, as Coppenger points out, they have unique responsibilities
which are wedded to unique benefits.[29] Specifically, non-Christian audiences feel no obligation but to watch movies they like. Christians, however, can have a fulfilling and remarkable role in supporting Christian
filmmakers *through funding*. Any middle-class Christian who would
otherwise have spent money on a movie ticket may be gratified to put
that money instead towards the development of a crowd-funded Christian film. Believers willing to supply between $1,000–5,000 could make
a tremendous impact on a movie, and the rare believers able to afford
$50,000–100,000 could literally fund an entire film. Coupled with the tal-
ent on display from current Christian filmmakers, the advent of crowd-
funding offers hope that a golden age of Christian filmmaking may be
just around the corner.

28. Cilliers, "Unveiling of Life," 2.
29. Coppenger and Shaffer, "Why Is Christian Film so Conflicted?"

Bibliography

Broch, Hermann. *Dichten und Erkennen: Essays.* Zurich: Rhein-Verlager, 1955.

Bullock, Philip Ross. "Andrei Platonov's *Happy Moscow*: Stalinist Kitsch and Ethical Decadence." *The Modern Language Review* 101.1 (2006) 201–11.

Cilliers, Johan. "The Unveiling of Life: Liturgy and the Lure of Kitsch." *HTS Theological Studies* 66.2 (2010) 1–5. https://hts.org.za/index.php/HTS/article/view/815.

Coppenger, Mark. "A Christian Perspective on Film." In *The Christian Imagination*, edited by Leland Ryken, 285–302. Grand Rapids: Baker, 1981.

Coppenger, Mark, and Todd Shaffer. "Why Is Christian Film so Conflicted?" *Ministry of Motion Pictures* (podcast), April 9, 2019. https://www.ministryofmotionpictures.org/2019/04/09/why-is-christian-film-so-conflicted.

Doss, Erika. "Makes Me Laugh, Makes Me Cry: Feelings and American Art." *American Art* 25.3 (2011) 2–8.

Dutton, Dennis. "Literary Theory and Intellectual Kitsch." *Literature & Aesthetics* 2 (2012) 23–34.

———. "Tomas Kulka on Kitsch." *Philosophy and Literature* 21 (1997) 208–11. http://web.archive.org/web/20210415132340/http://www.denisdutton.com/kulka_review.htm.

Eaton, Marcia. "Laughing at the Death of Little Nell." *American Philosophical Quarterly* 26.4 (October 1989) 269–82.

Eisenstein, Sergei. *Film Form.* Edited and translated by Jay Leyda. New York: Harcourt Brace Jovanovich, 1948.

Giesz, Ludwig. *Phenomenologie des Kitsches.* Heidelberg: Rothe, 1960.

Greenberg, Clement. *Art and Culture.* Boston: Beacon, 1989.

———. "Avant-Garde and Kitsch." http://www.sharecom.ca/greenberg/kitsch.html.

Harries, Karsten, ed. *The Meaning of Modern Art.* Evanston, IL: Northwestern University Press, 1968.

Kundera, Milan. *The Unbearable Lightness of Being.* Translated by Michael Heim. New York: Harper & Row, 1984.

Sidney, Philip. *Selected Prose and Poetry.* Edited by Robert Kimbrough. 2nd Ed. Madison: University of Wisconsin Press, 1983.

Solomon, Robert C. "On Kitsch and Sentimentality." *The Journal of Aesthetics and Art Criticism* 49.1 (1991) 1–14.

Ten Boom, Corrie. *The Hiding Place.* New York: Bantam, 1982.

Closing Thoughts

Today, Christians are much taken with the Transcendentals—Truth, Goodness, and Beauty. Of course, these three are essential and wonderful, but the notion of their necessary, interlocking eminence is problematic. So, too, is preoccupation with the beauty of God. Arguably, a better starting point for Christian aesthetics—and indeed for apologetical aesthetics—is the love of God, with prime focus on the Lord's beneficence rather than his winsomeness.

God's Love, the Key to Provenance

MARK COPPENGER

SCHOLARS AND FILMMAKERS HAVE been fascinated with the work of Hans van Meegeren, the Dutch forger who, during the days of German occupation, managed to fool Hermann Göring with a fake Vermeer. The Reichstag chief had traded over a hundred looted paintings for just one, *Christ with the Adulteress,* and hid it in an Austrian salt mine along with over 6,000 other stolen works of art. (The liberation of that treasure trove in 1945 has been told in *The Monuments Men*—a book and the movie it inspired.)

After the war, van Meegeren was charged with dealing a national treasure to the Nazis, and it took some doing to demonstrate that the work didn't originate with a seventeenth-century painter from Delft, but rather from a twentieth-century artist who did his forgeries in the town of Laren, about twenty miles southwest of Amsterdam. In van Meegeren's favor, they discovered that he'd used paint-hardening resins developed more than two centuries after the death of Vermeer.

A Good Abduction

The van Meegeren trial is an analogue to the apologetical aesthetics project—the examination of artistry and aesthetically arresting appearances for origin-indicators. From where and whom do these phenomena arise?

The approach I'm commending is called, in philosophical circles, abduction. It traces back to the work of Charles Saunders Peirce (pronounced "purse"), an interesting and sometimes difficult character, but a genius, who is commonly recognized as "the father of pragmatism," an American-born philosophy devoted to the practical implications of a concept or belief. For instance, he said that "hardness"[1] was not some transcendent property, but rather the ability to scratch something, as a diamond scratches glass, and, in turn, is not scratched by glass.

This fit his scientific temper, nurtured by a degree in chemistry and applied through years of service in the US Coast and Geodetic Survey. Intrigued by logic, he was familiar with the major classic forms of this discipline—deduction and induction. The former has the lockdown certainty of math, as in "If all men are mortal, and I'm a man, then I'm going to die." On the other hand, induction proceeds along the lines of "From reading books of eighteenth-century history, I see that all of the figures died, so I surmise that all men are mortal and that I will die." But Peirce saw that scientists did more than trace logical implications or bean count to arrive at summary statements. Their work involved educated guesses or hypotheses that extended beyond the evidence at hand, theories that tried to make sense of what was going on as the study unfolded. You can't smoothly program this sort of thing. Indeed, you might say that luck, intuition, and imaginative flashes are leading players in this enterprise. So Peirce introduced abduction as a term for this third kind of thinking, a word for which he sometimes substituted other terms and for which he ventured several definitions.

Over the years, the common use of abduction has connected to what's called "Inference to the Best Explanation" (IBE). It echoes Peirce and also draws on the ancient Greek criterion of "saving the appearances," coming up with a proposition or scheme that takes into account all the available phenomena, with nothing left over. It's not a matter of absolute certainty, for subsequent findings could spell trouble. The claims are falsifiable; a rival account could show up to challenge the overarching notion. So it comes down to whose theory does the best job of telling the big story.

In the work of apologetical aesthetics, we do well to consider what abduction can do to advance the Christian understanding of these matters and to undermine non-Christian, sub-Christian, un-Christian, and anti-Christian deliverances on this topic. And to strengthen our hand, I think it's important to craft a Christian account that is firmly grounded in both general and special revelation, that is to say, the witness of creation

1. Peirce, "How to Make Our Ideas Clear," 15.

and of Scripture, since honoring one to the neglect of the other hinders the cause of strategic clarity.

Apologists for the Christian faith fall into two camps—those who argue from the abstract conceptual heights and those who argue from the commonalities and particularities of experiential grounding; or, to put it another way, the rationalists and the empiricists; or, in yet another way, the *a priori* (before-experience) and *a posteriori* (after-experience) reasoners. Christian apologists are found in both groups (and, indeed, many individuals take turns operating in both ways). From above, we have philosophers who argue for God's existence on the basis of definition, as the greatest conceivable being, the impossibility of an infinite regress of causes (Aquinas's cosmological argument), or some other self-evident notion, such as the impossibility of an infinite concept's having a finite cause (deployed by Descartes in his *Cogito ergo sum* reasoning).

From below, we have the work of William Paley with his watch-discovered-in-a-field argument, inferring the existence of a watchmaker (the teleological or design argument) and two arguments deployed by C. S. Lewis—excuse making, which assumes an ethical law, which presupposes a law giver (the moral argument), and a longing for ideals (*Sehnsucht*), which points to their reality.

In these days, identifying with the bottom-up empiricists in this venture is a bit risky in Christian circles. Empiricists are charged with subjectivism and relativism and even suspected of impiety. The body of literature appearing in recent decades is frequently keen on the top-down notion that God himself is beautiful, entailing a range of applications to human experience, both explaining and evaluating the phenomena. Less appreciated is the aesthetician who says we need to focus upon what's happening around us and then draw the best conclusions we can about what this might teach us about God and his work—albeit consistent with, and indeed favored by, the teaching of the Bible. In this vein, I'll argue that the aesthetically freighted manifestations all about us point to God's *love* and *artistry* rather than to his *beauty*. You find thoughtful dissent from this conviction in this volume, but such is the way of earnest discourse.

Into this mix has come the notion of theological aesthetics, one enjoying wide currency these days. Unfortunately, some have intensified, or perhaps flipped, the enterprise in fashioning aesthetic theology. The latter locates aesthetics at the wellspring of theology in describing God and drawing implications from his beauty. Though there is overlap and often interchangeability of expressions, the former (theological aesthetics) more readily allows for discussing beauty without designating it a divine essence; it simply urges you to do your aesthetic work in light of biblical counsel, wherever that might lead—the sort of thing you'd expect in any seminary or Christian college.

Though Catholic theologian Hans Urs von Balthasar distanced himself from what I'm calling aesthetic theology, he was *de facto* a prime mover in that movement. He wrote,

> The word "aesthetic," in the latter expression [aesthetic theology in contrast with theological aesthetics], will inevitably be understood in the worldly, limited, and, therefore, pejorative sense. Even a glance at the whole tenor of the Bible will confirm our suspicion not only that "aesthetic," in this sense, is not one of the supreme Biblical values, but that it cannot seriously be considered as a Biblical value at all.[2]

It's gratifying to see that he finds our common understanding of aesthetic terms, e.g., beauty and loveliness, ill-suited to biblical theology. He insists on a more rarefied approach, but, if you'll forgive my empiricism, when you detach words from their earthly connections and soar into the rationalist aether, then you enter the realm of nonsense. Furthermore, I don't see the detachment he prescribes in much of the literature that takes its cues from his thinking.

In a volume aptly entitled *Balthasar: A Guide for the Perplexed*, Rodney Howsare observes, "Balthasar repeatedly warns that the person who is incapable of seeing worldly beauty will be the last one who is capable of seeing the glory of God when it appears."[3] So mundane aesthetics is, indeed, a key to going higher in theology. Or something. Balthasar is notoriously unclear, hence the operative expression, "for the perplexed."

If his basic claim is that, seen as a whole, salvation history has form and splendor and that, without delighted enchantment with the gospel and the Lord—and not just cold, rational demonstration—conversion is elusive, then fine. Both heart and head are essential. Any number of everyday Protestant pastors have said the same. But there's more, and that more encourages and equips a variety of scholars to elevate the aesthetic to perilous heights in their work.

---

2. Balthasar, *Glory of the Lord*, 79.

3. Howsare, *Balthasar*, 69.

Wadi Rum and Elbows

Let's take a quick look at the abductive playing field. Who is it that provides the best inference to the best explanation when it comes to matters aesthetic—the naturalists or the faithful? Well, certainly, the former have labored mightily to provide a purely material answer, for it's a real challenge to trace Beethoven's *Ode to Joy*, the *Tree of Jesse* window in the Chartres cathedral, and J. M. W. Turner's paintings of Venice back to single-celled organisms in the primordial soup.

Denis Dutton deserves special mention in this connection. His book, *The Art Instinct*, offers a Darwinian account of aesthetic appreciation, one that includes his report on a cross-cultural study on preferences. Ranging across the world, presenting interviewees with visual options, the researchers concluded that people prefer "blue landscapes" to geographical alternatives.[4] They favor scenes with verdant grasslands and vegetation, a winding river, and signs of human habitation. Those who migrated toward such venues were, so the story goes, naturally selected by survival of the fittest to pass along their preferences genetically.

My own experience suggests that Dutton did not adequately save the appearances, for one of the most engaging and memorable places I've visited would have been a Darwinian disaster zone—Wadi Rum in the desert region of southern Jordan. It rose to notoriety through its association with the movie *Lawrence of Arabia*, and has since has appeared as planet scapes in such films as *Star Wars: The Rise of Skywalker* (Pasaana), *Dune* (Arrakis), and *Red Planet* (Mars). As Matt Damon, star of *The Martian*, observed, "I was in awe of that place. It was really, really special. One of the most spectacular and beautiful places I have ever seen, and like nothing I've ever seen anywhere else on Earth."[5] Spectacular and beautiful, indeed, but ready to kill you quickly. I recall its hot sands burning our feet through the soles of our shoes, even as we were enthralled by the sight of granite cliffs rising from the desert. Not a blue landscape in sight.

While Dennett tries and fails, in my estimation, to give a plausible account of our aesthetic preferences, Scott Akin and Nicholaos Jones, take a more aggressive stance. In "An Atheistic Argument from Ugliness," they provide what they call an "evil twin" to the theistic argument from beauty, claiming to walk away with either an "atheist win" or an "agnostic

---

4. Dutton, *Art Instinct*, 14–15.
5. Polowy, "Ridley Scott and Matt Damon," para. 3.

tie."[6] To fill out their bill of particulars, they mention Marcus Aurelius's aversion to disgusting "liquid, dust, bones, filth"; Schopenhauer's tour through "operating theaters . . . prisons, torture-chambers and slave hovels . . . battlefields and . . . places of execution"; "songs by the 1980's rock group Ratt . . . the harsh call of crows, or the unsightly leaking of sap from a splintered tree limb . . . the insipid and unwieldy elbow . . . [with its] awkward hinged angularity . . . sticky and stinky swamps, boring groupings of trees, misplaced shrubbery, and intermittent villages filled with sticky and stinky children . . . And, of course, there is vomit, puss, bile, phlegm, and faeces." As for me, I don't think that elbows and sap leaks are that off-putting, but you see their point. There's a lot of nasty stuff in the world, and fair is fair. If you're going to cite sunsets and Handel, you have to take into account fingernails on the blackboard and running sores. True, but atheists have a lot more trouble explaining *Messiah* than Christians have in giving an account of an abscessed tooth.

Rome, Byzantium, and Points West

Roman Catholic and Eastern Orthodox theologians have been leaders through the centuries in the God-is-beautiful movement. As evangelical theologian Millard Erickson notes that "the Catholic tradition has made much of the idea that in heaven we will have a beatific vision of God," a concept he observes "may have been overemphasized."[7] In discussing the Cappadocian father, Gregory of Nyssa, Orthodox philosopher David Bentley Hart observes, "For Gregory God is to be understood first as . . . an unanticipated beauty, longed for but without certain hope, and so evoking desperation."[8] Hart adds, "God's glory . . . is neither ethereal nor remote, but is beauty, quantity, abundance, *kabod*; it has weight, density, and presence."[9] As Gregory himself put it, "We must contemplate the beauty of the father without ceasing and adorn our own souls accordingly."[10] We also find this sort of language repeatedly in Augustine, e.g., "O God, the Good and the Beautiful, in whom and by whom and through whom all those things are good and beautiful which are good

6. Aikin and Jones, "Atheistic Argument," 209–17.

7. Erickson, *Christian Theology*, 1228.

8. Hart, *Beauty of the Infinite*, 186.

9. Hart, *Beauty of the Infinite*, 28.

10. *Catechism of the Catholic Church*, 668.

and beautiful."[11] And, in our day, Catholic philosopher Peter Kreeft pro-claims boldly, "There are three things that will never die: truth, goodness and beauty . . . the only things we never get bored with, and never will, for all eternity, because they are three attributes of God, and therefore of all God's creation: three transcendental or absolutely universal properties of all reality."[12]

The *Catechism of the Catholic Church* uses this language as well: "God created the world to show forth and communicate his glory. That his creatures should share in his truth, goodness, and beauty—this is the glory for which God created them."[13] And, again, we have Hans Urs von Balthasar, whose program of theological aesthetics has two phases—vision and rapture. He observes, "Besides examining God's beauty as manifest by God's actions in his creation, his beauty would also be deduced from the harmony of his essential attributes, and particularly from the Trinity."[14] Then there are mystics—much given to sensory talk of God—like St. Teresa of Jesus (1515–82), who reported, "One day, when I was at prayer, the Lord was pleased to reveal to me nothing but His hands, the beauty of which was so great as to be indescribable."[15]

Among Protestants, we read apologetics professor Philip Tallon to say that "if the Christian God exists, who is beautiful in His very nature, we would expect there to be objective beauty. Because this God is the creator of the world, and it reflects His nature, we would expect the world to be invested with a great amount of objective beauty."[16] In this camp, Jonathan Edwards is often cited. As Owen Strachan and Doug Sweeney observed in their book on the subject, "Edwards identified seven attributes that demonstrated God's excellency, or beauty"—eternality and self-existence, greatness, loveliness, power, wisdom, holiness, and goodness. In their treatment of "loveliness," they quote him to say, regarding creation, that "it is all deformity and darkness in comparison of the brighter glories and beauties of the Creator of all."[17]

11. Augustine, *Soliloquies,* 30.

12. Kreeft, "Lewis's Philosophy of Truth," 23.

13. *Catechism of the Catholic Church,* 84.

14. Balthasar, *Glory of the Lord,* 125.

15. Teresa of Jesus, "Religious Experiences," 8.

16. Tallon, "Theistic Argument," 334.

17. Strachan and Sweeney, *Jonathan Edwards on Beauty,* 26, 30.

Baptist theologian Augustus Strong resonates with this, favorably quoting Edinburgh moral philosopher James Seth: "Both physical and moral beauty, in finite things and beings, are symbols and manifestations of Him who is the author and lover of beauty, and who is himself the infinite and absolute Beauty."[18] Jonathan King includes Reformed theologian Herman Bavinck in this group, though with qualification. He quotes Bavinck to say that God is "the apex of unchanging beauty," but notes that, recognizing "the Neoplatonic association such language carries," he preferred to speak in terms of God's "majesty and glory."[19] Then, in recent years, Protestant publishing houses have joined the chorus; for instance, InterVarsity's *The Beauty of God* features a chapter called "The Apologetics of Beauty," written by a Jesuit, who tracks with von Balthasar.[20]

"Resembles a Vermeer," Not "Resembles Vermeer"

To see one problem with the trickle-down-from-God's-beauty approach, let's go back to van Meegeren. At trial, his defense attorney didn't build his case on the claim that one of the figures in the painting resembled the artist. "Look at Jesus' nose, and then look at the defendant's. Uncanny resemblance," or, "Look closely at the figure behind the woman. Notice the eyes and mouth. He could be the man sitting right here before you in court. Right?" Of course, van Meegeren could have painted himself into the scene, as did Raphael, who placed his face in *The School of Athens*, peeking out beside Ptolemy at the far right side of this massive painting. But that would have been an odd distraction. And this line of defense would not have worked at all had the painting been a still life or landscape.

Equally odd would have been a macro, rather than a micro, approach: "Blur your eyes a bit as you look at the defendant. See the prevailing earth tones in his hair, visage, and dress? Now, check out the painting. Again, eyes blurred. See?! Same general impression." Or, "Don't you think the gray/white look of his hair and forehead echo the gray/white components of the place setting on the table cloth?"

No, the point was not to demonstrate that figures in *Christ and the Adulteress* somehow featured resemblance cues to either Vermeer or the

---

18. Strong, *Systematic Theology*, 61.
19. King, *Beauty of the Lord*, 36.
20. Oakes, "Apologetics of Beauty," 209–26.

counterfeiter. The question was whether the painting looked like their *work*, not their constitution or countenance.

Athenians and Hellenists

Granted, beauty is an exalted, desirable quality, whose very existence depends upon the Creator, who is himself exalted and desirable, at least to the faithful. And surely one does not want to suggest that God is in the slightest ugly or unseemly. So why not put beauty right up at the top along with other desiderata? Well, one must be careful about what or whom to position in the pantheon, and I fear we've stumbled in this connection. The problem is with the Transcendentals—Truth, Goodness, and Beauty. We already have the Trinity. Do we need another three in the highest? Yes, this smacks of apples/oranges talk, but it does raise the question: Is God answerable to, or constrained by, these three?

Straight off, the puzzle arises whether all God's features and ways are truthful, good, and beautiful. What shall we make of the time he prompted Gideon to deceive the Midianites, causing them to mistake a small force for a mighty army? And what of his drowning countless babies in Noah's flood? And why include the nasty story of Judah and Tamar in his Genesis account or weave Ruth the Moabitess (with Moab, the tribe's ancestor, the fruit of drunken incest) into the Savior's genealogy? "How deceptive, how vicious, how tacky!" Did God thereby shortchange the Transcendentals?

Of course there is nothing wrong with these three qualities, per se. As philosopher Arthur Danto observed *truthfully*, "The annihilation of *beauty* would leave us with an unbearable world, as the annihilation of *good* would leave us with a world in which a fully human life would be unlivable."[21] And, granted, they enjoy an impressive pedigree, with a host of classical thinkers advancing the notion. In his book, *The God Who Is Beauty*, Catholic professor Brendan Sammon observes at the outset, "The roots of the association between beauty and the divine reach well into the soil of ancient Greek philosophy."[22] Chapter by chapter, Sammon traces the development of this notion from Plato and Aristotle, through the Neoplatonist Plotinus, Dionysius the Areopagite, and Albertus Magnus,

---

21. Danto, *Abuse of Beauty*, 60 (emphasis mine).
22. Sammon, *God Who Is Beauty*, 15.

to Thomas Aquinas, most distinguished for wedding Christian theology to Aristotelian philosophy.

The Hellenists' enshrinement of beauty at the highest station should come as no surprise. Students in the humanities are regularly briefed on the difference between Greek and Roman sculpture, the former favoring idealized figures, the latter preferring earthier, candid portrayals. Consider, for instance, the contrast between the sculpted busts of Zeus (Greek) and Vespasian (Roman)—the god, timeless and resplendent with an ornate head of hair and beard, the emperor quite bald with wrinkled brow above a near squint.[23]

To be clear, there have been other Transcendental lists, with, for instance, *unity* a mainstay before *beauty* took its place.[24] And one could imagine Spartan alternatives or additions to the Athenian list, ideals that better fit the military mindset, one that resonates with Scripture commending "the whole armor of God" (Eph 6:11) (e.g., the Marine Corps' leadership traits of courage, decisiveness, initiative, endurance, bearing, and enthusiasm).

Still, the ones already mentioned seem to be the big three in common parlance among Christians and nonbelievers alike. They cover metaphysics (Truth), ethics (Goodness), and aesthetics (Beauty). But how did Beauty find its way into that august company, especially since

23. Laszlo, "Ancient Roman Sculpture."

24. Kilby, *Balthsar*, 50n.

the Bible warns that it can lead you astray? For starters, Eve was addled by a tree which was "delightful to look at" (Gen 3:6).[25] And as Proverbs 31:30 puts it, "Charm is deceptive, and beauty is fleeting; but a woman who fears the LORD will be praised."

Scripture doesn't post equivalent danger signs for Truth and Goodness. Yes, the Bible insists that declarations of truth must be marinated in love, and it denounces the soul-killing "goodness" of the Pharisees. Without love, your truth-speaking is hollow; with legalism, your goodness is a dangerous sham. But beauty can be all the more dangerous the more beautiful, the more beguiling, it is. (An obvious example is the aesthetic excellence of Leni Riefenstahl's film, *Triumph of the Will*, produced as Nazi propaganda.)[26]

Granted, some venture to write moral goodness into the very definition of beauty, thereby, making instances of beauty in the cause of evil the null set. But this would make beauty a subsidiary of goodness, leaving only two full-blown Transcendentals—Truth and Goodness—on the dais.

Suggested Connections and Disconnections

The Transcendentals are said to be closely, indeed essentially, intertwined. For instance, Catholic priest and mentor Thomas Dubay (1921–2010) observed that "Truth beauty and goodness have their being together; by truth we are put in touch with reality which we find is good for us and beautiful to behold."[27] In saying that truth links us with reality, which is salubrious and delightful, Dubay reflects the thinking of Augustine and Aquinas, who deployed a fascinating response to the Problem of Evil, a challenge to the faith which rhetorically poses the question, "How could a God who is perfect in power and goodness, permit or facilitate the seemingly gratuitous wickedness and suffering we see before us in the world?" Their answer was something on the order of "Nothing to see here." According to Aquinas, nothing can be essentially bad, but, rather, what we call "bad" is only a "privation" of good.[28] And addressing the question of whether God is responsible for evil actions, Augustine explained that evil

25. All Scripture citations are from the HCSB.

26. Devereaux, "Beauty and Evil," 125–29.

27. Dubay, *Evidential Power of Beauty*, 23. See also Guernsey, "Educating to Truth, Beauty and Goodness," para. 4.

28. Aquinas, *Summa Theologica*, I.49.1, 3.

volitions suffer from a lack of "positive actuality," neutralized by a "causal deficiency."[29] On this model, evil has its place as a foil for the perfection of virtue and is a role player in the cosmic drama, but it's not real, per se. Instead, it's something along the lines of a shadow, being merely an absence of light. Still, the untutored might venture the observation that the knife being thrust into him by the mugger, though essentially a matter of deficiency in goodness and causality, is plenty real to him.

Of course, there are Christian thinkers who find the Transcendental package less compelling. Carl F. H. Henry writes, "Neither in the Old Testament nor in the New does one find the humanistic ideal so prevalent in ancient Greek literature of beauty as a goal of life and learning. Throughout the biblical heritage it is God's will revealed in the law that determines the comprehensive content of the good."[30] And the Dane Søren Kierkegaard was impatient with those who lingered in the aesthetic shallows, unable or unwilling to move up to the ethical and religious planes. As he put it in *Fear and Trembling*, "Of all the branches of knowledge, esthetics is the most faithless."[31] Hence, "von Balthasar credits Kierkegaard with the banishing of aesthetics from nineteenth-century theology . . ."[32]

No doubt people have been led by beauty into inquiry about and encounter with God. Chinese philosopher Kai-Man Kwan quotes British philosopher F. R. Tennant in this connection: "'God reveals Himself . . . in many ways; and some men enter His Temple by the Gate Beautiful.' There are several other gates: Gate Meaning, Gate Goodness, Gate Truth, and Gate Love, Gate Rainbow, in addition to Gate Religion."[33] But this proliferation of gates tends to water down the special status of beauty, making it one of a half-dozen ports of entry to the divine, alongside love, purpose in life (meaning), and ritual (religion).

Dorian and Phrygian Innkeepers

Procrustes was a legendary Greek thug who, on his island, invited passersby to rest on a bed he'd make sure they'd fit in. If they were too short, he'd stretch them; too long, he'd lop off a foot. A wide range of writers

---

29. Augustine, *City of God*, XII, 6–7.

30. Henry, *God, Revelation, and Authority*, 252.

31. Kierkegaard, *Fear and Trembling/Repetition*, 97n.

32. Bush, *God, Morality, and Beauty*, 164.

33. Kwan, *Rainbow of Experience*, 238–39.

have used him as a metaphor for efforts to force agreement and compliance on matters calling for dispassionate inquiry. As admirable as Plato was, he waxed Procrustean in his top-down approach to nation building. For instance, in *The Republic*, Book III, he specified which musical modes were fruitful and which were counterproductive. For him, the words were a separate issue since they were true or false, reasonable or sophistical, whether spoken, written, or sung. As for the music itself, he goes on to say that, in his ideal republic with a philosopher king, "dirgelike" Lydian music must be done away with, for it is "useless even to women who are to make the best of themselves, let alone men." Also harmful was "lax" Ionian music, whose tonality and rhythms encouraged "drunkenness . . . softness and sloth," which proved debilitating for "warriors." The answer, he concluded, was to stick with the Dorian and Phrygian modes, which "fittingly imitate the utterances and the accents of a brave man who is engaged in warfare . . ." That being said, there would be no use for "instruments of many strings" and no reason to "maintain makers of triangles and harps." Better to stick with a simple "lyre" in the city or "a little piccolo" for shepherds in the fields.[34]

Of course, there are normal linkages between certain musical forms and types of behavior. Soldiers on parade do better with marches than waltzes; you don't hire a polka or mariachi band for a memorial service. But Plato's legislative approach to music reflected a peremptory take on the phenomena, one which might well miss the warrior's need to unstring the bow with some lax music.

Perhaps it's not a stretch to ask what Plato would have made of Adolf Hitler's defamation and destruction of "degenerate art." With his focus on *mimesis*, which was, at best, third-rate—a copy of a copy of an ideal form—the philosopher would likely have shared the Führer's disdain for modern art, which he denounced under the terms, "Cubism, Dadaism, Futurism and Impressionism." He despised Modernism because it was "thought-provoking, unconventional, uncomfortable, shocking, abstract, pessimistic, distorted, cynical, enigmatic, disorderly, freakish. It was exactly what you do not want if what you want for yourself—and for your nation—is an escape into a world of security, conventional beauty, conformity, simplicity, reassurance."[35] (Of course, this isn't to say Plato

---

34. Plato, *Republic*, 643–44.
35. Spotts, *Hitler and the Power of Aesthetics*, 159–60.

would have applauded the Nazis' bonfire of paintings by Klee, Miro, and Picasso, works hauled to the *Jeu de Paume* in a military truck.)[36]

Rookmaaker and Dyrness; Wolfe, Gay, and Danto

Incidentally, there is a cognate dispute in Christian music, with one party saying that certain tonal and rhythmic patterns are inappropriate for worship, while others say that all sorts of music can be fruitfully enlisted for use in church.[37] And the Christian family tussle over the worth of certain genres has extended to the visual and plastic arts, with the tension reflected in the conflicting titles, *Modern Art and the Death of Culture*[38] and *Modern Art and the Life of a Culture*.[39] In this connection, many remember Francis Schaeffer, who figured large in the fight against modernism with his film series and book, *How Should We Then Live?*, wherein he typified the movement as an accelerant to spiritual and social fragmentation beset with absurdity.[40]

To be sure, non-Christians have had their complaints as well. Novelist and essayist Tom Wolfe charged that modernism had fallen into servitude to specious ideology, no longer mindful of the painter's true calling.[41] Yale's Peter Gay added his take in *Modernism: The Lure of Heresy*, showing how obsession with transgressive novelty derailed artistic ideals in the personages of, for instance, Marcel Duchamp, Pablo Picasso, Virginia Wolff, and Arnold Schoenberg.[42] Also, in *The Abuse of Beauty*, Columbia's Arthur Danto put this in historical context, noting that while admiration for beauty and sublimity were regnant in the eighteenth century, "beauty had almost entirely disappeared from artistic reality in the twentieth century, as if attractiveness was somehow a stigma, with its crass commercial implications."[43] He pointed to the 1993 Whitney Biennial in New York as the thorough outworking of "a period of intense

---

36. Edsel, *Monuments Men*, 247–48.

37. For a discussion of this disagreement, see Hodge, "Influence of Harold Best's Music."

38. Rookmaaker, *Modern Art and the Death of a Culture.*

39. Anderson and Dyrness, *Modern Art and the Life of a Culture.*

40. Schaeffer, *How Should We Then Live?*, 187.

41. Wolfe, *Painted Word*, 91–92.

42. Gay, *Modernism.*

43. Danto, *Abuse of Beauty*, 7.

politicization" in the artistic community, a show "in which nearly every work was a skillful effort to change American society."[44] In this milieu, "beautiful" was stripped of its special content, rendering it purely "an expression of generalized approbation" on the order of "a whistle someone might emit in the presence of something that especially wowed them."[45]

So what shall we make of this region of dispute and even defamation? In doing our theological triage, should we designate artistic differences as first-, second-, or third-order matters? I'd suggest that, absent clear biblical counsel, we'd better look toward the tertiary rather than the primary. There are many topics Scripture does not address firmly with decrees or normative commendations. We don't have prooftexts on a preference for democracy, cable TV subscription packages, electric cars, mask mandates, social media options, or, aesthetically speaking, Georgian architecture. Make no mistake, there are plausible standards in all these areas, and we have both broad biblical principles and the counsel of reason and experience to help us—the deliverances of special and general revelation. But we need to go easy in writing off each others' scruples and genres.

We've all seen how aesthetic judgments can go nuclear, scorching Kenny G or Thomas Kinkade fans or, alternatively, Verdi and Salvador Dali enthusiasts. And sometimes it seems that an artistic version of Sayre's Law—"The politics of the university are so intense because the stakes are so low"—is in play. There's room for humility and charity. Remember, for the sake of analogy, both Calvinists and Arminians can be saved. Both believe in the authority of the Great Commission, the vital importance of prayer, biblical preaching, evangelism, and discipleship, even though they disagree over how they work and what approaches are optimally seemly and sensible. So let us call our various angles on God and beauty disagreements among friends. Besides, at base, all believers say that everything flows metaphysically from on high, for without God's creative and sustaining work there is nothing on earth to talk about (and nobody to talk to) on matters transcendental and otherwise.

That being said, let's continue to tease out some ways in which the differences might count.

---

44. Danto, *Abuse of Beauty*, 8.

45. Danto, *Abuse of Beauty*, 7–8.

Exegesis or Eisegesis

Catholic priest and professor Richard Viladesau observes of Karl Barth's theology, "Although the concept of 'beauty' does not play an important or autonomous part in the Scriptures, it is essential to the theological explanation of God's glory . . ."[46] Well, indeed, Scripture alone is reluctant to erect a towering theological edifice grounded in beauty. Granted, there is a verse which speaks of the beauty of God, Psalm 27:4: "I have asked one thing from the LORD; it is what I desire: to dwell in the house of the LORD all the days of my life, gazing on the beauty of the LORD and seeking Him in His temple." While a range of translations go with "beauty," other English Bibles render or unpack the word in question, *noam*, as "delightfulness," "gracefulness," "pleasantness," "goodness," "delightful loveliness and majestic grandeur," "sweet attractiveness," "incomparable perfections and glory," and "splendor." And elsewhere in the Old Testament, in Isaiah and Ezekiel, you find other "beauty" words in and around talk of God—*tsebi, tiphereth,* and *yophi*—regarding his kingship, crown, and branch.

Clearly, God is not repellant to his children; rather, they find him enthralling, splendid, and gratifying. But I think we need to be careful about putting great theological weight on the translation "beauty" when the alternatives are plentiful and sometimes oddly juxtapositioned (e.g., "majesty" marks a sunrise, while "pleasantness" sounds more twilight). And there's the matter of common usage, implying visual allure, as in "beauty contest," "beauty shop," and the magazine, *House Beautiful*—tricky business when the Bible cautions against physical conceptions of the Lord, who is "dwelling in unapproachable light; no one has seen or can see Him" (1 Tim 6:16). Indeed, when Moses asked to see God's glory, he was told, "You cannot see My face, for no one can see Me and live" (Exod 33:20).

Into the mix, we should also add the *Westminster Larger Catechism*, in its commentary on the Second Commandment at Q.109, when it proscribes "the making any representation of God, of all or of any of the three persons, either inwardly in our mind, or outwardly in any kind of image or likeness of any creature whatsoever; all worshiping of it, or God in it or by it." Clearly, this was a reaction to Catholic and Orthodox iconography, and I would suggest an overreaction, but the warning is there

---

46. Viladesau, *Theological Aesthetics*, 27.

just the same: "Proceed with caution on the sensory portrayals, whether imaginative or physical."

Nevertheless, the Bible uses experiential language in Psalm 27:4, but "glory" rather than "beauty" seems a better center-of-mass descriptor for God. Witness Exodus 16:10 (where his glory appeared in a cloud), Psalm 113:4 (where it's positioned "above the heavens"), and Ezekiel 43:5 (where the prophet's vision reveals it filling the temple). The word "glory" speaks more of heft and the power to dazzle and discombobulate, more akin to what Immanuel Kant and Edmund Burke call the "sublime" (Burke ties it to astonishment).[47] Like the encounters with El Capitan in Yosemite National Park, the array of stars seen on a moonless night in the wilderness, and the cataclysmic terminus of Kīlauea's lava run to the Pacific, an encounter with the Living God is more nearly stunning than delightful. Recall that Isaiah's reaction to God at the moment of his calling was more nearly "Oh, no!" than "Sweet!"

Once you make much of a sensate descriptor, you open yourself to some cringe-inducing counsel. Consider Psalm 34:8: "Taste and see that the LORD is good." Do we build theology on the deliciousness of the Lord? And what about Genesis 6:6, which says that "the LORD regretted that He had made man on the earth, and He was grieved in His heart?" Does this mean that God is moody, inclined to second-guess himself? Or consider Exodus 20:5–6, which says the Lord is "a jealous God, punishing the children for the fathers' sin." Are we to build a theology on the petulance of God?

Indeed, any number of examples should warn us against this exegetical tack, building problematic doctrines on single verses or even a small cluster of verses. Some took Paul's emphasis on justification by grace through faith to open the door to antinomianism; the Catholics have harnessed "This is my body" to the doctrine of transubstantiation; Jesus' talk of himself as a mother hen wishing to gather Jerusalem under his wings has been marshalled by some feminists to dismiss gender complementarity.

Right, but you don't have to mean visual beauty. Mathematical formulae such as the quadratic equation have a beauty or elegance in their simplicity. Oxbridge mathematician G. H. Hardy explained, "The mathematician's patterns, like the painter's or poet's, must be beautiful; the ideas, like the colours or words, must fit together in a harmonious way. Beauty is the first test and there is no permanent place in the world

47. Burke, *Philosophical Enquiry,* 57.

for ugly mathematics." He adds, "Chess problems are the hymn-tunes of mathematics."[48] Physical scientists also speak of elegant or beautiful theories, but there's no consensus on the weight of this factor. As British philosopher of science David Miller notes, "[A]esthetic considerations may point us in the right direction, but again they may deceive us. The truth may not be beautiful, or it may not be beautiful in a way that can be captured by beautiful theories."[49] The failure of Alfred Kempe's Four Color Theorem is a case in point.[50]

Still, the analogy is useful. If we're to speak of the beauty of God, we do have nonsensory options.

The Beatitudes and the Truly-Trulies

We might ask, "Where is the warrant to enthrone beauty when its absence is conspicuous among traditionally cherished and instructive verses?" It's "faith, hope, and love" (1 Cor 13:13), not "faith, hope, and beauty"; "God is love" (1 John 4:8), not "God is beauty"; the gifts of the Spirit in 1 Corinthians 12:4–11 and Romans 12:3–8 don't include "artistry" (though I don't think it's ruled out, for the list is suggestive rather than exclusive); the fruit of the Spirit in Galatians (5:22–23) don't include beauty along with patience and kindness. And consider the Sermon on the Mount (Matt 5–7). The text is big on truth—with commands to let "yes" be genuinely "yes"; warnings against false prophets and false professors; five occurrences of "truly" (*amen*); and a litany of contrary-to-what-you've-heards. The sermon is also fixed on goodness, with plaudits for those who "hunger and thirst for righteousness" and who do "good works" that shine. In this same ethical vein, it speaks against anger, lust, materialism, worry, judgmentalism, and easy divorce, as well as against ostentatious giving, praying, and fasting; also, it commands love for enemies, turning the other cheek, and persistence in prayer. It doesn't say, "Blessed are the aesthetically acute," or "You have heard that beauty is unimportant, but I tell you that tackiness is loathesome," or "Don't be like the purveyors of kitsch."

In this context, consider for a moment the aesthetics of the biblical text itself. Yes, there are soaring, Zeus-like passages, such as Psalm 23, Mary's Magnificat, and the christological pictures in Philippians 2:5–11

48. Hardy, *Mathematician's Apology*, 85, 87.
49. Miller, *Out of Error*, 183.
50. Ball, "Beauty ≠ Truth."

and Colossians 1:15–20. But there are many slow-going and even un-pleasant verses, whether the status of running sores in Leviticus 22:22, the dismemberment of the Levite's concubine in Judges 19, or the relatively soporific first ten chapters of 1 Chronicles. While you may attribute Vespasian's aging to the effects of the fall, the Bible is not in the least fallen, but is rather an inerrant revelation of God's will. The book's warts-and-all nature is not the product of papilloma viruses or depletions of androgen collagen, but rather of the breath of God (2 Tim 3:16). Of course, it all reflects his truth and goodness, but the passages are not always so beautiful in themselves. The Lord didn't care, because he wasn't driven by the protocols of enchantment and pleasingness, but rather by Truth, Goodness, and, yes, Love.

Isaac Watts and Fanny Crosby

Not surprisingly, our hymnody doesn't home in on the beauty of God. We sing of God as "a mighty fortress, a bulwark never failing"; as extending "amazing grace"; of the fact that he is "holy, holy, holy," a "fount of every blessing," and the "high king of heaven." Yes, the hymnal does touch on beauty, but not so much on the beauty of the Godhead. The referent is typically to Jesus, with focus on his righteous bearing—"Beautiful Savior, Lord of all nations, Son of God and Son of man!" ("Fairest Lord Jesus") and "May his beauty rest upon me, As I seek the lost to win" ("May the Mind of Christ My Savior"); or elements of God's creation, reflected in the hymn titles "For the Beauty of the Earth" and "All Things Bright and Beautiful."

Not surprisingly, there are hymns keyed specifically to Psalm 27:4. The psalters ensure it. For instance, *The Bay Psalm Book*, the first book written and published in what would become the United States and Canada, appeared in 1640, only decades after the publication of the King James Version of the Bible. It reads,

> One thing of God I have asked,
> Which I will still request:
> That I may in the house of God,
> All days of my life rest:
> To see the beauty of the Lord,
> And in his Temple seeke.[51]

---

51. "Psalm 27:4."

Isaac Watts (1674–1748) took up the challenge with his "Psalm 27, Part I"—"There shall I offer my requests, And see thy beauty still; Shall hear thy message of love, And there inquire thy will." Similarly, it shows up in a Scottish version of the Psalter under the designation Zebulon, written by Lowell Mason (1792–1872), best known for the musical arrangement we use for "Blest Be the Tie" ("To see the beauty of the Lord and in his temple seek his word"); the work of the Scot John Brownlie, whose 1911 treatment of that verse ("Light of My Life, O Lord, Thou Art") yielded, "And see the beauty of His face, whose love inspires my praise"; and, more recently, Keith Green's "O, Lord, You're Beautiful," with linkage to Psalm 27:4, though it's not clear whether he was celebrating Jesus or the Father.

Nevertheless, the weight of hymnody, and, indeed, psaltery, is disinclined to attribute beauty to God. Instead, we get, as in the writing of Fanny Crosby (whom we thank for "To God Be the Glory," "Rescue the Perishing," "Blessed Assurance," and a host of other beloved hymns), talk of the beautiful star, morning, bells, country, hills, mansions, Sabbath, sea, songs, sunshine, and way. Again, if the beauty of God is the key to theology, she missed it.

Some will exclaim, "Exactly! That's the reason we're putting so much effort into rectifying things. We have shortchanged, willfully or not, this great feature of divinity. This neglect has worked its way down into the churches, where artfulness has atrophied and the philistines have triumphed, but also into the public square, where evangelicals especially have left the field to the enemy, with terrible consequences." Hence, the zeal to lift up aesthetic interests to the highest station. But pendulum swings can send us to extremes.

Count Orlok and Sméagol

One problem with fixating on beauty is that it shortchanges the artfully ugly, aesthetically arresting villains and monsters. For instance, I'm chilled by the characters of Count Orlok in *Nosferatu* and Hannibal Lecter in *The Silence of the Lambs*, but not so much by Arthur Conan Doyle's Moriarty in the Sherlock Holmes films. And while we can appreciate the loveliness of Arwen Undomiel, played by Liv Tyler in *The Lord of the Rings*, the character of Sméagol/Gollum is arguably more striking and memorable. If our focus is on the beautiful and the pleasant to the neglect of artful ugliness, we can start to sound like the proprietor of Bob's Country Bunker in *The Blues Brothers*, who had a very limited artistic palette: "We got both kinds of music, Country and Western."[52] Or, analogously, "God deploys both kinds of things, Beautiful and Pretty." Anything else is our nasty fault and not worth acclaim.

The failure to do all sides justice has plagued the film industry. Hollywood is more inclined to make a scoundrel charming, whether Butch Cassidy or a hooker with a heart of gold, while rendering men of the cloth and churchgoing folks as cartoonish deplorables. But Christian filmmakers can slide down the other slope, candy-coating the life of disciples while demonizing the lost world. Both can lack verisimilitude. The Bible does neither. We see Moses, David, and Peter engaged in unsightly acts and such nonbelievers as Cyrus and Gamaliel with admirable deeds and qualities.

Though Arthur Danto spoke not as a believer, he had a point when he said, "I regard the discovery that something can be good art without being beautiful as one of the great conceptual clarifications of twentieth-century philosophy of art . . ."[53] Actually, he casts it as a rediscovery, providing an example from the fourteenth-century St. Sebaldus Church in Nuremberg, a Lutheran congregation since the Reformation. There, a statue called *The Prince of the World* "looks comely and strong from the front" but "is displayed in a state of wormy decay when seen from behind."[54] One thinks also of the ominous ugliness of Hieronymus Bosch's *Hell*, the cautionary spectacle of William Hogarth's *Gin Lane*, and Thomas Nast's lacerating, cartoon portrayals of the corrupt Boss Tweed—admirably artful without beauty.

Aunt Voula and Miss Nevada USA

Once a person has determined that Truth, Goodness, and Beauty are the supreme, interlocking ideals of all reality, then you find yourself saying some odd things. Isaiah 53 paints an ugly picture of Calvary, of a Jesus stricken, marked by the lash, bruised, crushed, lacking beauty. Yet we're assured this was a beautiful event. But surely the power of the cross lies in large measure with the stark ugliness of the event, the abject repulsiveness

52. Landis, *Blues Brothers*, 1:07:45—1:08:18.

53. Danto, *Abuse of Beauty*, 58.

54. Danto, *Abuse of Beauty*, 51.

of the spectacle. Clearly, it's the *narrative* and not the visuals that make the atonement beautiful, the same thing that leads us to speak of Good Friday. (And no, we never speak of Beautiful Friday.)

We see this language in the crucifixion chapter of Jonathan King's *The Beauty of the Lord: Theology as Aesthetics*. Though he majors on "glory" and "fittingness" rather than "beauty" in the text, the chapter head and a subhead read, "The Cross: *Beauty* Redeeming" and "The Already But Not-Yet *Beauty* of God's Reconciling Work Through Christ the Exalted King."[55] Of course, the cross is fitting. Of course, what was accomplished there was glorious, as was the sacrifice of the Son of God. But again, context is the thing.

This brings to mind Leibniz's theodicy, wherein he argued that, with all things considered, under God's sovereignty, "this universe must be in reality better than every other possible universe."[56] It wouldn't be a stretch to pick up the theme, insisting that this universe is "in reality more beautiful than every other possible universe."

Arthur Danto brings an interesting observation to this matter. He draws on Hegel's claim that there was a dramatic shift in depictions of Jesus on the cross. The Byzantines pictured him sagging, with bloated belly, slack and twisted knees, and a bowed head, but the tendency of the Italian Renaissance was "to beautify the crucified Christ," to "classicize Christianity by returning the tortured body to a kind of athletic grace . . ."[57]

Again, as gratifying as capacious categories may be, they run the risk of robbing perfectly good words of their usefulness. In this connection, I'm reminded of an exchange in the movie *My Big Fat Greek Wedding*. When Toula Portokalos introduces her beau, Ian Miller, to the family at a big dinner, her relatives are astonished and appalled to hear he's a vegetarian. Aunt Voula exclaims, "What do you mean he don't eat no meat?" but then adds, "Oh, that's okay. I make lamb."[58]

The flip side comes when we deny beauty to something arguably beautiful. Today, I read that a transgender contestant was crowned Miss Nevada USA. She is, at first glance, attractive in a womanly way. But appearances can be deceiving. For here we can have *falsehood* (not

55. King, *Beauty of the Lord*, 212–50 (emphasis mine).
56. Leibniz, "Theodicy," 510.
57. Danto, *Abuse of Beauty*, 56–59.
58. Zwick, *My Big Fat Greek Wedding*, 56:45—57:20.

a woman) and *wickedness* (gender bending in defiance of God's created order), but *beauty* nonetheless.

The same goes in the literary vein. The devastatingly false Qur'an has been credited with drawing even hostile listeners into Islam: "The Arab, already besotted with the beauty of language, suddenly heard an oration like none he had ever heard before. Everything about it was pleasure to him: its alluring melodies, its exquisite expressions, its harmonious structure, its novel style, and its argument too."[59]

The Blobfish and the Deep-Sea Angler

I regularly ask our theology-and-the-arts students whether God could create something ugly, such as the blobfish or the deep-sea angler. (The former scarcely has musculature and just drifts along with the bottom currents, mouth open to whatever might float in.)[60] It's not as though these creatures are unfortunate mutations of something beautiful. They're perfect for their environment, splendid handiwork.

So where's their beauty? Following Nicholas Wolterstorff, Jonathan King homes in on "fittingness-intensity,"[61] and, by this standard, the

59. Kermani, *God Is Beautiful*, 25.
60. Lidz, "Behold the Blobfish."
61. King, *Beauty of the Lord*, 14.

blobfish is beautiful. Its form is wonderfully conformed to its function. But it isn't beautiful, is it? And what of Roger Scruton's take on the Transcendentals: "Why do I believe *p*? Because it is true. Why want *x*? Because it is good. Why look at *y*? Because it is beautiful."[62] But that's not what's happening here. Rather, the blobfish is off-putting, yet it is God's good creation.

Closer to the surface, we find the crocodile, of which Steve Irwin might say, "She's a beaut!" (Snaggle teeth and gnarly plates, notwithstanding.) But there's the key. To another crocodile, she is charming and enticing. God's creatures are wired differently, and what may satisfy one could disgust or wreck another. (Don't share your delicious Hershey's bar with a cat; it could be lethal.)

This brings us back to God's love: He made us to find certain things attractive, and then he made sure to provide those things in the world. We love the smell of a rose—Voilà! Roses. We're soothed by the sound of a babbling brook—Presto! Babbling brooks (and corresponding sound apps on our smart phones). We're charmed by the appearance of the opposite sex. Boom! Eve. (My paraphrase of Genesis 3:23: "Now you're talkin'. The hawks and elephants and chipmunks have been amazing, but *this*! Wow!) Such charm is the base for rapturous descriptions of the beloveds in the Song of Solomon.

Turns out there are generalities that undergird these preferences, the sorts of algorithms that artists and patrons can employ and enjoy, whether the rule of thirds in photography, the nature-based Golden Ratio of 1.6180339887, or the never-ending, never-repeating number, evidenced in the spiral structure of the chambered nautilus and designated as *phi* in mathematics in honor of the fifth-century Greek, Phidias, who is thought to have employed it in his sculpture.[63]

Ah, but back to the crocodile, and even the blobfish. Might we not call them beautiful in their own way? Well, I suppose if by beautiful you mean well-constructed or ingenious. But that would seem to qualify it more as good, which is the most general term of approbation, applying to a good hammer as well as a good night's sleep and a good quiche. It vitiates the special meaning of beautiful.

We've spoken of eisegesis, and Genesis 1 provides an example. Here, there's an effort to tease out the aesthetic angle in the Hebrew word *tov* ("saw it was *good*"), but the blobfish works against that reading. Yes, there

---

62. Scruton, *Beauty*, 2.

63. Livio, *Golden Ratio*, 4–6, 8.

is much in creation that pleases the human eye, but not the created blob-fish (on day five). Rather it is good in terms of functionality, which is quite good enough for God to declare it good.

Stockhausen and Elastic-Side Boots

The old fable is told of the Bedouin who lets his camel stick his nose in the tent during a horrific sand storm. No problem. And then the camel's entire head appears inside. Not a big problem. But so on and so on until the whole camel is in the tent and the Bedouin is outside in the storm. Its applications are manifold, and I think one surfaces in our current discussion. Good and reasonable things are granted places of honor at the highest table, and, if you're not careful, they start hogging the food, reaching over others to grab the choicest portions, even knocking over their neighbors' chairs.

Consider the great Reformation doctrine, *sola scriptura*. Yes, the Catholics honor *Scripture*, but they added the authority of *tradition* and the *Magisterium* (teaching authority of the current church) to keep it in line. But the latter two have a way of "improving on Scripture," adding such doctrines as purgatory with indulgences, the immaculate conception and perpetual virginity of Mary, priestly celibacy, papal infallibility, and transubstantiation. And somewhere along the way, they lose track of *sola fide* and *sola gratia*.

The Wesleyan Quadrilateral has had its problems as well. Certainly, Christians should exercise their God-given *reason* and consult *tradition* as well as *experience* as they sort things out under the authority of *Scripture*, but honoring the four in the same breath has too often put a trump card in the hands of those who've gotten smarter than the Bible (e.g., those who've found insistence on male pastors *unreasonable*, especially after *experiencing* a fine sermon by a woman preacher, a lady who testifies to having *experienced* a call and the blessings that have followed as sweet confirmation of that call).

The same sort of thing can happen when beauty is conceptually hardwired to truth and goodness. Insisting on the tri-partite package, people will leave a church saturated with truth and moral rectitude but aesthetically challenged to join one with delightful artistic appointments but questionable if not downright scandalous teaching and practices. They become aesthetes for Christ. Of course, there are also those who give up on congregational worship altogether, saying they feel closer to God through walks in the forest—aesthetes for themselves, if you will.

C. S. Lewis offers a humble word of counsel at this juncture. As a new Christian, steeped in erudition and other refinements in the highest universities of England, he made his way to the local Anglican church:

> I disliked very much their hymns, which I considered to be fifth-rate poems set to sixth-rate music. But as I went on I saw the great merit of it. I came up against different people of quite different outlooks and different education, and then gradually my conceit just began peeling off. I realized that the hymns (which were just sixth-rate music) were, nevertheless, being sung with devotion and benefit by an old saint in elastic-side boots in the opposite pew, and then you realize that you aren't fit to clean those boots.[64]

Driven by the aesthetic, you might fall into infatuation with the picturesque quality of rundown peasant dwellings and scenes, as if seen through a Claude Glass, which, held up to the eye, turned the objects into tidy paintings. John Ruskin snapped out of it on a walk along the Somme River:

> [A]s I looked to-day at the unhealthy face and melancholy mien of the man in the boat pushing his load of peats along the ditch, and of the people, men as well as women, who sat spinning gloomily at the cottage doors, I could not help feeling how many suffering persons must pay for my picturesque subject and happy walk. [65]

Both Lewis and Ruskin needed to snap out of the aesthetic mode and pick up on truth and goodness. In contrast, it would be unfortunate to read the testimony of someone who snapped out of the moral mode and went all aesthetic. In fact, that's what happened when German composer Karlheinz Stockhausen described the 9/11 attack on the Twin Towers as "the greatest work of art imaginable for the whole cosmos." Of course, there was backlash, with, for instance, the cancellation of a four-day Stockhausen festival in Hamburg.[66] Yes, 9/11 was quite a sight, but the Stockhausen comment was like "Sure, Absalom stabbed

---

64. Lewis, *God in the Dock*, 61–62.

65. Costelloe, *British Aesthetic Tradition*, 240.

66. Castle, "Stockhausen, Karlheinz," paras. 4–5. UK rabbi Sir Jonathan Sacks took Stockhausen to task for his remarks in his book, *Home We Build Together*, 76–77.

his father David in the back, but, wow, he was handsome, and what a great head of hair!"[67]

The problem doesn't stop with choice of worship styles. Aestheticism or insistence on beauty and charm has truncated preaching, evangelism, discipleship, and apologetics. Raw-boned biblical prophets are thrown under the bus (e.g., Elijah's saying very rude and sarcastic things to the prophets of Baal on Mount Carmel; Amos's including "fat cows of Bashan" in his list of malefactors; Jeremiah's issuing baleful jeremiads; a rustic John the Baptist's provoking his own execution by calling out an adulterer; Jesus' table-tossing in the temple; Paul's saying he hoped the Judaizers' circumcision knives would slip). And, fast forward: would Jonathan Edwards get away today with preaching "Sinners in the Hands of an Angry God?" Would a Mordecai Ham or a Vance Havner pass contemporary muster with talk like this, from a Havner sermon?: "There is a Trend today that would put a new robe on the prodigal son while he is still feeding hogs. Some would put the ring on his finger while he is still in the pigsty. Others would paint the pigsty or advocate bigger and better hogpens."[68]

Mark Galli of *Christianity Today* had an implicit word of counsel for Elijah, Paul, Edwards, and Havner. Channeling his appeal through the Transcendentals, he said, "Christians believe that our longing for the good, the true, and the beautiful finds its completion in Jesus Christ—the Way, the Truth, and the Life." He then proceeded to rank down those who obscure the loveliness of Christ in their zeal for truth. To make his case, he told of a friend who attempted, in a world religions class, to "argue his college classmates into the Christian faith" using "unassailable logic." He was disappointed that nonbelievers were "either bored or hostile." But then the light went on:

> Only years later did he finally grasp that while he may have presented the abstract truths of Christianity cogently, he had failed to also present the person of Jesus Christ in a way that winsomely conveyed that our faith is first and foremost an intimate encounter with the God of truth. When we don't frame our apologetics, teaching, and preaching in this way, our presentation of Christ will not be fully true, let alone attractive.[69]

67. Cf. 2 Sam 14:25–26.
68. Havner, *In These Times*, 45.
69. Galli, "Beautiful Orthodoxy," 36–38.

Well, Jonathan Edwards conveyed the truth that sinners would have an intimate encounter with the God of truth: he was angry, and they'd be in his hands unless they repented. But I don't think that's what Galli had in mind. Is he saying that a more attractive presentation would have more likely melted the classmates' hearts? Or that by sticking with orthodoxy he'd even slighted truth somehow? At this point, therapeutic publicists and patrons for the Christian brand would murmur with Galli, "I don't think that's a good look," or "I don't believe that was helpful," or "I hope you feel better." And so, today, the platformed popularity of those who preach cultural sensitivity to the faithful outstrips the honor accorded to those who preach fastidious biblical faithfulness to the culture.[70]

Prussians and Brits

Some would have it that Prussians/Hessians (in the persons of Kant and Baumgarten) and Brits/Redcoats (such as Hutcheson, Addison, Hume, and Burke) have invaded our fair land with vulgar conceits, what with their fixation on what Baumgarten called the "science of sensual cognition." Thanks to them, the focal term "beauty" was subsumed under the broader, more experiential expression "aesthetic," coined by the aforementioned Alexander Gottlieb Baumgarten in 1740s Germany, picked up by Immanuel Kant in his *Critique of Judgment* in 1790, acknowledged for its growing currency in England in the early 1800s (by, for example, Coleridge and Ruskin), and first used as a university course name in America in the 1870s by Harvard's George Santayana. [71]

Though the emphasis was on the experience of the beholder (and, so, seemingly mired in subjectivity and relativism), intersubjective objectivity or universality was a mainstay of this thinking, based on the conviction that there is common human nature, such that critical judgments are defensible.

I took this position in a paper for an American Philosophical Association meeting back in 1978, and it strikes me as still plausible. Entitled "Redness and Aesthetic Goodness," it "presents an analogy" featuring "subjectivity without aesthetic anarchy and objectivity without aesthetic elitism." By my lights,

---

70. We're too often reminded of Schleiermacher's unseemly appeal to the church's "cultured despisers."

71. Costelloe, *British Aesthetic Tradition*, 2–3.

A particular appearance, perceptual conditions, and consensus are all involved in a thing's being red. The same three features are involved in a thing's being aesthetically good. The experiential component, the "appearance," is fascination, and the "condition" is a community of focus. Consensus carries over as is. [72]

Though the color judgment is grounded in an experience, that of redness, we attribute the property to the thing observed, whether the apple or the fire engine. (We say, "The apple is red," not "I'm having a reddish experience.") Of course, that experience is keyed to daylight. Sodium vapor won't work. Under it, a red car appears black. And even if the lighting is right, a few, the colorblind, won't get it. We don't have to wait for unanimity to make the call. As British philosopher and C. S. Lewis-foil C. E. M. Joad observed, "I believe that there is in fact no recorded instance of a man who did not find something beautiful in a fine sunset." Still, as Joad concedes, if some were to be found, we must simply conclude that they were blind.[73] And if someone appeared claiming to love the smell of the durion fruit, whose odor is so off-putting that it's banned on Singapore's mass transit system, we would not say that olfactory judgments are therefore purely relative. Rather, we'd ask what went wrong with that man's sensory equipment or whether he might be homing in on a less repellant part of the fruit.

72. Coppenger, "Redness and Aesthetic Goodness," 57.

73. Joad, *Essays in Common-Sense Philosophy,* 122–23.

Analogously, a fine painting, folk song, sitcom episode, al dente risotto, or Victorian home has the power to fascinate, charm, or arrest the beholder. Or you might think of a sermon that is engaging rather than boring. But, as with redness, the conditions are important. If, like Cameron in *Ferris Bueller's Day Off*, you get so fixated on the dots in the pointillist Georges Seurat's *A Sunday on La Grande Jatte* that you don't take in the whole scene, you're standing or looking too closely to evaluate the painting. Also, aesthetic attention (as opposed to medical, paternal, scientific, or ideological focus) is the key. That's why those trying out for symphony chairs often audition from behind a screen, so that their artistry can be judged without regard to race, gender, dress, or hairstyle. Some would add that the engaging quality of a piece is best judged over the course of repeated viewings or listenings, the sort of thing that leads to declaring it a classic.

Hebrew University philosopher Eddy Zemach speaks of "standard observation conditions" (SOC), which, for instance, in the judgment that someone is kissing someone, require that the conclusion be made "in daylight, at a distance of a few yards, when you are awake and not drugged, your eyes open and your eyesight good."[74] In this vein, one must not be confused to think that "every moral, economic, and military evaluation"[75] is aesthetic. It's not enough to like a picture because it reminds you of your mother or to like certain flowers because their scent repels mosquitoes. And he cautions us not to be waylaid in our aesthetic judgments by "time-sensitive properties," such as being "original . . . conservative, revolutionary, classic, surprising, conventional, etc."[76] The splash of a work might well have been its novelty and not its intrinsic excellence.

Yes, there are cultural variants, but as Hong Kong Baptist University philosopher Kai-Man Kwan observes,

> [M]any popular English songs are recognized to be beautiful by most Chinese. Moreover, the Chinese by and large will not dispute the status of the works of Shakespeare, Beethoven, Da Vinci, and Van Gogh as artistic masterpieces. Of course, the Chinese are also admirers of natural beauty, such as a beautiful sunset or mountain. In fact, this is one of the major themes of Chinese poetry and paintings.[77]

74. Zemach, *Real Beauty*, 50.

75. Zemach, *Real Beauty*, 12.

76. Zemach, *Real Beauty*, 77–78.

77. Kwan, *Rainbow of Experience*, 229.

Notice that he sticks with matters of sight and sound for examples. In his treatment of the God-pointing aspect of aesthetics, Kwan says that "eating a delicious steak" is not an aesthetic experience.[78] But I dissent. Yes, aestheticians typically focus on the senses that can carry a propositional payload through visual and auditory artistry—a painting that details aspects of a battle; a Churchillian wartime address to the nation. The gustatory, olfactory, and tactual capacities are typically relegated to lower status. Yes, they can signal truths—"This fish is spoiled" or "This hair shirt is incompatible with comfort"—but they don't go much beyond that conceptually. And they are hardly prone to elevate the spirit or ground a worldview. Still, the culinary, textile, and perfumer arts are admirable, while those unable to appreciate their renderings are unfortunately anesthetic.

Granted, this talk of experiential consensus raises the specter of pure subjectivism and herd aesthetics. In his brief against the aesthetics of Leo Tolstoy, who said that good art promoted a sense of wholesome community among the beholders, Joad wrote,

> The countryman who contemplates Botticelli's Round Madonna in the National Gallery and passes it without a second glance, finding it to be productive of less pleasure than the "Bubble Boy" advertisement of Pears' Soap, has passed as correct an aesthetic judgment as that of the connoisseur who prefers the Madonna and labels the country man "Philistine."[79]

(To clarify, the painting and not the Madonna was round. And the "Bubble Boy" was featured in an ad that ran for decades. Painted in 1886 by Victorian artist John Everett Millais, it depicted an engaging young boy holding a bowl of soapsuds and a pipe, watching a bubble he has blown drift upwards. It was originally named *A Child's World*.)

To Joad, I'd say, "Not so fast." For one thing, *A Child's World* is right artful, though its attraction may well be more in sentimental association than in "significant form," to use the Roger Fry/Clive Bell ideal. But Madonnas are freighted with sentimental associations as well. So what makes the latter the gold standard? Is it the studious and fastidious attention to artistic detail that sets it apart? Well, it's unlikely that Mallais dashed out his piece. Besides, so what if it took a lot of work? If an artist did an exhaustive study of the tensile characteristics of cat hairs before

---

78. Kwan, *Rainbow of Experience,* 226.
79. Joad, *Essays in Common-Sense Philosophy,* 113–14.

painstakingly plucking a cat and then tying each hair into a bow to be glued to a board from a tree he journeyed to Madagascar to fell, would that make the collage worthy? Would it add aesthetic value? Ah, but Millais had financial gain in mind. Surely that cheapened his product. But Botticelli had rich patrons for his work, including a Medici and a pope. Does that diminish the value of this work?

In other words, Joad has kicked the can down the road. We still have to ask why the Botticelli scores in a way the Millais does not. After all, haven't elites deceived us again and again over what is admirable? Why should we swallow their judgments on matters of taste? And if a work, indeed, tickles their palate, might we count their palate exotically defective, akin to those who relish revolting culinary delicacies from around the world, including dishes prepared using execreta (e.g., from Ptarmigan dung in Greenland and the urine of young boys in Japan)?[80] Of course, I'm not putting Botticelli in this category, but when all is said and done, his work must pass the test of charm, if you will, the sort of thing that is, at base, *humanly* hardwired and not reserved strictly for a Brahmin caste.

AM and FM . . . and VLF

We've been focusing on *human* consensus. Animals have their own aesthetic, with buzzards delighting in the smell and taste of carrion and turkeys not at all repelled by prominent wattles in prospective mates. But for humans, Burke observed, when taste "operates naturally" everybody is "agreed to call vinegar sour, honey sweet, and aloes bitter." Outliers simply suffer from a "vitiated palate."[81]

Yes, there are those who deny that animals are capable of aesthetic appreciation in that they lack the disinterestedness necessary for contemplation. Rather, they just go with unreflective appetites. William Shedd claims that "[the brute] cannot experience religious emotions like joy in God or aesthetic emotions like delight in beauty or rational perceptions like the intuitions of geometry, because he has no rational nature like man."[82] But I think this sells humans long and animals short.

In "I Saw Her Standing There," Paul McCartney wrote (and the Beatles sang) of a boy's visceral and rapturous reaction to the sight of a

---

80. Serbin, "Nasty Food."
81. Burke, *Philosophical Enquiry*, 14–16.
82. Shedd, *Dogmatic Theology*, 652.

teenaged girl at a dance. I'm confident that this song would not have taken flight had the lady standing there been the stunningly homely mother (played by Anne Ramsey) in *Throw Mama from the Train*; aesthetic discrimination was in play in McCartney's *human* songwriting. On the other hand, I'd be hard pressed to downgrade the joy in play exhibited by young polar bears sliding down an icy incline. It's not survival training, the best I can tell, but, instead, *animal* aesthetic delight—tactual, inertial, and visual—something with which we humans can empathize.

Be that as it may, for the gratifying, aesthetic engagement to occur, you need both prompts and promptees—a sense of appreciation and things worth appreciating. As Francis Hutcheson observed, without this internal sense, "Houses, Gardens, Dress, Equipage, might have been recommended to us as convenient, fruitful, warm, easy; but never as beautiful."[83] Or as Hume put it, "[T]here are certain qualities in objects, which are fitted by nature to produce those particular feelings [of beauty and deformity]."[84] As for those "certain qualities" and "particular feelings," we can be sure that "All things bright and beautiful . . . 'Twas God that made them all." (And, of course, Genesis 3 explains how deformity enters the world, itself prompting the yuck factor, also God given.)

A radio analogy suggests itself. For you to enjoy an amplitude modulation program, there has to be an AM transmitter somewhere in range and an AM receiver at your side. The same goes for frequency modulation (FM). On this model, you might think of God as setting up both sorts of aesthetic transmitters in creation, with humans receiving AM and, say, cats FM.

And, to extend the analogy, we might mention Very Low Frequency (VLF) transmissions, which the United States uses to communicate with its nuclear submarines. Able to reach down through a few hundred feet of seawater, these electromagnetic waves escape the ordinary notice of humans and animals alike. Perhaps, then, we have here a way into understanding the "beauty of the LORD" in Psalm 27:4. When we read this verse, we speak equivocally and parochially of beauty, reserving it for those who are redeemed, whose spiritual sensors are attuned to appreciate God Almighty. It takes supernatural wiring to detect it. When Christopher Hitchens wrote *God Is Not Great*, he showed that he was *Elohim*-blind. He might be a connoisseur of sunsets and the fall colors

83. Hutcheson, *Essay on the Conduct*, 20, 74.

84. Hume, "Of the Standard of Taste," 401.

of New England, but oblivious, indifferent, or hostile to the excellencies of God in Christ. In his book, *Seven Types of Atheism*, John Gray devotes a chapter to "God-Haters" such as the Marquis de Sade, who was "the greatest modern prophet of misotheism" and William Empson, who compared heaven to a Nazi concentration camp, revealing the Christian God to be "nakedly bad."[85] Not only were they not spiritually equipped to pick up on the beauty of God, they were so constituted as to count the gospel as irritating static or worse.

In his book on the attributes of God, devoting chapters to the Lord's solitariness, foreknowledge, sovereignty, immutability, faithfulness, goodness, patience, grace, mercy, love, and wrath—and not his beauty— Arthur Pink still touched on Psalm 27:4 when he said the psalmist was talking in verse 7 of "the beauty of holiness," an expression he connects with Psalm 110:3.[86] Well, indeed, holiness resonates with the hearts of the redeemed, but is not in the least engaging to John Gray's rogues gallery, including John Stuart Mill, Bertrand Russell, Friedrich Nietzsche, Ayn Rand, and Arthur Schopenhauer.

Neither Aesthetic Theology nor Anaesthetic Theology

In 2003, Adam Palinski was convicted for setting ruinous fire to a Catholic church in Wheaton, Illinois. At trial, the prosecutor read from his journal, wherein, months before the blaze, he wrote that he wanted "to destroy something beautiful and just be bad."[87] Well, he has many fellow-travelers in the world today. They don't literally torch the tapestries, but they work out their badness though perverse artistry, vicious or snide criticism, and nihilistic patronage.

It's obvious that Christians should not hate or destroy beauty. But neither should they worship it. Nor should they ignore it. Rather, they should savor it within the bounds of truth and goodness, and steel themselves against its blandishments when it departs from that realm. Furthermore, they should grasp the significance of its testimony to the love of God, who has engineered a beautiful fit between sensory faculties and objects which he has strewn about his creation.

---

85. Gray, *Seven Types of Atheism*, 94, 119.

86. Pink, *Attributes of God*, 52.

87. *Adam Palinski v. Joseph Mathy*, 4.

Between the errors of aesthetic theology (keying Christian doctrine to artfulness and beauty) and anesthetic theology (ignoring, marginalizing, or demeaning artfulness and beauty), lies the healthy and paradoxically infectious appreciation (as opposed to adoration) of beauty. Rocks on both sides. And with a generous channel between for the work of apologetical aesthetics.

Bibliography

Adam Palinski v. Joseph Mathy. No. 08 C 4581 (US District Court for the Northern District of Illinois Eastern Division, May 28, 2009), 4. https://www.govinfo.gov/content/pkg/USCOURTS-ilnd-1_08-cv-04581/pdf/USCOURTS-ilnd-1_08-cv-04581-0.pdf.

Aikin, Scott F., and Nicholaos Jones. "An Atheistic Argument from Ugliness." *European Journal of Philosophy of Religion* 7.1 (Spring 2015) 209–17.

Anderson, Jonathan, and William Dyrness. *Modern Art and the Life of a Culture: The Religious Impulses of Modernism.* Downers Grove: IVP Academic, 2016.

Aquinas, Thomas. *Summa Theologica: First Complete American Edition in Three Volumes.* Translated by the Fathers of the English Dominican Province. New York: Benziger Brothers, 1947. https://www.gutenberg.org/cache/epub/17611/pg17611.html.

Augustine. *City of God.* Translated by Marcus Dods, 487–90. Edinburgh: T. & T. Clark, 1871. https://www.gutenberg.org/files/45304/45304-h/45304-h.htm#Page_481.

———. *Soliloquies.* In *Theological Aesthetics: A Reader*, edited by Gesa Elsbeth Thiessen, 30. Grand Rapids: Eerdmans, 2004.

Ball, Philip. "Beauty ≠ Truth: Scientists Prize Elegant Theories, but a Taste for Simplicity Is a Treacherous Guide. It Doesn't Even Look Good." *Aeon*, May 19, 2014. https://aeon.co/essays/beauty-is-truth-there-s-a-false-equation.

Balthasar, Hans Urs von. *The Glory of the Lord: A Theological Aesthetics. Volume 1: Seeing the Form.* Edited by Joseph Fessio SJ and John Riches. Translated by Erasmo Leiva-Merikakis. 7 vols. San Francisco: Ignatius, 1982.

Burke, Edmund. *A Philosophical Enquiry into the Origin of Our Ideas of the Sublime and Beautiful.* Edited by James T. Boulton. Notre Dame, IN: University of Notre Dame Press, 1968.

Bush, Randall B. *God, Morality, and Beauty: The Trinitarian Shape of Christian Ethics, Aesthetics, and the Problem of Evil.* Lanham, MD: Lexington, 2019.

Castle, Terry. "Stockhausen, Karlheinz." *New York Magazine*, August 27, 2011. https://nymag.com/news/9-11/10th-anniversary/karlheinz-stockhausen/.

Catechism of the Catholic Church. Second Edition. Rome: Libreria Editrice Vaticana, 1994.

Coppenger, Mark. Abstract of "Redness and Aesthetic Goodness." *Noûs* 12.1 (March 1978) 57.

Costelloe, Timothy M. *The British Aesthetic Tradition: From Shaftesbury to Wittgenstein.* New York: Cambridge, 2013.

Danto, Arthur. *The Abuse of Beauty: Aesthetics and the Concept of Art.* Chicago: Open Court, 2003.

Devereaux, Mary. "Beauty and Evil: The Case of Leni Riefenstahl." In *Aesthetics: A Reader in Philosophy of the Arts*, edited by David Goldblatt et al. 125–29. New York: Routledge, 2018.

Dubay, Thomas. *The Evidential Power of Beauty: Science and Theology Meet.* San Francisco: Ignatius Press, 1999.

Dutton, Denis. *The Art Instinct: Beauty, Pleasure, and Human Evolution.* New York: Bloomsbury, 2009.

Edsel, Robert M. *The Monuments Men: Allied Heroes, Nazi Thieves, and the Greatest Treasure Hunt in History.* New York: Center Street, 2009.

Erickson, Millard. *Christian Theology.* Grand Rapids: Baker, 1985.

Galli, Mark. "Beautiful Orthodoxy: What the World—and the Church—Needs Now." *Christianity Today* (October 2016) 36–38.

Gay, Peter. *Modernism: The Lure of Heresy, From Baudelaire to Beckett and Beyond.* New York: Norton, 2008.

Gray, John. *Seven Types of Atheism.* New York: Farrar, Strauss, and Giroux, 2018.

Guernsey, Dan. "Educating to Truth, Beauty and Goodness." *The Cardinal Newman Society*, October 17, 2016. https://newmansociety.org/educating-to-truth-beauty-and-goodness-2/.

Hardy, G. H. *A Mathematician's Apology.* London: Cambridge, 1969.

Hart, David Bentley. *The Beauty of the Infinite.* Grand Rapids: Eerdmans, 2003.

Havner, Vance. *In These Times.* Old Tappan, NJ: Fleming Revell, 1969.

Henry, Carl F. H. *God, Revelation, and Authority: God Who Stands and Stays, Part II.* 6 vols. Wheaton, IL: Crossway, 1999.

Hodge, Elissa. "The Influence of Harold Best's Music through the Eyes of Faith and Unceasing Worship on Select Worship Authors and Educators." PhD diss., The Southern Baptist Theological Seminary, 2021.

Howsare, Rodney A. *Balthasar: A Guide for the Perplexed.* New York: T. & T. Clark, 2009.

Hume, David. "Of the Standard of Taste." In *Aesthetics: A Reader in the Philosophy of the Arts*, edited by David Goldblatt and Lee Brown, 399–404. Third Edition. New York: Prentice-Hall, 2011.

Hutcheson, Frances. *An Essay on the Conduct of the Passions and Affections, with Illustrations on the Moral Sense.* Indianapolis: Liberty Fund, 2002. https://oll-resources.s3.us-east-2.amazonaws.com/oll3/store/titles/885/0150_LFeBk.pdf.

Joad, C. E. M. *Essays in Common-Sense Philosophy.* Port Washington, NY: Kennikat, 1969.

Kermani, Navid. *God Is Beautiful: The Aesthetic Experience of the Quran.* Translated by Tony Crawford. New York: Polity, 2015.

Kierkegaard, Søren. *Fear and Trembling/Repetition.* Edited and translated by Howard V. Hong and Edna H. Hong. Princeton: Princeton University Press, 1983.

Kilby, Karen. *Balthsar: A (Very) Critical Introduction.* Grand Rapids: Eerdmans, 2012.

King, Jonathan. *The Beauty of the Lord: Theology as Aesthetics.* Bellingham, WA: Lexham, 2018.

Kreeft, Peter. "Lewis's Philosophy of Truth, Goodness and Beauty." In *C. S. Lewis as Philosopher: Truth, Goodness, and Beauty*, edited by David Baggett et al., 23–36. Downers Grove, IL: InterVarsity, 2008.

Kwan, Kai-Man. *The Rainbow of Experience, Critical Trust, and God: A Defense of Holistic Empiricism.* New York: Bloomsbury, 2011.

Landis, John, dir. *The Blues Brothers*. Universal City, CA: Universal Pictures, 1980.

Laszlo, Zsuzsanna. "Ancient Roman Sculpture—Immortality through Statues." https://theancienthome.com/blogs/blog-and-news/ancient-roman-sculpture.

Leibniz, Gottfried Wilhelm Freiherr von. "The Theodicy: Abridgement of the Argument Reduced to Syllogistic Form." In *Leibniz Selections*, edited by Philip P. Wiener, 509–22. New York: Scribners, 1951.

Lewis, C. S. *God in the Dock: Essays on Theology and Ethics*. Edited by Walter Hooper. Grand Rapids: Eerdmans, 1970.

Lidz, Franz. "Behold the Blobfish: How a Creature from the Deep Taught the World a Lesson about the Importance of Being Ugly." *The Smithsonian Magazine*, November 2015. https://www.smithsonianmag.com/science-nature/behold-the-blobfish-180956967/.

Livio, Mario. *The Golden Ratio: The Story of Phi, the World's Most Astonishing Number*. New York: Broadway, 2002.

Miller, David. *Out of Error: Further Essays on Critical Realism*. Aldershot: Ashgate, 2006.

Oakes, Edward T. "The Apologetics of Beauty." In *The Beauty of God: Theology and the Arts*, edited by Daniel J. Treier et al., 209–26. Downers Grove, IL: IVP, 2007.

Peirce, Charles Sanders. "How to Make Our Ideas Clear." In *Pragmatic Philosophy*, edited by Amelie Rorty, 12–18. Garden City, NY: Doubleday, 1966.

Pink, Arthur W. *The Attributes of God*. Grand Rapids: Baker, 1975.

Plato. *The Republic*. In *The Collected Dialogues of Plato*, edited by Edith Hamilton and Huntington Cairns, 575–844. Princeton: Princeton University Press, 1961.

Polowy, Kevin. "Ridley Scott and Matt Damon on Going to Jordan to Recreate Mars." *Yahoo! Entertainment*, September 29, 2015. https://www.yahoo.com/entertainment/ridley-scott-and-matt-damon-on-going-to-jordan-to-230136329.html.

"Psalm 27:4." In *The Bay Psalm Book*. 1640. Reprint, Oxford: Bodleian Library, 2014.

Rookmaaker, H. R. *Modern Art and the Death of a Culture*. Wheaton, IL: Crossway, 1994.

Sacks, Sir Jonathan. *The Home We Build Together: Recreating Society*. London: Bloomsbury Continuum, 2009.

Sammon, Brendan. *The God Who Is Beauty: Beauty as a Divine Name in Thomas Aquinas and Dionysius the Areopagite*. Princeton Theological Monograph Series. Eugene, OR: Pickwick, 2013.

Schaeffer, Francis A. *How Should We Then Live? The Rise and Decline of Western Thought and Culture*. Wheaton, IL: Crossway, 1976.

Scruton, Roger. *Beauty*. Oxford: Oxford, 2009.

Serbin, Adina. "Nasty Food: 20 Disgusting Delicacies from Around the World." *Chef's Pencil*, October 23, 2019. https://www.chefspencil.com/nasty-food-20-disgusting-foods/.

Shedd, William. *Dogmatic Theology*. 3rd ed. Edited by Alan Gomes. Phillipsburg, NJ: P & R, 2003.

Spotts, Frederic. *Hitler and the Power of Aesthetics*. New York: Overlook, 2002.

Strachan, Owen, and Doug Sweeney. *Jonathan Edwards on Beauty*. Chicago: Moody, 2010.

Strong, Augustus. *Systematic Theology: A Compendium and Commonplace-book Designed for the Use of Theological Students*. Philadelphia: Judson, 1907. https://www.gutenberg.org/files/44035/44035-h/44035-h.html.

Tallon, Philip. "The Theistic Argument from Beauty and Play." In *Two Dozen (Or So) Arguments for God: The Plantinga Project*, edited by Jerry L. Walls and Trent Dougherty, 321–40. New York: Oxford, 2018.

Teresa of Jesus. "Religious Experiences." In *Philosophy of Religion: Selected Readings*, edited by Michael Peterson et al., 7–10. New York: Oxford, 1996.

Viladesau, Richard. *Theological Aesthetics: God in Imagination, Beauty, and Art*. New York: Oxford, 1999.

Wolfe, Tom. *The Painted Word*. New York: Bantam, 1975.

Zemach, Eddy. *Real Beauty*. University Park: Pennsylvania State University Press, 1997.

Zwick, Joel, dir. *My Big Fat Greek Wedding*. Beverly Hills, CA: Gold Circle Films, 2002.

Contributors

Ann Ahrens is a musician, teacher, and writer who serves on various ministry teams at One Family Church in St. Louis, MO. Ann teaches private piano at Dayspring Arts and Education, a university-model K-12 academy. Additionally, Ann serves at Washington University School of Medicine in St. Louis, MO as the Residency Pathways Coordinator. Currently, Ann is working on a project on lament, corporate worship, and soul care. Ann has a BA in church music from Missouri Baptist University, a masters in piano pedagogy and performance from Webster University, an MTS from Urshan Graduate School of Theology, and a PhD in Christian worship from Southern Baptist Theological Seminary in Louisville, KY.

Daniel Blackaby is a creator, teacher, and lover of the arts. As a fifth generation author, he comes from a rich literary heritage and has published several novels, children's books, and non-fiction works. He holds a PhD in "Christianity and the Arts" from Southern Baptist Theological Seminary, writing his dissertation on an apologetic argument from sublime literature. In 2019, he started The Collision, a multi-media ministry aimed at helping Christians engage with culture and think deeper about art and entertainment. He is an ardent J. R. R. Tolkien enthusiast and a voracious reader of classic literature.

Daniel Cabal's interests in art, ministry, and business have led to his working as an aid worker and adjunct professor in Afghanistan, a filmmaker in the United States, and a pastor in Texas. Then, to pay the bills of earning a PhD, with an emphasis in film from a perspective of Christianity and the arts from Southern Seminary, Daniel started working in data analysis and has been employed by Fortune 500 companies ever since. He and his wife Mendy are blessed with two children. Daniel's current academic interests include developing a Christian view of time-based art production and examining onto-logical implications of the Paradox of Fiction. In addition to modest contributions to books by Mark Coppenger and Beth Moore, he di-rected the first season of a children's sitcom and a feature film which has not been released yet.

Mark Coppenger (BA, Ouachita; MA, PhD, Vanderbilt; MDiv, SWBTS) is Retired Professor of Christian Philosophy and Ethics at Southern Baptist Theological Seminary. He's also addressed matters aesthetical and apologetical as a professor at Wheaton College and Midwestern Baptist Theological Seminary. Along the way, he's been a pastor, a campus minister, and an infantry officer. A selection of his publica-tions and talks appears at his website, markcoppenger.com (under Books, Chapters, Articles, and A/V), where he also posts comments and links under Encounters, Ruminations, and Browsings.

Matt Crawford is the Senior Pastor of Trinity Baptist Church in Cor-dova, Tennessee, and holds a PhD in philosophy from Southern Baptist Theological Seminary. His dissertation was on C.S. Lewis's concept of *Sehnsucht* and its application to aesthetics, evangelism, and Christian apologetics. Matt edited the study notes for the 2017 revision of the *Apologetics Study Bible*, and he has written articles for LifeWay Research, *Facts and Trends*, and erlc.com. His primary ministry calling is to pastor, although he loves teaching and writing. Matt is married to Christie and has five wonderful kids ranging from four to ten years old.

William E. Elkins Jr. was awarded an art scholarship to the University of Science and Arts of Oklahoma in 1984 where he received a BA. He went on to earn an MDiv from Southwestern Baptist Theologi-cal Seminary and a PhD in worldview and apologetics, with minors in philosophy and Christianity and the arts, from Southern Baptist Theological Seminary. William has served as a senior pastor in Oklahoma since 1993 and as a chaplain in the Oklahoma National Guard. He is currently the pastor of Chickasha Reformed Church in Chickasha, Oklahoma, where he lives with his wife, Crystal, and near his three boys, their wives, and four granddaughters.

Steve Halla currently serves as a professor of art at Union University in Jackson, Tennessee. His academic interests include art history, visual theory, Japanese aesthetics, the rural cemetery movement, and the intersection of art and faith. He earned a BA from Moody Bible Institute (1994), a ThM in historical theology from Dallas Theological Seminary (2000), and a PhD in aesthetic studies from the University of Texas at Dallas (2006). He is also a printmaker specializing in the art of woodblock printing, which he learned under the tutelage of the late sculptor Carl Bindhammer (1940–2006).

Michael A. G. Haykin is chair and professor of church history at the Southern Baptist Theological Seminary, Louisville, Kentucky, and the director of The Andrew Fuller Center for Baptist Studies at Southern. He is the author of a number of books dealing with Patristic and eighteenth-century Baptist studies and is also the general editor of a seventeen-volume edition of the works of Andrew Fuller (Walter de Gruyter). He and his wife Alison have their home in Dundas, Ontario. They have two grown married children, Victoria (and Mischa) and Nigel (and Sharon).

Rod Miller teaches art history at Hendrix College in sunny central Arkansas. Miller's publications include *23% More Spiritual: Christians and the Fad*, and the novel, *Merely Academic*. He is also the co-author of *Western Culture at the American Crossroads*, and is the editor of *C.S. Lewis and the Arts*. In school, Miller quickly became disillusioned with the vapid nature of art history. After being mentored by an enlightened professor who directed him towards Beauty, he started the long trek through graduate school. Now he spends time attempting to break students, and anyone who will listen, of the belief that art is only about emotional responses and what one likes.

Matthew Raley became lead pastor of Towamencin Mennonite Church near Philadelphia, PA in 2020. He teaches at Western Seminary, Corban University, and Cairn University. Matt is also a violinist who has performed in orchestras and chamber music festivals for many years in California. He especially enjoys playing string quartets because of how intimately the parts dialogue with each other. Matt's wife Bridget and their sons Dylan and Malcolm are enjoying their new lives on the east coast. They are still accepting recommendations for where to find a good cheesesteak.

George Scondras is currently a PhD student at Southern Baptist Theological Seminary pursuing a degree in Christianity and the arts and writing on theology in fantasy literature. He also hold an MDiv from SBTS and serves as a Bible teacher at his home church. George is a controls engineer and an artist, applying his love for visual aesthetics both in his profession and in his pastime. He thoroughly enjoys interacting with kids, and is collaborating on a series of Christian apologetics books designed for young children. He lives in the sylvan hills of North Georgia with his wife and their two children.

Paul Shockley is a Lecturer of Philosophy at Stephen F. Austin State University and adjunct faculty member in religious studies at The University of Miami. His philosophical specializations are aesthetics, ethics, history, and religion. Paul received his PhD in philosophy from Texas A&M University; an MA in humanities/history of ideas from the University of Texas-Dallas; a ThM from Dallas Theological Seminary; and a BA from Stephen F. Austin State University. He is co-author of *Thinking with Excellence: Navigating the College Experience & Beyond*, author of *Worship as Experience: An Inquiry into John Dewey's Aesthetics, the Community, and the Local Church*, and co-editor of *Evangelical America: An Encyclopedia of Contemporary American Religious Culture*. He is a member of the American Society for Aesthetics (ASA). His personal website is www.prshockley.com.

Richard H. Stark III has served as a youth and education pastor for nearly a decade and a half and currently teaches at Palmetto Christian Academy in Mount Pleasant, SC. He has also taught in the School of Christian Studies at Anderson University (SC) and at his alma mater, North Greenville University. He holds a PhD in philosophy from Southern Baptist Theological Seminary, where he focused on theological aesthetics. In addition to the present volume, he contributed to the dialogical book *A Skeptic's Guide to Arts in the Church: Ruminations on Twenty Reservations* (ed. Mark Coppenger). Whether in the church or in the classroom, Richard enjoys utilizing the arts to equip students to encounter the goodness of God in creation and salvation and to engage their worldview and the worldview of others.

Mark Warnock came to faith in Jesus while a freshman at Florida State University. He earned a Bachelor of Music Education there and added an MDiv and a PhD in Christian Philosophy along the way

(SBTS). A classically trained pianist, Warnock served as a worship pastor in Illinois for many years. He is author of *The Complete Seminary Survival Guide* and has edited and contributed to other books, including *A Skeptic's Guide to Arts in the Church.* Warnock now directs the church planting residency at Family Church in West Palm Beach, working to multiply disciples and churches in South Florida.

Brian James Watson is the pastor of West Bridgewater Community Church in Massachusetts. He is a PhD candidate in the philosophy of religion program at Southeastern Baptist Theological Seminary, and he received the Master of Divinity degree from Gateway Seminary. Prior to his work in ministry, theology, and philosophy, he studied, performed, and taught classical vocal music. He holds degrees in music from Brandeis University (Bachelor of Arts) and the University of Texas at Austin (Master of Music; Doctor of Musical Arts), and has served as an assistant professor of music at the University of Mount Olive in North Carolina.

Harrison Watters is a podcast technician and artist living in Louisville, Kentucky. Away from his editing software and ink pens, Harrison is an undergraduate student at Boyce College studying philosophy, politics, and economics. As senior intern for the Augustine Honors Collegium at Boyce College, he is writing his undergraduate senior thesis on the role of political caricature in American op-ed discourse. You can find more of his work at https://harrisonwatters.myportfolio.com.

Eric Williamson teaches philosophy and religion at Blue Ridge Community College in Flat Rock, North Carolina. He holds a PhD in philosophy and ethics from Southern Baptist Theological Seminary. He has taught courses in ethics and theology at Saint Leo University and Boyce College. Eric is a contributor to the forthcoming work in a pop culture and theology series, *Disney & Moral Theology* (Lexington Books). He has also presented papers on pedagogical approaches in higher education and the epistemology of disagreement in religious diversity. While he relishes every course he teaches, one of Eric's favorite classes introduces theology in popular culture. Along with looking at the theological messages of film, celebrities, and musicians, the course also discusses the nature of church architecture. This discussion draws students into the history of architecture as well as the modern influence on church design.

Name Index

This index majors on the names of cited authors and artists and is lightly salted with a selection of concepts and fictional characters. Where an article virtually exhausts this book's treatment of a topic (e.g., Neutra; lament; Kitsch), its title serves as the index.

Scripture Index

Galatians
5:22–23 — 262
6:2 — 177

Ephesians
6:11 — 254

Philippians
1:9–11 — 116
2:5–11 — 262
2:8 — 117
3:10 — 181

Colossians
1:15–20 — 263

1 Timothy
1:12–17 — 132
1:15 — 117
6:16 — 260

2 Timothy
3:16 — 263

Hebrews
4:14–16 — 181
5:8–9 — 116, 117
6:19–20 — 195

1 Peter
1:3–9

1 John
2:1–2 — 117
4:8 — 262

Revelation
4 — 83, 87
4:8–9 — 103
4:3 — 82, 86, 87, 88
5:8–14 — 103
21:24–26 — 103
21:3–4 — 179
21:1 — 103
21:18 — 103
21:21 — 103

Lightning Source UK Ltd.
Milton Keynes UK
UKHW021113200622
404686UK00008B/1985

9 781666 715088